PENGUIN BOOKS

GOING FOR BROKE

John Rothchild is the author of the acclaimed *A Fool and His Money* and co-author (with Peter Lynch) of the best-seller *One Up on Wall Street*. He has written for several national magazines, including *Harper's*, *The New Republic*, and *Esquire*. He lives in Miami Beach, Florida.

# GOING FOR BROKE

## How Robert Campeau

## Bankrupted America's

## Retail Giants

•

## by John Rothchild

Penguin Books

PENGUIN BOOKS
Published by the Penguin Group
Viking Penguin, a division of Penguin Books USA Inc.,
375 Hudson Street, New York, New York 10014, U.S.A.
Penguin Books Ltd, 27 Wrights Lane,
London W8 5TZ, England
Penguin Books Australia Ltd, Ringwood,
Victoria, Australia
Penguin Books Canada Ltd, 10 Alcorn Avenue, Suite 300,
Toronto, Ontario, Canada M4V 3B2
Penguin Books (N.Z.) Ltd, 182–190 Wairau Road,
Auckland 10, New Zealand

Penguin Books Ltd, Registered Offices:
Harmondsworth, Middlesex, England

First published in the United States of America by
Simon & Schuster Inc. 1991
Published in Penguin Books 1992

1  3  5  7  9  10  8  6  4  2

THE LIBRARY OF CONGRESS HAS CATALOGUED THE HARDCOVER AS FOLLOWS:
Rothchild, John.
Going for broke: how Robert Campeau bankrupted the retail
industry and brought the booming eighties to a crashing halt/by
John Rothchild.
p. cm.
Includes index.
1. Allied Stores Corporation. 2. Federated Department Stores. 3.
Leveraged buyouts. 4. Department stores—United States—Corrupt
practices. 5. Campeau, Robert. I. Title.
HF5465.U6A47 1991
381′.141′0973—dc20  91–29581
ISBN 0-671-72593-9 (hc.)
ISBN 0 14 01.7316 1 (pbk.)

Printed in the United States of America
Designed by Liney Li
Photo Editor: Cheryl Moch

# Acknowledgments

•

In addition to all the people who spoke to me on background and would prefer to be appreciated incognito, I would like to thank the following:

Carol Sanger, vice president of corporate communications at Federated, also Dixie Barker and Mary Ann Shannon; Paul Cowan, Canadian filmmaker working on a parallel track; Abby and Steve Solomon; Isadore Sharp; David and Martica Steele; Danielle Padwa and David Burr; Pat Jaffe and David Oppenheim; Rich Green and John Byczkowski of the Cincinnati *Enquirer;* Jacquie McNish of the Toronto *Globe,* Tony Van Alphen of the Toronto *Star;* Beth Dunlop and Joan Chrissos of the Miami *Herald;* Tim Smith, Tom Herman, Bryan Burrough and Jeff Trachtenberg of *The Wall Street Journal;* Bob Morosky; Ron Tysoe; Carolyn Buck Luce; Jim Roddy; Dick Wertheim of Campeau public relations; IDD Information Services; Joe Bencivenga of Salomon Brothers.

Joe Lesser; Kay Shadley; Ben Frank; Bill Fix; Jim Zimmerman; Bill Rubin; Kurt Barnard; Ben Holloway; Allen Finkelson and Joe Mullin at Cravath, Swaine; Jim Freund at Skadden, Arps; Richard Eittreim; John Helyard; Peter Chiappetta; Ann Luzzatto and Peter Fitts at Citibank; Cynthia Strauss; Tom Randall; Kim Fennebresque; Fred Garcia; Susan Miller; Jeff Branman; Dan Sullivan; Skip Sigel; Ira Gluskin; Don Tigert; Kevin Haggarty; Joele Frank;

## ACKNOWLEDGMENTS
·

David Olive; Ellen Forman; Jim Grant; Ann Stock at Bloomingdale's; Peter Rosenthal; Sally Schaadt of 14 Research; Liz Darhansoff and partners; Joe Nocera; Dan and Rebecca Okrent; Taylor Branch and Christy Macy Branch; Michael Aaron; Susan Feldman and Derrick Niederman at *Investment Vision* magazine; Bob Bender, my editor, and Johanna Li, his assistant; Gypsy da Silva, my copy supervisor; Adrienne Welles, my copy editor; and my family, for putting up with the usual.

*To Mel and Lee*

# A Note on Sources

•

I did not interview Robert Campeau for this book. I had every intention of interviewing him. Several exploratory phone calls to his lawyer in Toronto, including three messages left on an answering machine, were never returned. I also sent a letter through Campeau's PR man, requesting an interview so that I could "hear the story from the horse's mouth, instead of getting it only from the jockeys." I chose this horse analogy because I knew that Campeau had owned the Blue Bonnets Race Track in Canada, and also that his Toronto neighborhood was called the Bridle Path.

Getting no response from the horse's mouth, I followed up with a phone call to the private line at Campeau's Bridle Path residence —the number provided surreptitiously by an acquaintance. This call was intercepted by Julia Hidy, Campeau's latest personal secretary in a long string of personal secretaries. Ms. Hidy, I was told by the same source who'd given me the number, screened all of Campeau's phone calls as well as his mail, which lately she must have dreaded showing to the boss because so much of it concerned lawsuits against him.

As I talked to Ms. Hidy, I imagined that Campeau was nervously pacing the marble floors of his $5 million (realtor's estimate) or $10 to $12 million (his estimate) updated chateau with its Olympic-sized swimming pool purified without chlorine, wondering when it might be sold out from under him to satisfy one of many of his loans in default.

Ms. Hidy wouldn't put Campeau on the line. She said that only after I'd "described the tonality" of my book in a second letter would Campeau even consider the idea of our talking. She confided that Campeau was unhappy with recent press coverage of his troubles, particularly the June 18, 1990 *Fortune* article entitled "The Biggest, Looniest Deal Ever," and was considering filing some lawsuits of his own. I argued that articles could not be compared to books, which are longer and give the writer enough space to tell all sides of the story. She countered that Campeau had hated the tonality of the Canadian biography, *Campeau: The Building of An Empire.*

Since I'd read *Campeau: The Building of An Empire* and found it to be almost entirely complimentary, I concluded right away that my subject wouldn't like the tonality of *Going For Broke,* beginning with the title, which I discreetly held back from Ms. Hidy. I sensed from her that nothing short of Great Business Leader Suffers Loss from Unforeseen Circumstances would have pleased her employer.

I was further discouraged to learn that even in more prosperous times, Campeau had turned down a *Life* magazine interview because *Life* wouldn't agree in advance to put him on the cover. Moreover, no journalist had been granted any sort of session with Campeau since the bankruptcy. My choice seemed to be to lie about the tonality, which would only be the starting point in a series of likely futile negotiations, or to proceed without the horse's mouth and concentrate on the jockeys, instead. I chose the latter course.

So aside from my having observed the main character once from the audience at a corporate meeting in Toronto—his last, it appears—I've relied on information gained in 150 interviews with aides, partners, sidekicks, pilots, lawyers, gofers, and various bankers who lent Campeau the $11 billion to make the ill-fated purchases for which he has become notorious. That many of these people have spoken off the record is understandable, given the threats of lawsuits that hang over their heads. Consequently, I have cited numerous "First Boston sources," "Citicorp sources," "Prudential sources," etc. All of these sources had direct knowledge of the matters they spoke to me about.

Wall Street, that great pecuniary souk into which Campeau wandered unknown in 1985, only to come out the owner of a pair of giant U.S. corporations, is where much of this story takes place. I spent many pleasurable hours in the offices of investment banking firms, which for some reason are always outfitted in Empire furniture and decorated with prints of clipper ships. On three occasions, I had my shoes shined by bootblacks who pass from cubicle to cubicle, visiting the bankers at their desks.

On the whole, investment bankers turn out to be intelligent, articulate, and charismatic, and they look gangsterishly stylish in their monogrammed two-toned shirts and pleated pants clasped by suspenders. However, in person they hardly possess the diabolical prowess ascribed to them in recent movies and novels. They are ordinary human beings, as prone to error and to folly as the rest of us, only much better paid, despite their mistakes.

The retailers, who were doing perfectly well until Campeau took them over, were on balance less cooperative than the bankers and lawyers who were Campeau's advisers and accomplices. Though I finally did get some retailers to talk, their initial reluctance to share their outrage and their dismay was surprising. From what they tell me, they've been trying to forget this sorry episode and would rather pretend it never happened.

Almost everyone I did interview, from the top bankers and dealmakers down to the people who had no more than a passing acquaintance with Campeau, referred to the man as "Bob." It was never "Mr. Campeau" or even "Robert Campeau," just "Bob." Journalists who are accustomed to using last names only called Campeau "Bob." Ex-business partners, whether they liked him or not, did the same. This was so prevalent that I began calling him "Bob" in my questions, in spite of the fact that we'd never met. "What did Bob say," I'd ask a source, "when Citicorp discovered he didn't have any equity?" Or, "How often did Bob get his sheep injections in Germany?"

That so many individuals with whom Campeau was linked casually and/or professionally would call him "Bob" must mean something. From what I can gather, it wasn't the familiar "Bob" that is customarily applied to friends and neighbors, because Campeau remained aloof, an enigma even to his closest associates. It was more a bemused "Bob" offered in amazement at his endearing and baffling antics, not the least of which was taking over two major corporations with virtually no money down.

A majority of my sources say they are still fond of Bob, even though so many of these relationships have ended badly. They say he could be extremely charming as well as persuasive, and that these positive attributes ought not to be overlooked, in reflecting on the fiasco to which the name Campeau will be forever connected.

# *Introduction*

•

This is the story of a marvelous financial calamity. Not so wonderful if you happen to be a creditor, of which there are 50,000 at current count, but marvelous in the way that it happened: a stranger comes to Wall Street, borrows nearly $4 billion to acquire a company that six months earlier he'd never even heard of. This transaction is scarcely settled before he's allowed to borrow $7 billion more to acquire a bigger company, making him a major force in retailing, an industry he knows nothing about.

The stranger who was able to accomplish all of this in the latter half of the 1980s was Robert Campeau. Prior to these adventures on Wall Street, Campeau was a successful Canadian real estate developer. The companies he acquired—first Allied and then Federated Department Stores—were successful retail enterprises, which before Campeau's accidentally having taken an interest in them had a fifty-year unbroken record of paying their bills. They were also old-fashioned, that is to say, relatively free of debt.

"Acquired" is really too bland a word to describe the involuntary surrender of Allied and Federated to the newfangled corporate coup known as the leveraged buyout (LBO). In theory, the LBO was supposed to boost productivity and increase profits, once the new owner had supplanted the complacent, unimaginative, and overpaid former management. In practice, the Campeau LBOs landed both companies in Chapter 11 receivership.

Among other notable side effects from Campeau's joint ventures, abetted by the best and the brightest bankers and buyout specialists on Wall Street, are the following: 8,000 workers laid off; First Boston, the once-mighty investment firm, having to be bailed out after several of its bridge loans went kapooie; the collapse of the junk-bond market; a slump in profits for department stores nationwide, as they were forced to reduce prices to match the drastic markdowns at Allied and Federated; the dumping of merchandise on discount stores by manufacturers with no place to sell their goods; the cutback in department-store advertising, which spread the misery into the newspaper and magazine businesses; the recession on Wall Street; the recession in the garment district on Seventh Avenue.

Take this a bit farther, with the unemployed retailers failing to buy new cars and the stricken investment bankers forced to sell their collectibles and their apartments on Park Avenue, and the dealmakers no longer indulging in $150 lunches at Lutèce or the "21" Club, and the entire nation's economic troubles could be pinned on the Campeau acquisitions, which would hardly be fair. Campeau wasn't the only Debtor Baron on whom the banks unwisely showered a fortune; this was an era of Debtor Barons, when billions went out to all sorts of imaginative speculations from Donald Trump to Ohio Mattress to Brazil. Campeau, in fact, arrived in New York at the perfect moment, in the final stage of the buyout frenzy, when playing it safe counted for nothing, and when all sorts of dreamers and connivers whose ambitions far outdistanced their assets were rewarded with huge sums.

The bankruptcy courts are clogged with the results of foolhardy endeavors now that the decade of big deals has given way to the decade of comeuppance, and Chapter 11 has become as familiar as Catch-22 or Route 66. Still, Campeau stands out, because he was a newcomer to Wall Street and because he and his lenders took each other to the extremes of wishful number crunching, while ignoring the many danger signs, not the least of which was Campeau himself. That the lenders kept on lending, after all Campeau put them through, is an inspiration to any working stiff who ever tried and failed to get a mortgage.

As the witty saxophonist Paul Desmond once observed, when

he saw a former girlfriend on the arm of a pin-striped financier: "this is the way the world ends, not with a whim, but a banker." What follows is a detailed account of how, in Campeau's case, the whims and the bankers somehow got together.

# One

In the spring of 1985, when the tulips had sprouted in Toronto, Robert Campeau was about to embark on two new projects: a major corporate acquisition and a face lift. (I bring up the face lift not only as interesting gossip, but because it will have a determinative effect on the future course of American retailing, and perhaps even banking, as we shall see. If it weren't for this cosmetic surgery, Campeau might well have gotten into the S&L business.)

At the time he was considering these two new projects, Campeau was sixty-one years old. There was a comic intensity about him that suggested Peter Sellers as Inspector Clouseau. He walked in brisk, purposeful strides. He spoke in a commanding, gravelly basso. He was a millionaire several times over. His company, the Campeau Corporation, specialized in all forms of real estate.

Campeau, pronounced "Compoh" in French-speaking Quebec, from which he hailed, owned apartment buildings, office towers, shopping centers, and condominiums in Ottawa, Toronto, Montreal, Houston, Dallas, San Francisco, and Florida. Only recently had he taken up permanent residence in Toronto, where in 1981 he had bought a mansion on the prestigious Bridle Path, torn it down, and then spent three years building a 25,000-square-foot chateau replacement. The hole for the pool had already been dug, when he decided to have the pool on the other side of the property.

Campeau subjected himself, no less than his residence, to a barrage of improvements: first a toupee and then hair transplants; capped teeth; face lifts; sheep-brain injections for longevity, which he flew to Europe to receive; Rolfing rituals; health-food diets; the daily swim in his specially purified pool; all of which produced a vigorous and dashing figure, slim and deeply tanned, with bright, prominent uppers and a healthy crop of medically harvested gray hair.

A photograph taken for a Canadian magazine in 1983 showed him dressed in lederhosen, sitting in a chair in his log cabin in the middle of his thirty-square-mile retreat, directly under the head of a moose he had killed. He and the moose shared a bemused, yet forlorn, expression.

The urge to supersede, to win, to maximize his every opportunity ("even on the ski slopes," said an observer, "where he'd supposedly gone to relax, the man was always competing") was a constant theme in the Campeau personal history, the Horatio Alger version of which was told and retold in Canada, more or less as follows:

Campeau entered the world in 1923 as the son of a blacksmith/mechanic in Sudbury, a mining town in the outback of Ontario. Sudbury was dominated by the International Nickel Company (INCO), which over the years had so thoroughly polluted the landscape that of all the desolate spots on earth, U.S. astronauts chose Sudbury as the place to practice their moon landings.

Here in the shadow of the INCO smelters, Campeau was raised with seven siblings (seven others died) in a French-speaking Catholic household. His earliest known entrepreneurial venture was peddling newspapers on the street corner. In the eighth grade, he quit school to take a job at INCO, sweeping floors for fifty cents an hour. The only hint that Campeau was somehow being prepared for the modern leveraged buyout comes in this description of his father from the biography *Campeau: The Building of an Empire,* written by Michael Babad and Catherine Mulroney:

"He [the father] didn't make an awful lot of money always, but he spent money, spent money, spent money. Then the revenues were not as large as he thought they would be."

Campeau's career in real estate was launched somewhat accidentally in 1949, after he'd tried a variety of jobs: millwrighting, hauling logs, running a small grocery store. His cousin Tony, a police officer, had built a house in his spare time, then sold it and doubled his money in a few months. Impressed with these results, Campeau suggested a partnership, and Tony joined him in Ottawa, where Campeau was living with his wife, Clauda. Clauda Leroux had worked as a waitress and packed bullets in a munitions plant. They were married in 1942 when Campeau was nineteen and Clauda was seventeen, and in a few years they had a daughter, Rachelle.

Campeau and his cousin Tony invested $5,000 in a house, doing most of the carpentry themselves, and sold it for $7,500. This soon led to the buying and selling of more houses, which led to the carving of subdivisions from the apple orchards on the far edges of Ottawa. With remarkable prescience, Campeau foresaw the great postwar migration to the suburbs and put himself in the middle of it. He advanced from homebuilding to subdividing, from subdividing to building apartments, from building apartments to putting up officer towers first in Ottawa and then in Montreal.

From a yokel in plaid lumberjack shirts, Campeau metamorphosed through flashy vests and bell-bottom pants into a sophisticate in fashionable European-cut suits. A local Professor Higgins smoothed the rough edges of his *joual* dialect, so he could speak respectable French as well as semi-intelligible English.

By the 1950s, Campeau had become a comfortably wealthy man, and his Lincoln Continental accompanied him abroad, scraping the sides of houses on the narrow European streets. In the 1960s, he became even wealthier, largely thanks to the half million square feet of office space he'd constructed in Ottawa, most of it rented to the Canadian government. He remade the skyline with high rises, the tallest in the city, taller than the historic capital buildings on Parliament Hill with its famous Peace Tower. There were height restrictions written into Ottawa's zoning laws to insure that nothing would exceed the height of the Peace Tower, but Campeau obtained variances. An ex–prime minister said that Campeau had "pygmatized" the national government.

In the condo boom of the 1970s, he expanded his operations in the United States, building condos and office towers in California, Florida, and Texas. He owned some shopping centers in Canada. In Toronto, he'd gone out to the waterfront, a wasteland of rotting docks and empty warehouses, and put up a fancy hotel, the Harbour Castle, along with some adjoining Harbourside condominiums. The local business community viewed this as a ridiculous project that was destined to fail, although the revival of the waterfront later proved Campeau had been right. But it wasn't just Campeau's hotel in the wasteland that raised eyebrows in Toronto, it was what people perceived as his insufferable grandiosity.

His coming-out party, a self-sponsored gala opening for the waterfront project, was an event that Toronto would not soon forget. Leaders of government and industry, most of whom had never met Campeau and scarcely knew who he was, responded out of curiosity to the engraved invitation. They arrived at the hotel too see Toronto's Royal Regiment Guard of Honour decked out in their summer uniforms, lined up at the entrance. Barbara Amiel, a writer for Toronto *Life* magazine, describes the scene:

"At 8 P.M., with the sun still high in the sky, the Guards' commander decided the time had come. The crowds, gathered along the driveway to watch the festivities marking the opening of the hotel, murmured expectantly. At the main door, Robert Campeau stood, surrounded by a group of half a dozen intimates. His eye caught the commander's. Campeau nodded. Moving briskly toward the saluting stand, his moire tuxedo shimmering subtly, just a hint of frilled shirt showing . . . Campeau stepped in front of the crowds. Solemnly, he acknowledged the presentation of arms by the commander and, with a little skip that brought him in step with him, he slid his feet in an imitation of all those inspections he had seen performed by countless members of the House of Windsor."

All this for a builder from Ottawa. Inside the new hotel, uniformed guides gave tours of the Roman-style baths in the royal suite; miniskirted waitresses maneuvered platters of venison around the gilded marble columns, and human sculptures struck poses on the staircases. The guest of honor worked the crowd, greeting wellwishers and forgetting their names until the lights dimmed, drums rolled, the curtains parted, and an emcee appeared on a stage to announce "the moment you've all been waiting for." Campeau ascended.

The moment they'd all been waiting for turned out to be what amounted to a lecture that resembled the opening argument in a intercollegiate debate. "The deeper that governments get involved in economics, the deeper the trouble we're all in . . . the trouble with universities and sociologists and teachers is that they're openly creating and leading up to a lot of problems and disasters on the part of the public," Amiel reported Campeau as saying. Gathering steam, Campeau railed against government handouts, government rigging of the public balance sheets, national politicians, and then local politicians.

As Campeau carried on with his diatribe, an embarrassed hush fell over the audience, followed by murmurs of disapproval. Several of the local politicians headed for the exits.

Ever since that coming-out party in 1976, the VIPs of Toronto had been asking each other: "Just who in the hell does this guy think he is?" When Campeau moved onto the Bridle Path in 1984, where there was another gala opening, with singer Paul Anka flown in by helicopter, the business community still didn't know what to make of him.

"Find me an acquisition," Campeau was telling Austin "Firpo" Taylor, a robust financier, thoroughbred expert, and gourmand-about-town in the spring of '85. They were sitting in Taylor's office at the investment banking firm of McLeod Young Weir in Toronto. Around the desk, easels displayed the banker's favorite paintings.

"Firpo" Taylor, a clever and kindhearted chap whose nickname derived from the fact that as a child he was already big enough to remind people of Argentine heavyweight boxer Luis "Wild Bull of the Pampas" Firpo (a comparison that a lifetime of meals now rendered inadequate) harbored mixed feelings about working with his enthusiastic visitor.

On the one hand, who could deny that Campeau was a force with whom to be reckoned? Right outside the window, there was new evidence: construction on the Scotia Plaza high rise, second tallest in the city, was about to begin. This metallic sliver, squeezed out of an undersized lot, was destined to rise above the squatter black granite headquarters of Toronto's major banks. This latest Campeau project exceeded the height restrictions in the planning and zoning codes, the same as Campeau's high rises in Ottawa had. Scotia Plaza was a perfect symbol of Campeau himself, a maverick structure, taller than the codes allowed, mocking the rules, imposing itself on the Establishment's Bay Street.

Hadn't Campeau surrounded Ottawa with suburbs over the violent objections of its female mayor, Charlotte Whitton, who once stood in front of one of his bulldozers in a futile attempt to stop the advance? (Campeau later reciprocating by stopping *her* advance at a formal gathering, with a foot planted firmly on the train of her dress.) As a developer, Campeau was a formidable force, who by cajoling, browbeating, and knowing the right politicians usually got what he wanted. In his Harbour Castle project and elsewhere, he had proven he had vision. He was also a valuable client of Taylor's loan department.

On the other hand, Firpo Taylor was also aware of Campeau's wild-card reputation, his quick temper, his absurd grandiosity, his tendency to veer off on exotic tangents outside of real estate, many of which were pursued wholeheartedly and then dropped: a water-powered dishwasher; cardboard-box houses for the Third World; the investments in technology companies announced with great fanfare as "Campeau Tech" in the 1981 annual report, then abandoned in 1982; his sudden urge to own a TV station, nixed by the Canadian broadcasting authorities; his insistence on running the Harbour Castle Hotel (allegedly, he once said he wanted to be the next Conrad Hilton) as opposed to simply building it; and the most exotic of all tangents that led to the famous showdown on Lt. Col. Kenneth White's lawn.*

This latter tangent is worth examining in some detail, for it explains a great deal about the role that Campeau would soon play on Wall Street. It was 1980, summertime, a sunny morning near Bromont, a resort area in the far reaches of Quebec. Lt. Col. White, the CEO of Royal Trustco, Canada's largest trust company as well as its largest real estate brokerage firm, was having his breakfast on the lawn. An agitated Campeau, who'd hired a seaplane and then a taxi to get there, stumbled Walter Mitty–like onto the scene.

Lieutenant Colonel White, a military veteran of the stiff-upper-lip school who couldn't imagine why this relatively parochial developer had come all this way to see him, invited Campeau onto the lawn for some coffee. Campeau's taxi driver waited outside the gate, as Campeau explained the purpose of his visit. He was taking over

---

* The meeting on Lieutenant Colonel White's lawn has passed into Canadian lore, the way that the meeting between, say, Pocahontas and Captain John Smith has in the United States. Many versions have been published in articles and books.

Royal Trustco that very afternoon. He'd dropped by to seek the CEO's cooperation and to congratulate him on his fine leadership, and hoped that White could visualize the exciting synergies that would result from the Campeau/Royal Trustco merger, once Campeau had purchased the outstanding Royal Trustco stock.

Try as best he could, White could not visualize any exciting synergies between Canada's premier financial institution, which had $7.5 billion in assets and managed $19 billion in trust fund and pension accounts for a million Canadians, and a middling-successful girder jockey from Ottawa. A Rockefeller or a Morgan couldn't have been more surprised if Tom Carvel had stopped by one of their mansions to inform them he was taking over their oil companies or banks.

Gripping the impossible dreamer by the arm (Campeau was several inches shorter than White), the CEO of Royal Trustco reportedly escorted him to the edge of the property and threw him off. "Pull the bid! Pull that damn bid!" were White's parting words, as later quoted in the press.

But neither the size and power of Royal Trustco, nor the ejection from White's lawn scared Campeau into pulling his damn bid—in fact, just the opposite. If this couldn't be a friendly merger, as Campeau had politely suggested, then he was perfectly willing to do a hostile deal and take over Royal Trustco that way. Once again, Campeau was several years ahead of his time. Here it was the summer of 1980, and Campeau was making the rounds of Canada's biggest banks, urging them to lend him billions so he could buy up all the Royal Trustco shares.

Campeau might have been regarded as a pipsqueak, but Toronto's Bay Street Establishment was taking the threat of a Campeau-owned Royal Trustco so seriously that a Who's Who of Canadian finance joined together in a giant back-room conspiracy to grab all the loose shares before Campeau could get his hands on them. Banks, insurance companies, industrial companies, even the billionaire Reichmann brothers, Paul and Albert, Orthodox Jews, were enlisted in the national effort to save this Waspy old-guard enterprise from the clutches of the upstart owner of the Harbour Castle Hotel.

•  •  •

Beginning in 1984, Campeau once again was talking about making acquisitions, in between at least two lengthy and somewhat mystifying disappearances—one to get a face lift, and the other, the story goes, to recuperate from an emotional crisis. As one corporate officer alleges, "Bob was gone so much that the running of the real estate operation was being handled by others. When he was around, dreaming up possible acquisitions gave him something to do."

By 1985, when Firpo Taylor was actively engaged in helping Campeau find an acquisition, Royal Trustco was still fresh in the banker's mind. Taylor, in fact, had been the spearhead of the anti-Campeau faction. But in the banking world, neither lenders nor borrowers could afford to be vindictive. Campeau, for his part, wasn't holding any grudges, and Taylor and his partner, Daniel Sullivan, had done some Campeau real estate financings in the interim. They both admired Campeau's offbeat chutzpah. They enjoyed speculating what unpredictable thing he was going to do next. They were reluctant to turn down an assignment from a big real estate client. So they agreed to cooperate.

What sort of acquisition did Campeau have in mind? the bankers wanted to know. Campeau said he wanted to go after another Canadian trust company. "We were surprised," recalls Sullivan, "that after Royal Trustco he hadn't given this idea up. Here it was five years later and he was still thinking about trust companies. But Taylor and I liked Bob, and we'd said we would help."

By the summer of 1985, Campeau's two consultants had identified a possible target, Canada Trust Ltd., a smaller operation where a large block of stock was rumored to be available at a good price. Making a discreet inquiry, they discovered that this stock would not be available. "This is when Bob got tired of beating his head against the wall in Canada," says Sullivan. "This is when he decided he wanted to take over a bank in the United States."

Take over a bank in the United States? Wherever Campeau had gotten that idea, the Toronto duo thought it lacked "essential realism." There were many regulatory problems with a foreigner's taking over a bank in the United States. "We informed the client," says Sullivan, "about these drawbacks, and suggested that he consider taking over a savings and loan instead. Campeau got very excited at the prospect. We told him he'd need some U.S. expertise that we didn't have, and we put him in touch with Shearson Lehman in New York.

Shearson Lehman in New York owned a 10 percent stake in Sullivan and Taylor's company, McLeod Young Weir, in Toronto, so that both sides would benefit from whatever fees this latest Campeau adventure might produce.

Shearson Lehman then sent an emissary to Canada to meet with their prospective client and discuss the pros and cons of his acquiring an S&L. Campeau was still excited, and agreed to pay Shearson a $100,000 finder's fee. Shearson prepared an engagement letter to formalize these arrangements, and Campeau quietly flew off to Brazil for an as yet unknown reason that turned out to be cosmetic surgery.

Meanwhile, Shearson had found an S&L for Campeau to take over, but the client had vanished. Phone calls to his office were not returned, and Campeau aides and secretaries offered no clue as to the boss's whereabouts. Back in New York, Shearson began to wonder if the poor man had been kidnapped, but the less dramatic truth, known only to a chosen few, was that the would-be owner of the S&L was hiding in his house, getting accustomed to his new look.

Frustrated that a lucrative opportunity was about to be lost, Shearson wandered off to find another buyer for the S&L it had earmarked for Campeau. Shearson was still expecting to receive its $100,000 fee, to be split with McLeod Young Weir, but Campeau had never signed the engagement letter and refused to pay.

This entire episode—the face lift, the disappearance, the refusal to pay—embarrassed the Toronto bankers who had recommended Campeau to Shearson in the first place, and they apologized to their New York counterparts for this unfortunate waste of everyone's time. Sullivan and Firpo Taylor hoped this was the last they'd hear of Campeau's acquisitions in the United States.

A few weeks passed, summer had turned to fall, and neither Taylor nor Sullivan had been contacted by their mercurial client. Sullivan had all but forgotten the Campeau assignment, when he got an urgent message that brought him down off the ski slopes.

"I'd gone away for the weekend. Unreachable, or so I thought. Bob, though, had managed to find out where I was. An emissary of his phoned my sister-in-law, who gave him the number of the chalet where I was staying. I got an urgent message there that Bob wanted to talk to me and to Taylor immediately.

"So I called Taylor, who in turn called Bob right away, and Bob said to him, 'I can't talk to you now, I'm eating my breakfast. Call back later,' and hung up. Taylor waited then until he was sure that Bob had finished his breakfast, and all Bob said was, 'I want to continue the search.'

"I never figured out why all of this urgency—which wasn't urgent enough for Bob to interrupt his breakfast—couldn't have waited until Monday."

Campeau's desire to continue the search gave Sullivan a ticklish public relations problem. Campeau was acting as if nothing unusual had occurred, and meanwhile, Shearson had told Sullivan it wanted nothing further to do with Campeau. Aware of Campeau's volatile reaction to bad news, and also of his aversion to paying fees, Sullivan took a diplomatic approach and told Campeau that Shearson had backed out because "the costs of their search would be more than you're willing to pay."

Now Campeau was calling at all hours, suddenly obsessed with owning an S&L, as Sullivan reluctantly tried to find another U.S. investment bank to represent him. After the last fiasco, who could guarantee there wouldn't be another? Who could guarantee that the bankers would even be paid?

Putting such trepidations aside in the interest of helping a client, Sullivan recommended Campeau to Morgan Stanley, but Morgan Stanley declined the assignment as well. "We don't think he's serious," Morgan Stanley told Sullivan. The way Sullivan explained it to Campeau was that Morgan Stanley "wasn't interested."

"So maybe you can do the search for me yourself?" asked Campeau, refusing to give up.

As a last resort short of showing a valuable customer of real estate loans the door, Sullivan and Taylor decided to introduce Campeau to Tribco Partners, a start-up investment boutique that was subletting a corner of McLeod's New York offices at State Street Plaza.

Off Wall Street, no less than Off Broadway, attracted numerous hopeful enterprises whose enthusiasm exceeded their resources, and whose impact on the financial markets was as yet only marginal. Tribco Partners was one such enterprise. The staff consisted of Thomas Randall, one colleague, and a secretary. Randall, the founder and CEO, had worked for Paine Webber before striking out on his own earlier in 1985. He had an agreement with the Toronto bankers to pursue joint ventures.

Randall was competent, hardworking, and honest, but his operation could hardly be mistaken for a major investment bank's.

"Shearson and Morgan Stanley aren't really interested in working with him," was what Sullivan in Toronto told Randall in New York, in throwing the Campeau assignment Tribco's way.

Campeau did not succeed in real estate by being pessimistic, and he wasted no time fretting over the difference between Shearson and Tribco Partners, any more than the celebrated Don Quixote fretted over the difference between a knight in armor and a windmill. With the same verve with which he'd tracked Sullivan to the ski slopes to tell him to "continue the search," Campeau told his Toronto adviser to pack his bags—they were leaving for New York. He'd made an appointment to meet Tom Randall at the Waldorf Towers.

Having arrived promptly for the 1 P.M. engagement and sat in the lobby of the Waldorf Towers until 2:30, Randall was preparing to give up and go home, when a man wearing a porkpie hat bounced into view. It was Campeau, with Sullivan the banker close behind, and behind Sullivan was Pierre, the chef from Campeau's fish camp in the provinces.

Frightened by the noises of the city, Sullivan recalls, Pierre had spent the limo ride in from the airport with his hands over his ears.

"Follow me," said Campeau as soon as the introductions were exchanged. With the earnest lope of a man on the move, he led Randall, Sullivan, and chef Pierre across the lobby and into an elevator that took them to the upstairs suite that Campeau had reserved.

Depositing his entourage in the living room, and giving no further explanation, Campeau headed for the bedroom and closed the door. His three companions were left alone to make small talk, which was difficult for the chef, since he spoke no English. Eventually, Campeau emerged from the bedroom, offered everyone a drink, and began to discuss his plans for making a major acquisition in the United States.

Campeau, who by this time had expanded his list of possible

targets, said it could be an S&L or a life insurance company, or perhaps something to do with real estate, which was his main focus. He asked Randall to explain how Tribco Partners operated and how Randall would carry out the investigation. Randall, who'd been previously briefed about Campeau's interests, was in the middle of giving a report on what he'd learned about various S&Ls and insurance companies when Campeau cut him off abruptly in mid-sentence.

"Fine. I think you'll do fine," Campeau said, with obvious impatience. "I've got to go now. I've got an appointment to see John Reed, the CEO of Citicorp." Gathering up his winter coat and his hat, Campeau exited with a wave of his hand, leaving a mystified Randall to wonder what sort of impression he'd made. "Show Pierre the city," Campeau commanded. Pierre was too frightened, still, Sullivan recalls, to set foot outside the door.

Having landed his first big client in this unusual fashion, Randall busied himself with researching possible undervalued situations, including three S&Ls and four insurance companies. Regularly, he called Campeau with progress reports, leaving messages with the secretary in Toronto. Campeau returned these calls from places like Acapulco or Germany, and to a lesser extent from his house in Toronto, seeming to make every effort to reach Randall just before dawn.

It was not unusual for our Tribco Partner to be aroused from a deep sleep at home by the telephone ringing close to his ear at 4:30 A.M., and to pick up the receiver in a stupor only to find that instead of a breather it was Campeau on the line, wide-awake and eager to discuss some minor detail in one of Randall's calculations. Randall admired Campeau's amazing grasp of numbers and the fact that he seemed to do some of his best thinking in the middle of the night.

To all of the many fateful coincidences that have changed people's lives, such as the accidental spill in the laboratory that led to the discovery of radium, or the monkey bite that caused a civil war in Greece, add this one: Randall had an acquaintance who worked at Allied Stores.

At this point in our story (January 1986), Randall wasn't even dreaming of putting Allied Stores on Campeau's potential acquisitions list. A sensible man, Randall knew that Allied Stores was a department- and specialty-store conglomerate with a market value of $2 billion and 24 divisions, 670 separate outlets and 70,000 employees nationwide. He knew, also, that Campeau Corporation had a market value of $200 million and was a real estate enterprise with fewer than 1,000 employees. That the one could be overcome by the other was the farthest thing from his mind. Besides, Campeau had never mentioned retailing as one of his interests.

No, Randall's hunch was that Campeau, who owned shopping centers in Canada, might be interested in buying the five shopping centers owned by Allied Stores that his source inside the company told him might be for sale. Or failing that, perhaps some smaller deal might be arranged, such as getting Brooks Brothers, a division of Allied, to put an outlet in one of Campeau's malls.*

In one of their off-peak phone conversations in the spring of 1986, Randall brought up Allied Stores for the first time. Campeau had never heard of it. Randall assured Campeau he'd heard of the parts.

"What are the parts?" asked Campeau.

Randall named some of the parts: Brooks Brothers, Ann Taylor, Jordan Marsh of Florida and Boston, Garfinckel's of Washington, Bonwit Teller, the Bon Marché of Seattle. Campeau recognized Brooks Brothers. He'd been in Brooks Brothers.

Perhaps, Randall suggested enthusiastically Campeau could work out a deal to bring a Brooks Brothers store into one of his Canadian properties.

"That's an idea," said Campeau.

Randall brought up Allied Stores again at a meeting in Campeau's office in Toronto, where the interior was tastefully decorated in oriental rugs and walnut, and the area around Campeau's desk was elevated above the general level of the floor. There was a blizzard outside. Firpo Taylor, who had a bad hip and walked with a cane, wasn't thrilled to be dragging his outsized frame through the snow and down the street to Campeau's office to listen to more talk about acquisitions, which he didn't take entirely seriously.

---

* At his initial meeting with Campeau, Randall had also brought up the possibility of Campeau's buying some shopping centers from Macy's.

Sullivan was also present; he recalls that at an earlier encounter he and Campeau and Randall had looked up Allied Stores in the *Moody's Guide,* hoping to learn the locations of the five shopping centers. By this meeting, they'd found the locations, but Campeau seemed not to be particularly interested in shopping centers. He was more excited about the S&Ls and insurance companies that Randall had been analyzing.

But by late November, in another complete about-face, Campeau had lost interest in S&Ls and insurance companies that Randall had dutifully researched. Suddenly, he had a new interest: R. H. Macy & Co.

"Get me Finkelstein," he commanded Randall out of nowhere. "I want a meeting." Finkelstein was Edward Finkelstein, CEO of Macy's, a public company that was about to be "taken private" in a leveraged buyout.

Why a meeting with Macy's? Randall wondered. The subject of Macy's had come up in one of their discussions, because Macy's also had some shopping centers to sell. But Campeau wasn't thinking about the shopping centers. He was thinking about the Macy's leveraged buyout, which he'd been following in the newspapers. Randall had brought retailing companies to his attention, and he could see that Macy's was onto something lucrative. Finding an acquisition was no longer his priority; now he wanted to participate in the Macy's LBO.

From the tone of "get me Finkelstein," it sounded to Randall as if a summit conference between two businessmen of great stature was a foregone conclusion.

Putting his research aside in favor of trying to reach Finkelstein, for after all his job was to satisfy the client, Randall hit an immediate snag. He couldn't get Finkelstein. Perhaps if Campeau had met Finkelstein on some other occasion, Randall's task would have been easier, but Campeau didn't know Finkelstein, and Finkelstein hadn't heard of Campeau, and Randall was getting nowhere.

He tried to get to Finkelstein through Goldman, Sachs, Macy's investment bankers, and got the runaround there. Finkelstein's office was not jumping at the chance to convene a strategy session with a Tribco partner who represented a Canadian real estate developer who wanted to help out in the upcoming LBO, either. Campeau, meanwhile, seemed to think it was Randall's fault that he hadn't reached Finkelstein.

"He wants a meeting with Finkelstein," a harried Randall reported back to Sullivan and Firpo Taylor, after failing several times to set up the powwow. "This is very important to him. He wants to participate in the Macy's LBO. What can we do?"

After considerable effort, Randall was able to arrange a meeting with a member of Macy's board of directors, who in turn put in a word with Finkelstein, who in turn set up a "courtesy session" between the unknown developer and a Macy's senior vice president, James York. "Will Finkelstein be stopping by?" Campeau asked, when he heard this news.

The courtesy session, held at Macy's headquarters in New York around Christmastime in 1985, did not go particularly well. Campeau didn't appreciate being shunted off to a lower-level executive, nor being told that there was no role for him in the Macy's LBO, except perhaps in buying some Macy's mortgages. "Is Ed Finkelstein going to come around and say hello?" Campeau wondered out loud more than once. Finkelstein never did.

Spurned by Macy's, Campeau called yet another strategy session with Randall. "Let's delve into Allied," he told Randall, "a little bit more."

# TWO

Randall assumed at first that delving further into Allied meant the five shopping centers. But it didn't. It meant that Campeau was thinking about taking over the whole company, with its $4 billion in sales and its twenty-four divisions nationwide.

Having learned to expect the unexpected from this unusual client, Randall was nonetheless amazed. Just a few weeks back, Randall had figured that Campeau might be interested in attracting a single Brooks Brothers store into one of his malls. Now in a great imaginary leap, Campeau had vaulted himself into the ownership of all forty-five Brooks Brothers stores, plus all the Jordan Marshes, Bonwit Tellers, Ann Taylors, Garfinckel'ses, Bon Marchés, Stern'ses, and so on.

Suppressing his skepticism in favor of good relations, Randall went about the business of preparing a thumbnail analysis of Macy's versus Allied Stores versus other big retailers that Campeau directed him to make. It was clear what had happened. Having been rejected by Macy's in its LBO, Campeau had decided to do a Macy's-style LBO on Allied, putting himself in the role of Finkelstein.

Campeau's search for an acquisition had led him to the two Toronto bankers, the bankers had led him to Randall, Randall had led him to Allied, and Allied had led him to Macy's, which was going private. Putting one, two, and three together, Campeau arrived at the logical next step: taking Allied private.

As a developer, Campeau had learned to take the best ideas of his competitors and put them to use. Macy's became the blueprint for his acquisition. He quickly grasped the facts of an LBO, the cash flow, the added value, how you could sell off parts to pay the debts, the sum of the parts being greater than the whole. Randall realized that Campeau understood the Macy's LBO strategy down to the last detail and was intrigued the management had pulled it off. (Macy's completed its LBO in July of 1986).

Randall's thumbnail analysis showed that Allied Stores was indeed an undervalued situation, more undervalued even than Macy's had been, at the price at which it was taken private. Retailers in general, badly managed and wasteful, had for years been considered by Wall Street analysts to be undervalued, their stocks depressed because of chronically disappointing earnings, their sizable real estate assets unappreciated.

But discovering an undervalued Allied was one thing, and having the wherewithal to purchase it quite another, as Randall reminded himself. He'd have given long odds against a retailing company with a market value of $2 billion being taken over by a real estate company with a market value of $200 million, as his imaginative client now envisioned.


Of this entire exercise so far described, the trips to New York, the meetings with Sullivan and Firpo Taylor, the retaining of Shearson, the hiring of Randall, the Finkelstein episode, some of Campeau's key corporate executives were blissfully unaware. They were busy running the real estate operations for Campeau Corp., which was a challenging task on its own.

While Campeau Corp. was quite profitable and continued to benefit from Campeau's early decision to build high rises in Ottawa and rent them to the government as well as his more recent decision to build waterfront condominiums in Toronto, it had experienced notable failures in the United States. In the late 1970s, Campeau had built condos and office towers in Dallas, Houston, and on Florida's east coast, and the Texas market promptly went bust. In 1983, his company reported that $854 million worth of such "discontinued assets" would be sold.

As it was putting up condos and office towers at a time when America was being glutted with both, Campeau Corp. was overlooking the malls and shopping centers that were making other developers very rich. Reportedly, Campeau was irked with his advisers for allowing him to overbuild in Texas and for missing out on other opportunities. In the 1982 annual report, he had unveiled a stunning new plan: Campeau Corp. was phasing out of residential real estate to concentrate on commercial ventures.

The Texas problems suggested that Campeau, like many other foreign investors in the United States, was susceptible to making overly optimistic assessments and to coming in too late with too much. And since he'd failed to win the esteem he thought he deserved in Toronto, nobody was more bullish on America than Robert Campeau.

Like so many things in Campeau's life from his chin to his hair to his mansion, his executive staff had been done over, the early French-speaking retinue of relatives and associates from the building trades (names like Paradis, Cadieux) supplanted by Anglo-Canadians (McCartney, Carroll, King, Brown, Walker) with accounting and business degrees, who were better qualified to manage the complicated real estate portfolio of a large, publicly traded corporation.

At the time Campeau was making his side trips to New York, this relatively sophisticated inner circle included Don Carroll and David King, both of whom had worked for Campeau for over a decade; and two newcomers, the canny James Roddy, recruited as a financial expert from a jewelry company in Toronto; and the precocious Ronald Tysoe, a lawyer who came to work for Campeau in 1981, at the age of twenty-eight.

Campeau's brain trust was engaged in a continuous behind-the-scenes struggle to keep the boss's impetuosities in check. The man had had some great ideas—e.g., building on the Toronto waterfront —but from the earliest days in Ottawa, advisers had tried to subdue his wilder impulses. In the 1960s, an associate accompanied him to zoning hearings to keep him from jumping up and down. As the operation got bigger, the impulses got wilder. In 1970, Campeau ceded control in his own company to a fellow Canadian entrepreneur in a complicated exchange of shares, a decision he soon regretted.

Two years later, he was able to buy his own shares back at a much higher price, with the help of a loan from—of all places—the Vatican.

Against his sudden urges to rip out the stone flooring at the Place de Ville plaza, recently installed at great expense; or to take a flyer on cardboard houses; or to install a two-toned marble facade on his Scotia Plaza high rise; or to invest in high-tech ventures, the staff attempted (often unsuccessfully) to exert a modest counterforce.

Ron Tysoe, Campeau's youngest adviser, was the first to hear of the boss's interest in Allied Stores. In January 1986, Campeau left a packet on Tysoe's desk, which included some Allied annual reports, Randall's thumbnail analysis, and the pages copied from Moody's and the *Value Line Investment Survey*. "Evaluate this potential acquisition," the note on the packet had said.

Along with his Campeau Corp. colleagues, Tysoe knew that Campeau was keen on making acquisitions, and they'd even discussed certain Canadian companies as possible targets, but nothing had prepared Tysoe for Allied. A glance at the balance sheet revealed the problem: How could a company the size of theirs conquer a company the size of Allied? Tysoe's doubts were broached gingerly in a memo to the boss. "Surprised at the size of Allied," Tysoe wrote. "This is a retailing company. A BIG retailing company."

"I don't care," Campeau responded. "I still want to pursue this."

Tysoe and Roddy, the two newcomers to Campeau Corp., faced a ticklish dilemma. Campeau's fascination with the giant U.S. retailer seemed so preposterous that they couldn't really believe that the boss was serious. Yet Campeau sounded serious, and they were hardly in a position to argue the point. They were on less solid footing than Carroll and King, Campeau's older and more seasoned advisers. And Roddy and Tysoe knew about Campeau's short fuse.

The best course of action, they decided, was to relax, play along, and to hope that the Allied infatuation would pass. Even if it didn't, the banks surely would put the kibosh on such a project by refusing to lend money to it, and the "realities of the marketplace," as Roddy called it, would send Bob a message.

Later that same month, still unbeknownst to his board of directors, Campeau headed for New York to seek financial support for his LBO of Allied Stores. By now, he had developed a rationale for the project, "the synergy between retailing and real estate." He rented two suites at the Waldorf and brought along the reluctant duo Roddy and Tysoe, who expected that this wild-goose chase would end quickly.

But Campeau's timing couldn't have been better. Buyouts and takeovers, such as the one he'd precociously attempted on Lt. Col. Kenneth White's lawn in 1980, were now all the rage. Wall Street was uncovering one undervalued situation after another, as its investment bankers plotted a succession of corporate raids over hundred-dollar lunches at Manhattan's swankiest restaurants, or in private clubs like the Links, Down Town Association, or Union. Restaurants had taken over from golf course locker rooms as the incubators of deals.

Where a deal to an investment banker once had meant selling a company's stock or underwriting its bonds, in the mid-1970s those old-school activities had become passé. The gentlemanly and profitable profession of selling stocks and bonds had turned out to be neither. Price-cutting and discounting, so disastrous to the airline industry, had had the same effect on Wall Street. So had government deregulation. In 1975, the SEC abolished fixed commissions on stock trades in an effort to promote competition. This took the profit out of the business and caused securities firms to grope for new sources of revenue. In 1982, the SEC adopted its infamous Rule 415, which permitted corporations to alter their traditional relationships with their underwriters in issuing more stock or selling more bonds. Rule 415 was a terrible blow to investment banks; there was no longer any real money in underwriting stocks and bonds; even powerhouse firms such as First Boston were limping along on reduced profits.

It's often said that greed is the motivating force on Wall Street, but desperation, not greed, drove the so-called white-shoe firms such as First Boston and Morgan Stanley to undercut the competition and attempt to steal each other's formerly untouchable corporate clients. A long list of unthinkable practices from the Gentleman's Code had, by the time Campeau appeared, become very thinkable.

For instance, the Gentleman's Code had inhibited reputable Wall Street firms from engaging in hostile takeovers. Morgan Stanley, regarded as the most reputable of all, even had a rule against hostile takeovers. But this went out the window in the predatory world of buying and selling corporations, which had supplanted the more genteel world of buying and selling stocks and bonds *for* corporations. In the first major hostile takeover deal in modern U.S. history, International Nickel's 1974 raid on Electric Storage Battery (a pioneering effort right from Campeau's childhood backyard!), Morgan Stanley represented INCO.

Merger and acquisition departments, where takeovers and buyouts were conceived, didn't exist in most firms in the early 1970s; Morgan Stanley had a four-person department in 1974. In 1983, it had a seventy-five-person department, and M&A was the firm's major source of profit. By 1985, M&A was everybody's major source of profit, with $200 billion worth of deals being done on Wall Street every year. The business of America had become the business of taking over businesses.

After Morgan Stanley broke the taboo on hostile raids with INCO, the Gentleman's Code was further loosened by other unthinkable firsts: the first leveraged buyout of a major company in its entirety (Gibson Greetings, 1982); the first hostile takeover attempt financed by junk bonds (Boone Pickens, Mesa Petroleum, 1984); the first successful friendly takeover financed by junk bonds in which the acquirer was a financial Lilliput (Nelson Peltz, Triangle Industries, 1985); and the first successful unfriendly takeover financed by junk bonds in which a Lilliput swallowed a Brobdingnag (Ronald Perelman, Revlon, 1985).

In fact, Campeau's arrival at the Waldorf almost perfectly coincided with Ron Perelman's amazing bondquest of the cosmetics giant, using junk for money and tiny Pantry Pride as his "acquiring vehicle." Perelman represented a major breakthrough for all believers in pluck, luck, and no money down. That a former peddler of licorice extract, video cassettes, and cigars, whose skill in financial management was at one time concentrated on handling his wife's sizable fortune could—thanks to the cash infused by the fallen Drexel Burnham Lambert—snatch up a $4 billion enterprise ought to have been an inspiration to Campeau.

Drexel, after all, was the most popular bankroll—some would say the only bankroll—for maverick corporate prospectors such as Perelman and Peltz who, like Campeau, had come out of nowhere, and whose ambitions, like Campeau's, far exceeded their resources. By essentially inventing and then controlling the junk bond market, Drexel's Michael Milken had democratized capital. His was the shop where neophytes and underdogs could become players in the M&A game, a chance they would never have gotten from the clubby firms such as First Boston or Morgan Stanley. Drexel was the one place where an unknown like Campeau could have hoped to find a receptive audience for his wild idea.

Yet Campeau steered clear of Drexel. Why, nobody seemed to be sure. One theory was that he knew so little about Wall Street that Drexel represented nothing in particular to him. ("I got the feeling," Peter Slusser, an investment banker from Paine Webber, said later, "that at first Campeau had no idea what I did for a living. He kept referring to me as his broker.") A second theory was that Campeau put himself in a more serious and substantial class of people than the freewheeling predators who trafficked in Drexel's junk. But whatever the reason, Campeau bypassed Drexel and headed straight for the white-shoe investment banks on the Establishment side of the Street. On his list of potential financial backers was a small firm called Morgan Shiff; Goldman, Sachs; Merrill Lynch; Salomon Brothers; and later, First Boston. Neither Campeau nor his advisers really knew one investment bank from another. "It was basically a matter of looking up names in the Yellow Pages," one adviser recalls.

Rising before dawn to jog in Central Park and/or to swim laps, then breakfasting on bran muffins, fresh-squeezed orange juice, and Evian water, Campeau set out to knock on Wall Street's most prestigious doors. He brought along copies of Campeau Corp. annual reports and his two skeptical advisers.

Wearing European-cut suits, his horn-rimmed glasses dangling from a lanyard around his neck, this "who's he?" from Canada, clutching a few pages of analysis from "who's that?" Tribco Partners, began to seek funds for what would amount to the largest retail takeover in history, and of a company that Campeau himself hadn't ever visited. It's even possible that once Campeau became interested in Allied, he never entered an actual Allied store.

Fat chance of getting anywhere with Shearson after the face-lift episode; the Campeau team skipped Shearson. At First Boston, Tysoe had called the switchboard, but couldn't get an interview. No luck either at Goldman, Sachs—the Campeau people hadn't realized that Goldman, Sachs was Allied's regular investment banker.

At Merrill Lynch and Salomon Brothers, Campeau gave his

spiel, similar to the one he'd given Lieutenant Colonel White on the lawn in Bromont, about the "synergies between real estate and retailing." Like Goldman, Sachs, Merrill and Salomon said thanks but no thanks—they also did business with Allied Stores and saw no reason to ruin a profitable relationship for the benefit of strangers from Toronto who fancied themselves takeover artists.

It was zero for four at this point, a result that neither surprised nor dismayed Campeau's two sidekicks, who were somewhat relieved that the marketplace had given the right message, although they were trying to do a good job for the boss. As a last resort, they made an appointment at Paine Webber, where Tom Randall had gotten his start and still had connections. (Late on a Thursday night, Campeau had called Randall wanting him to set up the meeting with Paine Webber the very next day. Doubting that he could accomplish this feat on such short notice, Randall contacted his old firm in the morning, and got Campeau scheduled for the afternoon.)

Paine Webber was suffering from an extreme case of the pecuniary blahs. Since 1979, this large brokerage firm hadn't made much money in the brokerage business. This was not unusual on the Street. With the reduction in commission rates and the increase in competition, nobody was making much money in the brokerage business. From a net profit standpoint, Paine Webber might have been better off to dismiss the staff, sell the buildings, and put the firm's capital into a savings account.

In 1979, Paine Webber diversified into investment banking with its acquisition of Blyth, Eastman, Dillon, which had been Eastman Dillon Union Securities before it merged with Blyth, but whatever you called it, it hadn't done Paine Webber much good. According to IDD information services, which tracks such matters, Paine Webber ranked sixteenth, near the bottom in dealmaking in 1984, handling only $2 billion worth of M&A transactions to Morgan Stanley's $42 billion. In 1985, Paine Webber slipped to twenty-first, and was the principal adviser in only $1.4 billion worth of deals.

Competitors disparaged Paine Webber's M&A department as "rinky dink" or "the amateur hour." Paine Webber preferred to regard itself as highly principled—unwilling, for instance, to stoop to Drexel's level of grabbing other firm's clients or bankrolling greenmailers.*

Recently, Paine Webber had gotten into the swing of things with an ambitious attempt to peddle junk bonds for Carl Icahn, a pioneer greenmailer and a regular client of Drexel's. Icahn needed the money for his hostile takeover of TWA, and Paine Webber allegedly offered him a cheap introductory rate. But as is often the case when principles are compromised for practical advantage, Paine Webber ended up the loser. After staging an enormous "road show" at the Waldorf and luring prospective buyers with the unprecedented offer of free trips from California and Japan, Paine Webber couldn't sell Icahn's junk. A sadder but wiser Paine Webber was forced to bring Drexel back into the deal, and to accept a humiliating demotion to co-manager on the tombstone.†

The Icahn flop ‡ did nothing to improve Paine Webber's reputation, and the M&A department was far from overworked when Campeau called. An unknown Canadian who said he wanted to do a takeover was worth inviting to lunch.

In the formal upstairs dining room, Peter Slusser and J. T. Atkins, representing the firm, listened politely as the man who'd introduced himself as a developer from Canada explained for the fifth time in two days how Allied Stores was an undervalued situation, and how synergistic the merger between the retailer and his real estate operations could be.

Slusser was an honorable, Jimmy Stewart sort of chap, an old-fashioned investment banker who believed in the Gentleman's Code and who had a particular liking for Canadians. He told Campeau that Paine Webber was an old-fashioned and honorable firm that

---

* A greenmailer was someone who launched a takeover raid against a company with no intention of actually acquiring it. The idea was to scare the company into paying an inflated price for the greenmailer's stock, to be rid of him.

† The tombstone is the formal announcement of any deal, published in the financial press, and analyzed carefully for the placement of the names of the various participating firms. Upper-left corner is more prestigious than right, etc. Wall Street followed the tombstones the way that Washington watchers follow the embassy guest lists—a way to determine who was in and who was out.

‡ Icahn actually acquired TWA and as of this writing still owns the company, so in this case, his bid wasn't greenmail.

specialized in friendly takeovers, avoided hostile takeovers, and would have nothing to do with greenmailers.

Putting himself in the Paine Webber spirit, Campeau assured Slusser that he was not a greenmailer, but rather a serious contender for the ownership of Allied Stores, which was a great fit with Campeau Corp., and that a friendly takeover would be just fine with him. (Campeau's aides don't recall any prior discussion of "friendly" in their planning up to that point; but having gone zero for four, they were prepared to approve of anything Paine Webber suggested, even writing up a contract in Sanskrit). Campeau was adamant about one thing: he wanted nothing to do with junk bonds.

Slusser soon concluded that the real estate developer sitting across from him was not likely to take over Allied Stores in either a friendly or a hostile deal, with junk bonds or without, so the details were somewhat irrelevant. "At first," says Slusser, "we didn't necessarily think in terms of Campeau's actually acquiring this major U.S. corporation. We thought in terms of initiating some sort of bargaining session on his behalf, with uncertain objectives. Perhaps, in the end, Allied would have taken over Campeau's company. To us, that was more realistic than the other."

Regardless of who was trying harder to please whom—Campeau needed a banker at least as much as Paine Webber needed a client—both sides agreed to form a partnership. For an initial fee of $250,000, Paine Webber agreed to develop a plan for Campeau's friendly acquisition of Allied Stores, however farfetched that prospect seemed to Slusser.

Back at the Waldorf, Roddy and Tysoe shared their amazement that the wild goose chase, on the verge of having been called off, was still on. "Having Paine Webber," says Roddy, "allowed us to trudge along for another six months. Who else would have?"

At Campeau headquarters in Toronto, David King, president of the company and a regular voice of reason, was reportedly infuriated by the boss's continuing fixation with Allied Stores, and that Campeau had hired a major Wall Street firm to help him pursue his wacky objective. He called Toronto banker Sullivan. "What the hell," he wanted to know, "is going on down there?"

Exit Tom Randall. The hard-working Tribco partner who introduced Campeau to Allied in the first place, who did the preliminary research, who never complained about the late-night and early-morning phone calls, who had tried to get a meeting with Finkel-stein, and who had brought Campeau to Paine Webber, was banished from the transaction right after the get-acquainted lunch. Randall sensed that he was being cut out of the deal, and when he raised the issue with his client, Campeau blew up and stormed out of the room. It would be two years and a lawsuit before Randall received any money for his efforts, and his name was never mentioned on a tombstone. In spite of all this, he continued to feel fondly toward Campeau.

# Three

In March 1986, Campeau secretly began to buy shares in Allied through a dummy corporation called Perez Capital. Allied didn't know this, but there were a lot of things that the participants in this clandestine maneuver didn't know about one another. Campeau didn't know that Paine Webber didn't really believe he had any chance to take over Allied. And Paine Webber didn't know about Campeau's nervous breakdowns, or about his two families, with two wives and two sets of children, which he'd maintained for several years in a landlubber's Captain's Paradise.

News of the breakdowns didn't reach Campeau's Wall Street bankers until a year later, in 1987. And news of his two families didn't reach Wall Street until two years later, in 1988. Campeau has since contended that these personal details from an earlier time had nothing to do with his ability to run a business or to manage a leveraged buyout, but there are some, in wisdom of hindsight, who would disagree.

According to reporter Arthur Johnson, who wrote the story for Toronto's *Report on Business* magazine in March 1987, Campeau's first breakdown occurred in 1970–71, after he'd entered into the complicated joint-venture agreement that left him with no control over his own company, as earlier described. In the aftermath of what some called an act of corporate suicide, which Campeau regretted,

Campeau suffered several months of emotional gridlock during which time he was often unable to get out of bed.

On the advice of his brother, Father Oliva, a Catholic priest, Campeau had returned to working with his hands, building a four-car garage at his house in Ottawa. Later during his crisis, he retreated to Florida and spent additional months in therapeutic carpentry, building a house. He returned from Florida a rejuvenated man, and was able to buy back his company with the help of the aforementioned loan from the Vatican.

The second breakdown occurred ten years later in 1980, after Campeau lost the Royal Trustco fight. Johnson reports that Campeau had trouble "coming to grips with it all," and once again dropped out of corporate life, this time to travel for several months. A third breakdown, which allegedly landed Campeau in a sanitorium in 1985, only a short time before he came to see Firpo Taylor about finding an acquisition, is rumored.

These episodes—at least the first two—may have been related to Campeau's romantic oscillations, of which reporter Johnson was ignorant when he wrote his story in 1987, and which Campeau's bankers didn't learn about until the summer of 1988. But it seems that Campeau carried on an exhausting subterfuge during the mid-1960s, in which Clauda, his loyal wife of many years, was the centerpiece of his official above-ground family in Ottawa; while Ilse, his girlfriend, was the centerpiece of his clandestine family in Montreal.

It sounds like bigamy, but Campeau was technically not a bigamist. He was simply a very busy monogamist, who tried desperately to keep both factions satisfied.

A summary of this saga in its full complexity, taken largely from *Campeau: The Building of an Empire,* the 1989 Canadian biography, is as follows:

When Campeau married Clauda Leroux they were both teenagers—she was working in a textile plant and part-time as a waitress; he was working at a munitions plant. After their daughter, Rachelle, was born in 1947, Clauda was unable to bear more children, so they adopted two sons, Jacques and Daniel, from an orphanage in Montreal.

As Campeau's fortunes improved, Clauda continued to do her own housework and to chop her own wood, and apparently at one point even refused to hire a maid, but otherwise adapted well to her husband's growing prosperity. Friends regarded them as a solid, family-oriented pair, and very much in love.

In 1961, the year of the Campeaus' nineteenth wedding anniversary and Bob's thirty-seventh birthday, Ilse Luebbert (blond, German, twenty-one) was cycling around an Ottawa subdivision looking for a job. She stumbled into Allied Building Supply, a Campeau subsidiary (he liked the named Allied even then!), where the boss happened to be attending a staff meeting. Without identifying himself, Campeau took a special interest in Ilse's job application.

Ilse was hired as a stenographer in the fuel-oil division, and the kind man who helped her with her application asked her out to dinner. After a number of dinners, Ilse learned she'd been dating her married boss. The dates continued, and Campeau's Lincoln Continental could be seen parked in front of Ilse's house.

Distressed and confused, Ilse flew home to Germany. Campeau followed her there, and the two of them agreed to be sensible and call the whole thing off. But after Ilse returned to Ottawa, the whole thing started up again. This led to the birth of a son, Robert Campeau, Jr., in 1963.

By this time, Campeau had installed Ilse on a farm outside of Montreal, a convenient driving distance from Ottawa. Ilse knew about Clauda, but Clauda didn't know about Ilse. As far as Clauda was concerned, her husband went to Montreal on business trips.

Meanwhile, Ilse's parents had moved from Germany to Ottawa, but reportedly were kept in the dark about their grandchild. Nor did Campeau's three children in Ottawa realize they had a half-brother in Montreal. It was difficult for Campeau and Ilse to keep their stories straight.

For three years, Campeau kept up this exhausting Clauda-Ilse routine, while somehow finding the energy to do his real estate deals. At headquarters in Ottawa, key employees, aware of the situation, had begun to gossip, which eventually caused Campeau to summon them to a special meeting in which he admitted to his double life. At the same time, he made it clear that he'd never tolerate such behavior on the part of anyone else on the payroll, who'd be fired on the spot for pulling a stunt similar to his. Only an extraordinary person, he said, could stand up to the strain.

Soon, it was common knowledge among employees and friends

that Campeau had an extra family; everyone knew it except Campeau's wife. This made for uncomfortable dinner parties, and friends urged Campeau to tell Clauda the truth. He hemmed and hawed, apparently unable to get up the nerve. Clauda finally learned about Ilse as Ilse was about to have her second child.

This discovery left Clauda devastated, but Campeau now felt free to move in with Ilse. He installed her, along with Robert Jr. and their new baby, Giselle, in a new house in a Montreal suburb. This did not resolve the ambiguity; it only reversed the roles. Whereas Campeau had lived with Clauda and seen Ilse on the sly; now he lived with Ilse and saw Clauda on the sly.

In 1969, Clauda filed for divorce, hoping to resolve the confusion once and for all. It was this divorce action, more than Campeau's having lost control of his company, speculate the authors of *Campeau: The Building of an Empire,* that triggered his first breakdown. Associates said he "aged ten years in one," "looked like a ghost" and was "close to a vegetable." This emotional crisis, the authors argue, led Campeau to spend more time with Clauda back in Ottawa, a disappointment to Ilse in Montreal, who was now pressing Campeau to marry her.

Ilse's discovery that Campeau was seeing Clauda on the sly put him into a funk, deeper apparently, than had Clauda's initial discovery that he was seeing Ilse on the sly. During this period, when he was building the four-car garage in Ottawa, Clauda was trying to nurse him back to health. Not to leave Ilse out, he kept in touch with her by phone.

Accompanied by Clauda, Campeau traveled to Montreal for weekend treatments at the clinic of psychiatrist Alan Mann, later appointed to the Campeau corporate board. (Whether Campeau visited Ilse on these Montreal trips is a matter for conjecture). In 1971, when he retreated to Florida, as mentioned earlier, his daughter Rachelle went with him. Clauda remained in Ottawa with Jacques and Danny, the two adopted children; Ilse stayed in Montreal with Robert Jr. and Giselle.

Convinced that she and her husband were close to reconciliation, Clauda flew to Florida to see Campeau, who promptly flew off to New York to spend a weekend with Ilse on the sly.

By December 1970, the divorce papers had gone through, and Campeau returned to Montreal not to reconcile with Clauda but to marry Ilse. Clauda was crushed by this development, which she learned of from a third party, as Campeau apparently felt unable to tell her the truth directly.

After they were married, Campeau and Ilse moved to Ottawa and built a $600,000 home with an indoor pool surrounded by lounge chairs with built-in stereo headphones, a mile or so from where Clauda was still living. Campeau and his first wife frequently passed each other on the street.

Clauda developed breast cancer and died in 1979. Campeau's three oldest children were upset that their father never visited their mother in her final, dying months.


Allied Stores was oblivious to the fact that it had attracted Campeau's attention. It was the third-largest retail conglomerate in America outside of the chain stores (Sears, J. C. Penney, and K Mart.) Several of Allied's department-store chains had been in business for fifty years or longer, founded by local peddlers, pushcart vendors, or small shopkeepers who thought big. In major cities across America, the story was the same: local pushcart peddler invests modest profits in small store, small store becomes bigger store, bigger store becomes the great downtown emporium where "everything under the sun is sold under one roof," as the advertising often claimed, the name of the emporium becomes a household word, the owner grows very wealthy, his children take over the business, which is handed down to their children, and so on.

Customers speak of having "grown up" on Jordan Marsh or Maas Brothers as if these stores were part of the family, and loyalty to a local department store could be as strong and as enduring as loyalty to a neighborhood church.

A union of family-owned stores was an after-hours project of B. Earl Puckett, a bookkeeper at Loeser's store in Brooklyn. Several retail visionaries had this same idea at once. If the oil companies and the steel companies could combine for mutual benefit, the argument went, why not the so-called merchant princes? Working together, they could save money through centralized buying of merchandise, they could share promotional ideas, they could lobby for tax breaks, they could consolidate back offices and reduce overhead.

Allied was formed by Puckett in 1929, hardly a propitious year for new business ventures, but it survived the Depression and by the 1940s had grown into the nation's largest department-store conglomerate, with sixty-one stores in twenty-one states.

As much as it was a collection of stores, Allied was an expression of Puckett's belief in fair pay and fair play. Meyer's of Greensboro, North Carolina, one of the original stores in the alliance, was a typical example, staking its reputation on its policy that "no exaggerated statement shall ever be made about the merchandise." In speeches at annual meetings, Puckett talked less about profits than about "mutual obligations to the World of Tomorrow," and "standards of achievement below which we cannot—below which we dare not—fall." The Allied spirit was captured in its official logo, in which five well-groomed men dressed in business suits—representing management, stockholders, employees, customers, and manufacturers—stood at attention like male caryatids, supporting a sign that read "The Allied Partnership."

By the 1960s, the Allied partnership had lost its number-one ranking to the flashier Federated Department Stores, a rival alliance that had managed to attract the top retailers in several places where an Allied store was second-best. Where Allied sold clothes, Federated sold fashion. Federated was run by merchants, and Allied was run by a lawyer, the snappish and much-feared Thomas Macioce, whom the employees called the Bean Counter.

Like all department-store companies, Allied faced a series of dilemmas caused by the migration of millions of customers to the suburbs, where they preferred to shop in malls. Retailers in general were as unprepared for this exodus to the malls as U.S. automakers were unprepared for the arrival of the foreign car. They stood by, somewhat helplessly, as one department-store item after another— toys, books, appliances, shoes, sporting goods, stereos, pots, TVs, lawn furniture—made their debuts on the shelves of the discount specialty outlets.

Allied struggled to keep up with the trends. It put its own department stores into malls. It got into specialty retailing belatedly, by acquiring Brooks Brothers, Ann Taylor, and Bonwit Teller, along with Jerry Leonard's for big men and Catherine's for big women in all-cash buyouts. All cash was the primitive way in which takeovers were accomplished in the backward 1960s.

Since that time, under the conservative, tight-fisted rule of the

Bean Counter, Allied had continued to produce a steady, if unspec-
tacular profit. It had a solid balance sheet with almost no debt. It
provided safe and steady employment to 70,000 people. It owned
substantial real estate assets. The company was in some ways outmoded, but certainly in no danger of extinction.


Slusser of Paine Webber was invited by Campeau to visit the mansion in Toronto, where he admired the twenty-three hour clock from
the French Revolution and met Ilse. At Campeau's Fourth of July
celebration to honor Americans, Slusser gave a toast to Canadian-
American friendship. Campeau invited him to go moose hunting,
but Slusser declined. Slusser invited Campeau to visit the vineyard
country in California.

Though he and Campeau never discussed personal matters,
Slusser was impressed with Campeau's flair, his quick grasp of numbers, his "global vision," his impromptu lectures on world politics,
and his passionate commitment to taking over Allied Stores.
Granted, the 5 A.M. phone calls to which Slusser was now subjected
were bothersome, but in this honeymoon phase of the partnership,
Slusser considered the need to chat before dawn to be one of Campeau's charming eccentricities. "Clearly," Slusser recalls, "he was
not your typical Wall Street type."

More important, by checking with a few independent sources in
Toronto, Paine Webber had determined that Campeau was a respected real estate developer who could pay his bills—a perfectly
reasonable basis for representing him. Slusser had heard nothing
about nervous breakdowns or mistresses or double families.

Paine Webber's plan, as it evolved from the various strategy
lunches, was for Campeau to buy a sizable chunk of Allied stock, as
he was already doing, then approach the CEO, Macioce, about cooperating in some sort of friendly deal. Further study of Campeau
Corp. assets had reinforced Slusser's suspicion that a hostile takeover
was out of the question, since Campeau would have to borrow up to
$2.5 billion to buy all of Allied's nearly 50 million shares at a likely
final price somewhere near $50 a share, which was the top of what
Slusser thought was a sensible price range.

Not only did the potential price tag seem risky to Slusser, but he
didn't expect that Campeau could borrow up to $2.5 billion with

only $100–150 million for a down payment (equity), which is what Campeau had told Paine Webber that he could put up.

In order to give the appearance of being a serious contender—for otherwise nothing would come of this—Campeau needed a good lawyer. Not just any lawyer would do. He had to be a takeover specialist from a firm that handled important M&A deals. And the firm had to be one that didn't represent Allied Stores, a situation known on Wall Street as "being conflicted."

Around the Paine Webber office, Slusser used a code system adapted from his military days in the Air Research and Development Command to protect the secrecy of Express, which is the name that Campeau had given to his mission. In shopping for a law firm that wasn't conflicted with Allied, Slusser camouflaged his inquiry by sticking Allied's name in among other company names on a long list, then showing the list to various attorneys and asking them to indicate which of the companies they already represented.

It's a tribute to the industriousness of the New York legal establishment, and to Macioce's clever defensive tactic of engaging as many lawyers as possible (that way, whom could a potential corporate raider hire?) that Slusser couldn't find a big-name firm that wasn't doing business with Allied Stores. It seemed that every corporate attorney in town was involved in some fashion or another with this one company. It wasn't by accident that the legal profession was growing twice as fast as the GNP.

In desperation, Slusser contacted Samuel Butler, an old rugby pal from Harvard, and also a partner at prestigious Cravath, Swaine & Moore. Cravath had many famous clients, including IBM and Time Inc., but miraculously had avoided doing any legal work for Allied Stores. Cravath also represented Paine Webber itself, but Slusser had run out of options. He was willing to find another lawyer to represent Paine Webber's interest in this deal if Cravath would agree to represent Campeau.

As a favor to his old college chum, Butler agreed to a preliminary consultation with the representatives of the Canadian businessman whom Slusser had so highly recommended. Thus, the high school dropout from the moonscape of Sudbury became the unlikely beneficiary of a Harvard rugby connection. Butler handed off the assignment to Allen Finkelson, an in-house M&A expert and master takeover strategist.

Ushered to the fifty-seventh-floor waiting room at Cravath's headquarters, Campeau could see, affixed to the wall, the Cravath attorney's tree, which traced the firm's jurisprudential lineage back to the 1880s. A secretary escorted him to one of the conference rooms.

Campeau was wearing a large hat with a feather in it, giving him the dashing look of a French boulevardier, and he carried a sack of Bing cherries. It was the first time that anyone at Cravath could remember a prospective client bringing a bag of fruit to a meeting.

Finkelson watched with fascination as Campeau chomped on cherries while revealing his plan: a friendly takeover of Allied Stores. Finkelson, who'd once worked in the investment banking department at Lehman Brothers, was impressed by two things: the man's obvious, if naive, enthusiasm; and the absurdity of his proposition. There was no way, Finkelson thought, that Tom Macioce, Allied's combative CEO, would agree to be taken over by this condo builder from Toronto.

Those who doubted that Campeau could acquire Allied stores had grown into a large crowd that included Campeau's brain trust at the Waldorf; his advisers back in Toronto; his Toronto bankers, Sullivan and Taylor; his advisers from Paine Webber; and now his lawyer, Finkelson of Cravath. Finkelson's doubts were no more a deterrent to his accepting the assignment than Paine Webber's had been. Like Slusser, Finkelson was charmed by Campeau's quirky bravado, and besides, Campeau had come recommended by Paine Webber.

After hearing Campeau swear he wasn't a greenmailer (how everybody on Wall Street detested greenmailers!)* and making a couple of phone calls to Canada to confirm that Campeau was the big-time real estate developer he claimed to be, Finkelson accepted the job. One of America's best-known law firms was now in Campeau's corner.

To make a serious bid for Allied Stores, as Campeau intended, or even to make a chimerical bid that might lead to productive

---

* One reason Wall Street hated greenmailers was that the fees on a greenmail deal, where the intent was only to cow a hapless company into paying a big price to buy back the greenmailer's stock, were paltry as compared to the fees for doing complete takeovers. Some firms ultimately required a share of the greenmail profits if the "real deal" never took place.

barter, as some of his advisers expected would happen, required money. The cash itself didn't have to be there—needless to say, Campeau didn't have $2.5 to $3 billion. What was required was the promise of cash, which various reliable sources would provide for a fee.

So far, what Campeau had was Paine Webber's assurance that it could raise a considerable chunk of the necessary amount by selling junk bonds, the Icahn fiasco notwithstanding. The role of the investment bank was to provide the so-called unsecured or subordinated debt portion of the takeover funds, and the junk bond market had created a seemingly inexhaustible supply of capital for just this sort of undertaking. Campeau, however, insisted from the outset that he was opposed to junk bonds, and Slusser hadn't bothered to press the point.

Junk bonds in themselves weren't enough to launch a credible offer anyway. Along with this unsecured debt, which was called junk for a reason, Campeau would also need some secured debt— money that a commercial bank would agree to loan against the assets of the would-be target, Allied.

Before the Great Depression, commercial banks and investment banks were indivisible. They were separated by Congress during the national economic hangover from the pecuniary binges of the late 1920s. Bankers' reputations, in the aftermath, had fallen lower than those of croupiers.

This was not entirely undeserved. For instance, Citicorp, then called the National City Company, had underwritten and touted to the public two issues of Peruvian 7 percent bonds in 1927–28, which originally sold for $96.50 per unit and dropped to $5 by 1932. In the summer of 1929, National City had sold and recommended Anaconda Copper at $100 a share, which by June of 1932 was selling for $4.

These two well-publicized horror stories were given considerable attention at Senate hearings in 1933 as symbolic of Wall Street's reckless venality, which brought about the 1929 Crash. That banks could accept deposits through one door and fritter away the money in risky underwritings and speculations out the other was believed to be the principal culprit in the financial collapse that cost many Americans their life savings.

The U.S. Congress, responding to angry constituents, passed

the Glass-Steagall Act in 1932. This required each bank to declare itself a commercial bank (which would be permitted to take in deposits and make mortgage and business loans), or an investment bank (permitted to underwrite stocks and bonds). The bifurcation, in theory, would prevent bankers from gambling with depositors' money on rank speculations such as IOUs from Peru.

In practice, commercial banks were still free to make bad loans to Latin America directly, and also to loan money to endless real estate projects of dubious plausibility, as well as to many highly unprofitable real estate investment trusts (REITS). They were also free to loan money on the secured side of mergers, acquisitions, and/ or leveraged buyouts, where they joined forces with the investment bankers underwriting the junk bonds in a widespread reunion of forces.

In the Lark Ages of the 1980s, the commercial banks, the same as the investment banks, found the M&A business to be one of the bright spots on their balance sheets. The corporate loan departments had to compete with commercial paper and letters of credit, as more and more corporations borrowed from each other rather than from banks. As millions of once-captive clients of savings accounts abandoned the bank for money-market funds, banks were forced to offer higher rates of interest to hold on to their depositors. The fierce competition for deposits as well as loans created a double whammy: banks paid more for money, and they got back less.

By the time Campeau appeared on Wall Street, commercial banks were making their biggest profits from secured loans to corporate raiders. They charged huge fees, into the tens of millions, for simply writing commitment letters promising to make takeover loans, many of which never materialized.

But Campeau was having a hard time finding a commercial bank to commit itself to the Allied takeover. In Canada where the bankers knew him best, most wanted no part of it. There was no sense asking Toronto Dominion Bank. Its CEO, Richard Thomson, was engaged in a long-running feud with Campeau dating back to Royal Trustco. In fact, Thomson was holed up in a building that Campeau needed to demolish in order to begin construction on his Scotia Plaza high rise. Campeau reportedly had threatened to bring the walls down on Thomson's head.

Among the less acrimonious prospects, Canada's bankers generally shared the view that Campeau was foolish to lurch into retailing and was in no financial shape to produce the equity that surely would be required. Phrases such as "Tevye without a fiddle" were bandied about the mahogany-paneled men's clubs.

At the Canadian Imperial Bank of Commerce, where the bankers asked about the location of the Allied shopping centers, Campeau's chief financial officer, Jim Roddy, had to admit he didn't know. Even at the friendly Bank of Nova Scotia, which for years had been Campeau's lead bank in real estate, Cedric Ritchie advised Campeau against getting involved with Allied. Aware of Ritchie's position, Campeau's brain trust had set up a meeting between him and Campeau early on, as part of the "realities of the marketplace" campaign. Old-timers King and Carroll, especially, hoped that Ritchie would tell Campeau to blow off.

Undaunted by these Canadian rejections, Campeau flew to California with Roddy and Tysoe, to meet with commercial bankers there. "We were worried," said Roddy, "that banks in New York would be conflicted with Allied, so we went as far away as possible, the West Coast."

Visiting a bank with Campeau was an unnerving experience for his staff. His English wasn't perfect, and he didn't always hear well. He could be extremely ingratiating, then fly into a rage. At any moment, he might break into an economics lecture, or a Soviet politics lecture, or a lecture on the strength of the Deutschemark. He'd forget people's names. He'd spew forth facts and figures, some of which were highly fanciful, and if a banker challenged him, he'd bristle or worse. At First Interstate of California, he stormed out of the room. "Our idea," says one of his aides, "was to let Bob speak last at these meetings, and then hold our breaths."

Campeau had no luck in California; "nobody out there wanted to do 100 percent debt deals with unknown Canadians," Roddy recalls. In midsummer of 1986, the Campeau team returned to New York, hitting all the banks they'd tried to avoid in the first place. One of them was Citicorp, America's most prominent commercial bank, then under great pressure from Wall Street analysts to increase profits every quarter. Citicorp was doing a brisk trade in commitment letters.

The initial get-to-know-Campeau session, held in a windowless conference room in Citicorp's New York headquarters, did not go well. Campeau was charming to begin with, but threw a temper tantrum in the middle of the presentation after one of the younger bankers questioned his math. Campeau shouted, and the banker shouted back.

This was Citicorp's first clue they were dealing with a volatile character, who soon acquired the in-house nickname Mad Bomber. Whether the bank should have anything to do with this Mad Bomber was hotly debated. The pro-Campeau faction won the debate with three persuasive arguments: (1) if all went well, Campeau might use Citicorp as his banker in future real estate deals; (2) a peek at Allied's balance sheet showed there was more than enough collateral to cover a Citicorp secured takeover loan; and (3) Campeau intimated he could put up to $300 million of his own money on the table as equity.

In mid-July, Citicorp decided to formally back the Campeau bid for Allied Stores with a commitment to provide up to $500 million in secured loans, and to raise another $490 million from a syndicate of other banks. This was for the so-called Phase 1 of the acquisition, when Campeau would buy a controlling interest in Allied. (In Phase 2, Campeau would acquire the rest of the company and the entire deal would be refinanced. Citicorp said it could provide $500 million for that, and could syndicate another $1.8 billion from other banks).

Citicorp's role was very hush-hush. A team of young bankers, led by Jean Michel Gal, was recruited within Citicorp to work undercover on Project Express behind a so-called "Chinese wall." Even Gal's immediate boss knew nothing about it.

On July 25, while on a chartered boat at Expo '86 in Vancouver, Campeau received the news that Citicorp had offered its commitment—for three weeks! "This commitment shall expire at 5 P.M. on August 15," the letter read, "unless accepted and a copy of this letter is returned and you have sent to Citibank $3 million nonrefundable, of which $1 million is due on delivery of this commitment."

"Valid for only three weeks!" Campeau stormed. "A million dollars up front!" "He couldn't believe," says one of his advisers, "that a bank could hold somebody up for that much, for a three-week option to borrow money. It was worse than a neighborhood loan shark."

After further haggling, the term was stretched to five weeks, and Campeau paid the $1 million, and then the $2 million after that, his biggest out-of-pocket outlays since the Allied escapade had begun. Campeau was getting in deeper. His advisers reassured themselves that as the price of Allied increased, Campeau could always sell his stake and use the profits to pay the expenses of this lengthy misadventure.

# Four

By summer's end, Campeau had bought 2.1 million shares of Allied stock at an average price of $46.61, with funds borrowed from his own Campeau Corp. He owned 4 percent of Allied. He still had his commitment from Citicorp, plus a smaller $150 million commitment from the Bank of Montreal—one Canadian bank that did come into the deal. The plan Campeau developed with Paine Webber was that he would offer Allied shareholders a combination of cash and securities (paper) with a value of between $45 and $50 a share.

The next step was for Campeau to visit Tom Macioce, the CEO of Allied, and politely inform him of Campeau's interest in the company. "An LBO with Campeau financing," says Peter Slusser, "was the concept our client was prepared to tee up."

Slusser, who by this time was tiring of the predawn chats, set up a meeting for August 1. It took place in Macioce's office in the old W. R. Grace Building in midtown Manhattan, where the decor reflected Macioce's penurious touch, functional and unostentatious. In keeping with the spirit of her surroundings, Macioce's personal secretary had stuck with her manual typewriter.

Like Campeau, Macioce had grown up Catholic and poor, but there the similarities ended. Campeau took the independent route to riches; Macioce advanced in the certified way, earning a law degree from Columbia University, working up through the ranks of the legal department into Allied's top position, then running the company with a competent and heavy hand. Campeau was a maverick in Toronto in spite of his success; Macioce was a corporate fixture in New York. He raised money for Columbia University, and he sat on the board of several big corporations, including the Manufacturers Hanover Trust bank.

Macioce's connections were often cited as one of the reasons that Allied Stores had been left alone by corporate raiders—he'd already tied up most of the big law firms and the big banks. When executives of the May Department Stores Company of St. Louis were looking at possible acquisitions in 1985, they narrowed the choice to Allied and Associated Dry Goods. They chose the latter because they feared that Macioce was too formidable an opponent and would "only go out in a pine box," as one of them put it.

But where the May Company hadn't dared to tread, Campeau had rushed in. Macioce sat attentively behind his desk as Campeau introduced himself, then gave more or less the same speech he'd given on Lieutenant Colonel White's lawn, congratulating the CEO of Allied on his fine leadership to date, offering him an important role in the new, improved Allied, which under Campeau's experienced guidance would surely benefit from the synergies between retailing and real estate. Campeau also offered Macioce a 15 percent equity stake in the new enterprise, for him to split with Macioce's fellow executives.

The gist of Campeau's speech can be gotten from a letter to Macioce he wrote later:

Dear Tom:
    As you know from our recent discussions, we have great respect for Allied Stores and its management team and believe that a business combination with Campeau Corporation would serve the best interests of Allied and its shareholders. We have decided that it is appropriate for us to propose that Campeau Corporation acquire Allied stores. . . .

Macioce could afford to be gracious, an amused spectator at the stranger's entertaining little monologue. Prior to the meeting, he'd made some phone calls of his own, and learned things that somehow had eluded Campeau's Wall Street allies—that Campeau had suffered emotional breakdowns, that he flitted from one grand scheme to another, that he lacked the equity to back up a serious bid for a company the size of Allied. Around the office before the meeting, Macioce was saying that Campeau was a "flake" who was "as thin as a ham sandwich." He refused to get upset over nothing.

As Campeau rambled, Macioce tried to figure out what the Canadian had up his sleeve. Even a flake in Campeau's position, Macioce presumed, wouldn't delude himself into thinking he had a chance to take over Allied Stores, so there must be some other rationale for Campeau's visit, some hidden agenda behind the ridiculous cover story about a takeover. What about the shopping centers? Yes, that must be it, Macioce decided. Campeau was a real estate guy who owned shopping centers, and Allied had shopping centers it wanted to sell, so Campeau must be feigning a takeover to scare Allied into selling the centers at a cheap price.

These shopping centers were the very ones that had caused Randall to bring Allied to Campeau's attention in the first place.

"Allied isn't for sale," Macioce told Campeau. Then, at a second meeting held on August 15, when Campeau insisted he wanted to buy the whole company, Macioce tried to bring the shopping centers to the surface. "Allied isn't for sale," Macioce again declared, "but we've got some real estate."

A third meeting was held on August 18. Again, Macioce mentioned the shopping centers, again Campeau insisted he wanted to buy the whole company, again Macioce reiterated that the company wasn't for sale. But by this time a remarkable turnabout had occurred. Campeau agreed to consider buying the shopping centers, as Macioce had suggested.

This was an abrupt reversal, coming as it did after several months of Allied or Bust. Given the Campeau tradition of abrupt reversals, this one was not entirely surprising to Campeau's advisers, but it was unexpected. Round the clock they'd worked, through one setback after another, and Campeau remained steadfast: he wanted Allied Stores. They'd signed up with Paine Webber, they'd signed up with Citicorp, and now, after all this effort, Campeau was volunteering to settle for a shopping-center deal? Had reality finally set in?

But theirs was not to wonder why, theirs was to help Campeau negotiate for the five Allied shopping centers, which had become the newest objective. In late August, a flurry of exchanges between Macioce's office and Campeau's suite on the fortieth floor of the Waldorf Towers established the basic facts, such as the cash flow from these properties, and also their location—Tacoma, Kennewick, and Seattle in Washington; Paramus, New Jersey; and Peabody, Massachusetts.

As it turned out, there was no deal for the shopping centers, as Campeau had imagined out of the blue, because he and Macioce were unable to settle on a price. Campeau offered $300 million, which was $50 million less than someone else had offered previously, and Macioce, a veteran haggler himself, was not about to be low-balled by a flake from Canada.

Campeau wasn't budging, either—he hadn't gotten where he was by budging. Once, at a retirement party for a longtime employee, he tried to make a deal to buy back the man's Campeau Corp. stock at a favorable price. Once, the sale of his house in Ottawa to his own daughter was stalled over his insistence that the washer/dryer unit didn't come with the property and still belonged to him. Once, the sale of a $600,000 apartment building in Ottawa was held up while Campeau and the buyer argued over who got to keep the lawn mower.

According to his Canadian biographers, if the Ottawa zoning codes set a height limit of 325 feet for new buildings, as they did in certain sectors of the city in the 1960s, Campeau demanded 450 feet. When government officials acceded to 342 feet, Campeau offered to compromise at 375. When they held him to the 342-foot requirement, he put up a 342-foot building, but with an extra 28-foot "pimple" for rooftop equipment. Campeau argued that the extra 28 feet didn't count as part of the building's formal height. His opponents saw it as another example of his relentless oneupmanship. Eventually, he would be suing and countersuing his own children over voting rights to the stock in their trust funds. Could this man be expected to give in to Macioce on the price of five shopping centers? Three hundred million dollars, he told the CEO of Allied Stores, take it or leave it.

Macioce left it. "He's playing rope-a-dope," Finkelson advised his client in mid-September, referring to the famous stalling tactics of boxer Muhammad Ali. "He never had any intention of selling you the shopping centers in the first place."

Macioce's colleagues insist that this wasn't a rope-a-dope, and that Macioce would have sold Campeau the shopping centers if Campeau had offered a reasonable price. In any event, Campeau once again was spurned, his shopping center bid turned down on September 3, when Macioce called off any further discussion on the matter.

The list of spurners grew longer by the day: Lieutenant Colonel White of Royal Trustco, Ed Finkelstein of Macy's, Shearson Lehman, Morgan Stanley, Canadian banks, California banks, and now the Allied leadership. On September 4, a resolute Campeau, more determined than ever to take over Allied Stores, proposed a formal offer to Macioce: $58 a share for all the shares of Allied, 80 percent of which would be cash, and 20 percent securities—preferred stock in the new enterprise.

"We are confident that all necessary funding can be obtained and that there will not be any impediments to a rapid consummation of our proposed transaction," Campeau wrote in his letter. "Indeed, Citibank N.A. . . . will lead our banking syndicate."

For a brief moment after making this latest proposal, Campeau imagined that Macioce had capitulated and agreed to sell the whole company. "I think we've got a deal," he exclaimed one day to Tysoe, his corporate vice president, after leaving Allied headquarters where he'd discussed the formal offer with Macioce. "Where's a phone? We've got to call Finkelson. We've got to find a phone."

When a frantic search through lobbies failed to produce a phone that worked, Campeau ducked into a seedy-looking rooming house.

"A room for ten minutes," Campeau asked the day clerk, "how much?" "Twenty bucks," the clerk said, apparently accustomed to such requests. "Ten bucks," Campeau countered, never missing a chance to haggle. "Has it got a telephone?"

So for ten bucks, the CEO of Campeau Corp. and his vice president got a room for ten minutes, long enough for Campeau to call Allen Finkelson and alert him that the sale of Allied Stores was about to be consummated in friendly fashion.

Alas, the deal that Campeau imagined he'd made with Macioce did not coincide with the facts. Allied Stores had no interest in considering a friendly offer, just as Campeau's lawyer had predicted. There was but one course of action left short of going home: make a hostile bid to the shareholders, and conquer Allied against the management's will. What neither Paine Webber nor Finkelson had thought Campeau capable of doing, they were now helping him to do.

Slusser of Paine Webber had expressed his distaste for hostile deals at the initial meeting with Campeau in July—how quickly this resistance was overcome as soon as Campeau decided to do one in September. Paine Webber, in fact, was delighted to continue to participate in this zany escalation of the Allied/Campeau conflict. In fact, it was Campeau who wanted to be rid of Paine Webber. He'd become convinced that Paine Webber lacked the experience to mastermind a multibillion-dollar hostile.

Finkelson was also aware of Paine Webber's potential shortcomings in this situation. Initially, he had had his doubts that Campeau could pull off any sort of Allied takeover, hostile or otherwise, with or without Paine Webber, so it hadn't really mattered who the investment banker was. But since Campeau had decided to play hardball, Finkelson's job was to give good advice and improve his chances.

Those chances were bad enough as it was, and worse with Paine Webber involved. Granted, this was a sensitive issue, since Paine Webber was the only investment bank that had supported Campeau in the first place. Moreover, Paine Webber had introduced Campeau to Finkelson and gotten Finkelson this lucrative assignment, and Slusser and Finkelson's boss, Sam Butler, were good friends. But loyalty was one thing, and duty to bill-paying clients another, and as a frustrated investment banker himself, Finkelson acceded to Campeau's view that Paine Webber wasn't up to the challenge—however dubious—of Campeau's hostile bid.

The tricky public relations problem was how to find a replacement for Paine Webber before Paine Webber got wind of what was happening: otherwise, it might get mad and quit on its own, leaving Campeau with no investment bank at all. So, employing the same discretion with which Paine Webber had searched for Campeau's lawyer, Campeau's lawyer now searched for a substitute for Paine Webber. The first week in September, Finkelson quietly convened a "beauty contest" to which three prominent firms were invited.

·   ·   ·

A remarkable pilgrimage was soon on its way to Campeau's Waldorf suite—Eric Gleacher from Morgan Stanley; James Stern and J. Tomilson Hill from Shearson Lehman; and Bruce Wasserstein, Joseph Perella, and Kim Fennebresque from First Boston. These three firms had done more than $200 billion in M&A transactions in 1985 alone.

How things had changed in six months. Shearson had wanted nothing further to do with Campeau after the face-lift incident; Morgan Stanley had rebuffed him as "not serious"; and First Boston had refused even to grant him an initial interview. Now all three were competing for his business.

In spite of their up-to-date communications systems, neither the Shearson emissaries nor the Morgan Stanley emissary knew of their own firms' previous run-ins with Campeau during his S&L phase, and Wasserstein was likewise unaware that the Campeau team had attempted to see him at First Boston in early summer. None of them, in fact, had heard of Campeau at all. What sent them scrambling to the Waldorf was a tip from Finkelson: "a guy from Canada wants to do a hostile."

By the fall of 1986, merger fever had reached such a pitch that a tip from a lawyer that somebody was thinking of doing a deal caused the most prominent whizbangs in M&A to grab their calculators and their overcoats. Finkelson's word was particularly good with Wasserstein, since the two of them had worked together as junior partners at Cravath.

Perhaps sensing that the tables had turned, Campeau received Shearson in his jogging suit, and Morgan Stanley—according to Gleacher—wearing an open shirt with a gold chain, and the Rolex, the dictator's watch, on his wrist. When he received First Boston, Campeau sat on his couch with his legs tucked up underneath him. One of the buttons on his shirt had popped open, exposing a hairy navel that the First Boston team was forced to contemplate as they made their presentation.

Wasserstein's appearance at the Waldorf was particularly impressive. This portly, disheveled financier in Coke-bottle-thick glasses, about whom his colleagues joked behind his back "he plays tennis in black socks," was the recognized grand master of the M&A game.

Wasserstein's highly publicized successes—Texaco's $10 billion acquisition of Getty Oil, DuPont's purchase of Conoco, Occidental

Petroleum's purchase of Cities Service, the sale of Marathon Oil to U.S. Steel, the Capital Cities–ABC merger, Philip Morris's acquisition of Kraft—were principal reasons that one out of ten Yale graduates applied for a job at First Boston in 1986, and that 30 percent of Harvard Business School graduates ended up in the M&A departments of the top four firms. The M&A game, with billions of dollars at stake and admiring journalists on the sidelines, had come to play the same role in suburban white folklore as professional basketball played in the ghetto.

The salaries were phenomenal—a rookie just out of an MBA program could easily make $150,000 to $200,000 a year; a junior partner in his early to mid thirties, $1–2 million; a senior partner, $2–3 million, and all-stars like Wasserstein could get $6 million, $7 million, $10 million—there was no limit. Since most of this money came in the bonuses doled out at the end of the year, there was a salesman's pressure to produce, which meant doing deals.

The hours were like college hours—with a deal in progress, the bankers would stay up for days at a time, taking catnaps on couches, subsisting on adrenaline, caffeine, and leftover Chinese food. The vocabulary was the macho vocabulary of the locker room: "teeing up the concept"; "slam dunk"; coaxing a ridiculously high bid from a naive adversary was a "hat trick"; a successful junk bond sale was a "home run."* The offices of investment bankers were executive romper rooms, filled with balls and hoops and Lucite "deal toys," the souvenirs of victory.

Wasserstein wouldn't have fit in at First Boston in the stuffier, more complacent days when the underwriting department was called the House of Lords and the trading department the House of Commons. As a teenager, Wasserstein had lived on Park Avenue, but he was hardly what you'd call a Park Avenue type. His father was a small businessman and inventor from Brooklyn, who devised a method for turning velveteen into ribbon, and later made a sizable fortune in real estate. His elementary school was the yeshiva of Flatbush. His mother, reportedly, was the inspiration for Tasha Blum-

---

* In describing takeovers, the financial press often ignored the locker-room vocabulary of the participants, and chose instead to glorify deals with allusions from medieval chivalry—hence, white knights, crown-jewel stratagems, etc.

berg, the middle-aged fitness nut who carried her spare leotards in a briefcase in the highly acclaimed play *Isn't It Romantic?* written by Wendy Wasserstein, Bruce's sister.

In any event, the Wasserstein family of Brooklyn and later Park Avenue produced a genius playwright and a genius takeover strategist, as well as a second daughter who advanced to the presidency of the communications division of American Express. The late Paul Cowan once described this early-childhood scene in an article in *Esquire:*

"When Bruce Wasserstein was eleven years old, in the late 1950s, he and his kid sister, Wendy, used to spend their Friday nights in the living room of their parents' home in the Midwood section of Brooklyn watching TV and playing Monopoly. As Wendy recalls it, Bruce—now one of the most innovative, successful deal makers on Wall Street—used to deal the properties out instead of waiting for the tokens to land on them. According to the rules he'd devised, you could supplement the money you got from your opponent with cash borrowed from the bank—and risk building up to three hotels per lot. That way, Monopoly became a game between real estate moguls, not between children whose fate was determined by a roll of the dice."

The Talmudic method that Wasserstein learned in the yeshiva, the paternal money gene, the free spirit of Tasha Blumberg, and playing Monopoly by made-up rules were all perfect preparation for a career in the M&A game, which required a legal mind, a strong urge to get rich, and a creative playfulness with corporate regulations. But Wasserstein was not aware he'd been preparing for Wall Street. First, he had to get through the sixties, when he edited the student newspaper at the University of Michigan, and spent his summers working in poverty programs and then for Ralph Nader. Then he got a law degree and an MBA from Harvard.

At one point, Wasserstein's great ambition was to own a small-town newspaper or to become a lawyer in Alaska, but he settled in New York instead, and there, for want of anything better to do, he took a job at Cravath, Swaine & Moore, the same law firm whose curious destiny it was to represent Campeau.

Mergers and acquisitions hardly existed when Wasserstein signed on with Cravath. M&A was more experiment than career when Wasserstein was hired away from Cravath by the recently organized M&A department at First Boston.

There, Wasserstein was the acclaimed inventor of several ploys and counterploys that won him the grudging admiration of his peers in the merger business, who regarded him as the Clausewitz of deals. In 1983, a formal portrait of Wasserstein and his two children, floating in an extravagance of white space that you'd normally see in an art publication, appeared in *Fortune* under the headline "The Innovator," alongside this fawning text:

"First Boston's merger and acquisition department 'wasn't even on the charts' in 1977 when Bruce Wasserstein, 35, handled his first major deal, Combustion Engineering's takeover of Vetco, an oil and gas equipment and services company: Shortly afterward, Wasserstein became a new father. The mergers department and daughter Pamela—perched in Wasserstein's chair beside her two-year-old brother Ben—have grown up together. Wasserstein is proud that First Boston participated in four of the top five deals of 1982. Wasserstein is widely credited with inventing maneuvers like the two-tier tender and the crown-jewel stratagem, in which a company tries to make itself unappealing to a raider by selling off prized operations to a white knight."

What deals he and his sidekick, Joe Perella, who first hired Wasserstein for this sort of brilliance and then was condemned to labor in his shadow, had done. The M&A department they established at First Boston, which some likened to an ongoing student uprising in the midst of a catered party at a polo club, helped the firm to a record $125 million in earnings in 1985, a long way from the $1 million it had earned, before M&A gathered its lucrative momentum, in 1978.

That the great Wasserstein had bothered to come to the Waldorf to confront Campeau and his hairy navel we can take as strong evidence that no possible deal was being ignored. But Wasserstein and Perella were not impressed with the details of Campeau's plans. Campeau's people wanted to raise some of the money by selling "preferreds with warrants," a type of security used occasionally in small buyouts, but not applicable to this kind of transaction. That Campeau would suggest such a thing, which apparently Paine Webber had gone along with, struck the First Boston team as particularly yokelish.

Famous for giving would-be clients a rousing "dare to be great" speech, Wasserstein instead wondered out loud if Campeau was in this for greenmail. (How Wall Street continued to hate representing greenmailers!) He also observed semipolitely, "Your description of what you are doing and how you are doing it makes me realize you aren't serious. Come back when you are."

Leaving the Waldorf convinced of Campeau's lack of sophistication, and asking themselves, "Who is this guy that Finkelson recommended?" the First Bostonians were halfway down the block when they ran into Sam Belzberg, whom Perella recognized.

This was Samuel Belzberg of the notorious Canadian greenmailing Belzbergs, who'd recently held up Lear Siegler and Ashland Oil for millions. "Hey, Sam," Perella chirped, "know anything about a guy named Campeau?"

"Yeah, I've heard of him," said Belzberg. "But I don't know much about him."

"When you have to ask Sam Belzberg for a reference, you're already in trouble," was the joke that went around First Boston.

Gleacher of Morgan Stanley was even less impressed with Campeau's plan to do a hostile than Wasserstein was. "As I sat there listening to him," Gleacher recalls, "it occurred to me that nothing the man was saying made any sense."[*]

It was Shearson's high-powered representatives, Tom Hill[†] and Jim Stern, who hit it off with Campeau. Unsophisticated or not, the

---

[*] Campeau's aides say that the $25–30 million that Gleacher threw out as an estimate of the possible fees made them think it was Gleacher who wasn't making any sense. "Bob almost fainted at those numbers," says a Campeau team member. "He didn't get mad, he just said, 'We'll have to get back to you.'" Gleacher said, "Look, this is the big leagues. Here's the kind of money you are talking about.' Turns out Gleacher was right."

Gleacher denies having this conversation.

[†] Hill and Wasserstein were professional rivals who earlier worked together at First Boston. Wasserstein, the story went, had sold Hill on the advantages of both of them leaving First Boston and going elsewhere, but when Hill accepted a job at Smith Barney, Wasserstein stayed put. Hill watchers suspected that this was Wasserstein's clever way of getting rid of him.

guy in the jogging suit had charisma, he seemed to be serious about his bid for Allied Stores, and perhaps most important, he seemed to react favorably to Hill and Stern. Elated that they'd made a positive impression with a new potential source of revenue, the two Shearson bankers returned to headquarters at the World Financial Center. There, they found an even bigger potential source of revenue sitting in the corporate dining room.

Edward DeBartolo, worth more than $900 million by *Forbes*'s count, had come to Shearson to discuss a rival bid for Allied Stores. Tom Macioce, his old friend and a fellow Italian-American, had enlisted him as a white knight to rescue the company, now that the flake from Canada was about to launch his stupid tender offer. "He's had nervous breakdowns," Macioce told DeBartolo.

Even at this point, Macioce didn't regard Campeau as a realistic threat. Campeau's financing was suspect for one thing; where would such a meshuggener get the money? But once Campeau's offer was made public, the company would be officially put in play, and other more serious bidders would surely be attracted by the commotion. And if the company was doomed to be sold off, better it be sold to a good friend, a good Catholic, a man of his word, a man who understood retailing, a man who'd actually visited an Allied Store, a man who owned fifty-nine major shopping malls from Florida to California and one-tenth of all the retail mall space in the country, not to mention the San Francisco 49ers, the Pittsburgh Penguins, and a sizable slice of Ohio.

Perhaps it was fitting that a shopping-mall magnate was recruited to defend Allied Stores. The malling of America, some of which was DeBartolo's doing, contributed to the predicament of department-store retailers that made companies like Allied vulnerable to takeovers in the first place. Malls had lured customers away from the downtown areas, where department stores maintained their flagship outlets. Unable to fight the malls, department stores were forced to join them, with costly expansion programs that often diminished returns.

The philosophy behind the department store—everything under one roof—which triumphed over mom and pop on Main Street—small shops under separate roofs—was in turn superseded by the philosophy of the mall—small shops under one roof. The malls were "anchored" by famous department stores, while at the same time providing a lucrative beachhead from which specialty retailers, such as The Limited and The Gap, could compete.

The upshot was that companies like Allied lost whatever preeminence they might have had in the retail markets, which depressed their earnings and helped create the chronic malaise that held down the stock price, resulting in the undervalued situation that attracted corporate raiders.

The would-be rescuer of Allied, DeBartolo, was a courtly octogenarian who worked seven days a week at his office in Youngstown, Ohio. Stylistically, he couldn't have been more different from the bon vivant who'd put Allied into play. DeBartolo was rarely seen dressed other than in his dark business suit. He continued to occupy a modest ranch house in Boardman, a suburb of Youngstown. His favorite restaurant was Paonessa's, a friendly neighborhood place in Boardman that he owned. He'd never had a face lift or a hair transplant. He'd never been to Europe. A friend once invited him to Florida to stick his feet in the ocean; DeBartolo confided that he'd never stuck his feet in the ocean. His idea of a wild time was ordering a Scotch with an orange peel, which he never seemed to finish.

When his house in Boardman was being redecorated, DeBartolo, who could have gone anywhere, chose to rent a room at the local Holiday Inn. He *owned* the local Holiday Inn. Except for the corporate jet, whose main purpose was to return him to Boardman as often as possible so he wouldn't be stuck spending the night in trendy cities, DeBartolo had few extravagances. This was a multibillionaire who preferred to live the life of an overworked clerk.

DeBartolo's surprise appearance in Shearson's dining room was exhilarating to its M&A department, which had been divided by intracubicle warfare. One faction was led by Campeau's new friend, Tom Hill, a splendiferous dresser described in *Barbarians at the Gate* as "an oiled-back Gordon Gekko haircut atop five feet ten inches of icy Protestant reserve." The pressures of M&A, like the pressures of gold prospecting, caused normally sociable individuals to threaten to cut each other's balls off.

In less contentious times, Shearson had served as the regular investment banker for Allied Stores. But it blew the account, losing it to Goldman, Sachs. This was an in-house embarrassment. It wouldn't have happened, an insider says, if Shearson's people hadn't "bored the hell out of Tom Macioce." Now, in an incredible stroke of luck, the Wall Street gods had dropped DeBartolo into Shearson's lap. This was a chance not only to haul in a huge commitment fee for representing DeBartolo in his white-knight rescue of Allied, but also to recapture the profitable Allied account if the DeBartolo rescue succeeded.

Actually, the Wall Street gods had less to do with DeBartolo's appearance at Shearson than Paul Bilzerian did. Bilzerian, DeBartolo's partner in a number of stock-market deals, had been Shearson's best M&A client, and was instrumental in convincing DeBartolo to use Shearson here. Bilzerian subsequently was convicted of criminal charges for unrelated financial transgressions.

Meanwhile, Campeau, with whom Shearson's emissaries Hill and Stern had been eager to formalize a pact just before lunch, was entirely forgotten by mid-afternoon. The Shearson people didn't even bother to show up at a follow-up meeting with Campeau already scheduled for later that day. Why should they?


Back at the Waldorf suite, Campeau and his advisers, jilted by Shearson, their first choice in the beauty contest, quickly called First Boston to inform that firm that it was Campeau's first choice, and that Campeau wanted to meet with Wasserstein again.

But Wasserstein had something better to do that afternoon, and Perella and Michael Rothfeld, a First Boston managing director, were dispatched to show Campeau how a deal could be done. Rothfeld was a highly intelligent, highly opinionated, highly principled thirty-nine-year old investment banker who'd just returned from a vacation in France. "There's a guy from Canada," Rothfeld was told by Perella. "Finkelson knows him. He thinks he's going to buy Allied Stores. See if you can figure out whether the deal is financeable and we'll go over there and visit him."

Rothfeld spent a couple of hours looking through the public files, Allied annual reports, and so forth, and produced a rough sketch of how a takeover could be financed.

The meeting between Campeau and Rothfeld didn't begin well. Campeau explained his plan to take over Allied Stores with a combination of newly issued "preferred stock with warrants," plus commercial bank loans, as he'd developed it with Paine Webber. Rothfeld, who'd already been briefed on this amateurish strategy by

Perella, chimed in: "You can't do a hostile on Allied with cram-down paper* and bank loans. You need subordinated debt. And you'll have to sell assets to pay down this debt."

"You mean junk bonds," Campeau exploded. "I don't need any junk bonds. Citicorp will lend me money on my name. And I don't have to sell any assets."

Rothfeld blithely suggested that in raising money for billion-dollar transactions, the Campeau name wasn't likely to open many doors. "Nobody knows you in the financial markets in this country," said Rothfeld. "You aren't exactly a Henry Kravis or Boone Pickens."

"Does this mean I have to put in more equity?" Campeau asked Rothfeld, calming down a bit. Assured that it didn't, as long as his promised $300 million personal contribution was real, Campeau was greatly relieved.

Convinced of Campeau's eagerness to do business with First Boston in spite of his snippety attitude, Perella and Rothfeld returned to the office to discuss the matter with Wasserstein. Perella was still skeptical about Campeau, and Rothfeld had his reservations as well. "I think the guy is a clown," Perella said. But Wasserstein smelled a deal. "Well, Joe, you have other things to do, so why don't I go to the next meeting with him," Wasserstein responded to his partner.

Wasserstein himself returned to the Waldorf that evening, to close the deal with his famous "dare to be great" speech, the gist of which was that to be great, you had to be willing to take on huge debts and pay huge fees. Campeau was impressed. He and his aides said they wanted to hire First Boston, but Paine Webber's role was still an issue. Campeau wasn't willing to cut his old firm loose. Plus, he was still annoyed at First Boston's Rothfeld for calling him an unknown.

"I don't mind Paine Webber's name still being on this deal," Wasserstein told Campeau. "But they aren't sharing our fee. If you want to use Paine Webber, it's going to cost you more."

Campeau and Finkelson went out into the hall to discuss this.

---

* "Cram-down paper" was the generic term for various kinds of stock offered to the shareholders in a takeover deal as a substitute for cash. "Cram-down" was the salvation of corporate raiders who lacked resources and couldn't attract enough loans to pay for their purchases outright.

When they came back, Finkelson said: "We still want to hire you to do the deal, but we want Paine Webber to do the junk bonds."

Wasserstein reminded Campeau and Finkelson of Paine Webber's unimpressive record at doing junk bonds. "If you want me," he said, "You are going to need First Boston at every level to get this accomplished."

Finally, it was agreed that Paine Webber's name would appear on the right side of the tombstone, the subordinate spot in the advertisement for the deal. Otherwise, Paine Webber would play an entirely passive, if not nonexistent, role in the planning. Wasserstein seemed to want it that way.

Campeau said he would pay Paine Webber separately, a noble sentiment that later turned out to be greatly exaggerated.

At a Dear John luncheon at the Waldorf, Campeau tried to break the news as gently as possible to Paine Webber's Peter Slusser. He was using junk bonds. He'd hired First Boston. He'd hired Wasserstein.

"If I have to hit some people over the head with a baseball bat, I'm going to do it," said Campeau by way of explanation, referring, of course, to Slusser's oft-stated aversion to doing hostile transactions. "I needed some teeth."

Slusser argued that Paine Webber had plenty of teeth, and was perfectly capable of hitting some people over the head with a baseball bat if the situation warranted, as this one obviously did. Campeau was conciliatory but insistent. "First Boston is going to take the lead on this one," he said. "But you'll still be on the tombstone. You'll be part of the deal. You'll be paid your full fee."

Slusser had no choice but to accept the diminished role. Exit Paine Webber, the loyal bankers who'd taken over where Randall had left off, now dropped as unceremoniously as Randall had been. A separation agreement, stipulating that Paine Webber would receive $6.5 million from Campeau for its services on his winning of Allied was signed by both parties. Campeau didn't pay, however, contending that Paine Webber hadn't done anything to deserve the fee, and at a meeting set up later by the Paine Webber people to resolve this problem, the Campeau people didn't show up. Paine Webber had to sue to get its money, and eventually the case was settled in Paine Webber's favor.

Campeau's final overture to Macioce, which everyone involved knew was futile—an offer to acquire Allied in a friendly merger at $58 a share—was rejected by Allied's board on September 11. Then, on September 12, Campeau went public with an offer to all shareholders to purchase 30 million of Allied's shares for $58 a share in cash. This was enough shares to give him solid majority control, and he could worry about buying the remaining shares in a merger agreement later. He also announced his financing for this initial phase: Citicorp would provide up to $990.5 million in a commercial bank syndicate; $150 million would come from the Bank of Montreal (one of two Canadian banks that went along with Campeau, once he had Citicorp); $600 million of junk bonds would be sold by First Boston with an assist from Paine Webber; and $50 million in equity from Campeau himself.

At the bottom of the first page of the offer, where the dealer managers are acknowleged, "The First Boston Corporation" was listed on the left and "PaineWebber Incorporated" was relegated to the right.

Back at the DeBartolo camp, another set of lawyers, investment bankers, and commercial bankers was being quietly recruited to support DeBartolo's bid to counteract Campeau's bid—one small example of how takeover battles could stimulate the monogrammed-shirt economy. Shearson was wooing DeBartolo, but hadn't yet gotten him to sign a contract.

That the funereal billionaire had shown up for lunch was a good omen, but a rumor that Merrill Lynch was trying to snatch the Allied assignment threw the Shearson office into a general panic. "People were running around," says one ex-Shearson banker, "muttering about how we couldn't afford to lose this deal."

But what *was* this deal? Was Allied Stores worth $58 a share, the amount of the Campeau tender offer, which DeBartolo would surely have to top? Could the company generate enough cash to make the interest payments on the whopping debt that the bankers were obligated to raise? Cash-flow numbers, earnings numbers, numbers for the market value of the various Allied divisions all had to be collected and then "crunched" by the number crunchers to

produce a plausible scenario in which a $58-plus buyout by De-
Bartolo made sense. Most important, this plausible scenario had to
be discovered right away, before DeBartolo took his business to
another investment bank.

So in the third week of September 1986 it was final-exam time
for a team of Shearson's best number crunchers as they pored over
the entries in Allied's books—to which they were given free access,
since the company was favoring a DeBartolo bid. They made a
disturbing discovery. There weren't enough numbers to crunch.
Where were the daily balance sheets? The divisional income statements? Without crunchable numbers, what could they possibly put
into their cash-flow model? Without a cash-flow model, how could
they possibly do the deal?

In a series of meetings between Shearson's staff and Macioce's
staff, the investment bankers tried to get Allied to produce more
numbers. "We were exasperated," says a Shearson source. "The
whole system seemed to be in Macioce's head."

But Macioce explained that a retail company didn't require such
a detailed scorecard as, say, an oil company. The retail business was
too unpredictable, too seasonal, for a daily scorecard to be of any use.
"What, are you guys crazy?" Macioce argued in one of the meetings.
"In retail, it all comes down to Christmas, when you win or lose
everything in five weeks." But after Macioce finished saying this,
Peter Chiappetta, one of the exasperated bankers, had a prophetic
second thought:

"You know, we've never done a leveraged buyout deal on a retail
company. Maybe we shouldn't be doing one now. Maybe the whole
idea of doing an LBO in retail won't work. To do a safe LBO, you
need predictability, regular cash flow, but here, with everything
happening at Christmas, what are we going to base it on?"

Chiappetta's second thoughts were easily forgotten in Shearson's
mad scramble to get DeBartolo's signature on a commitment letter.
If the Allied numbers weren't crunchable, then they had to be made
to crunch, and with that goal in mind, Shearson hired a consultant
from Touche Ross, who had done Allied audits in the past, to assist
in constructing a viable cash model.

The numbers problem flared up in a meeting at which Shearson's bankers and lawyers attempted to close the deal with De-
Bartolo. In the middle of a raucous impasse, with bankers screaming

for more numbers that Allied's executives said they couldn't provide, Chiappetta, Macioce, DeBartolo, and a few others decided to escape to Il Menestrello, one of DeBartolo's favorite New York restaurants. A good Italian meal was more influential than a dozen viable cash models when it came to doing business with the Ohio billionaire.

In a quiet corner at Il Menestrello, the banker from Shearson, the CEO from Allied, and the white knight came to emotional terms. "That son-of-a-bitch Campeau," said Macioce. "He's not going to run my company. He's had a nervous breakdown."

A day later, the pact was agreed to: Shearson was highly confident it could raise $1.2 billion to help finance the DeBartolo bid for Allied Stores. It was the biggest such commitment Shearson had ever made, and the first, as Chiappetta described it, "north of a billion dollars." It was also the biggest commitment fee Shearson had ever received, $26 million, all thanks to a meal at Il Menestrello and Chiappetta's friendship with DeBartolo's pal Paul Bilzerian.

# Five

First Boston had attached its name to Campeau's public offer, apparently on the basis of two or three encounters, not entirely pleasant, with a new client about whom the firm had less biographical information than it would gather on an applicant for a janitorial job.

During the early days in September, when it had signed up with Campeau but before the announcement of the $58-a-share proposal, First Boston did a detailed study of Allied through annual reports and other public documents.

Representing the hostile bidder, First Boston had limited access to the detailed information that Shearson got for representing the friendly bidder, but gradually more information came into First Boston's hands. Ironically, First Boston's number crunchers, knowing less, were more satisfied with Allied's numbers than Shearson's number crunchers, who knew more. From First Boston's vantage, an Allied takeover at $58 looked promising.

Being a collection of separated divisions, Allied was at least a very convenient target. Its parts could be easily sold off to raise cash to pay the debts from the acquisition itself. In a pinch, Campeau could always sell another part. Moreover, by scuttling the least profitable divisions, Campeau would be left with an attractive core of assets—including Boston's Jordan Marsh, Florida's Maas Brothers, Seattle's Bon Marché, Ann Taylor, and Brooks Brothers—that might well be worth more than the whole. First Boston's number crunchers were confident that the so-called retained divisions would generate enough cash to cover Campeau's interest payments, and then some. Also, they were reassured to discover that going back to World War II, department-store companies "blew through recessions as well as the supermarkets," as one cruncher put it. "Allied was a potential slam dunk."

First Boston also studied the financial condition of Campeau Corp. In looking over these annual reports, as well as private valuation studies, the bankers were impressed with Campeau's $700 million (Canadian) equity in real estate. That the Campeau properties could serve as collateral in the event of a pecuniary mishap—such as Campeau's not being able to pay his takeover bills—weighed heavily in favor of doing business with him. So did the fact that Campeau rented office space to the government in Ottawa. Governments, First Boston figured, were stable tenants who never forgot to send the rent check, and Campeau had to be well-connected politically to have attracted his.

Considerably less research was done on Campeau as a person— in part because the bankers were inclined to favor math over gossip, and in part because the Toronto press hadn't written about the curious episodes described earlier. (That Campeau had two families was common knowledge in Ottawa, but not in Toronto, where no journalist had thought of Campeau as an important enough story to investigate).

Only after First Boston had appeared on the Campeau tombstone did the first bit of Campeau personal history surface in the office. It was a chapter in a book entitled *Men of Property: The Canadian Developers Who Are Buying America,* mostly devoted to dull real estate transactions, but which, in the Campeau section, reported on several Campeau feuds. The most memorable of these had the mayor of Ottawa, Charlotte Whitton, standing in front of one of Campeau's bulldozers to protest his latest apartment project in the mid-1960s.

As this anecdote was told and retold around First Boston, Campeau himself ended up in the driver's seat of the bulldozer, where he was trying to run down Ms. Whitton! The First Bostonians already had witnessed enough of their new client's supercilious snits so that his running down the mayor didn't seem out of character. Also, Campeau had begun making his predawn phone calls.

"Sit down, you're not going to believe this," First Boston's Robert Cotter told a colleague who had stepped into Cotter's office one day to ask a question. "Campeau's got a fortune-teller."

"Bullshit. How do you know?"

"He just told me himself on the phone. A German fortune-teller. He thinks he's destined to take over Allied. The fortune-teller says so."


DeBartolo the challenger had not as yet appeared, although he had engaged Shearson as his investment banker and Citicorp as his commercial lender. Citicorp, not called a "common carrier" for nothing, had assigned yet another team to work secretly on the DeBartolo bid, behind yet another Chinese wall. So Citicorp support was playing both sides. (By this time, the Citicorp support of Campeau was, of course, public knowledge).

First Boston was not yet formally committed to giving Campeau any money, although it had said it was "highly confident" it could sell $600 million worth of junk bonds. "Highly confident letters" were Drexel's stock in trade, and everybody had begun using the phrase—in this case, as one banker put it, "as part of the bullshit of Campeau's initial financing." With no rival bidders, there would be time to devise a more credible financing package as things went along. But rumors of a possible white knight reached Wasserstein in the third week of September.

Wasserstein was in Campeau's suite along with Mike Rothfeld and several First Boston underlings, worrying about the bullshit of Campeau's financing, including the inadequacy of the so-called "secured loan facility" from Citicorp. (First Boston didn't know, of course, that Citicorp was fiddling with DeBartolo behind Campeau's back!) "Maybe," Wasserstein suggested to Rothfeld, "we don't need to rely so much on banks. Why don't we use our own money?"

"If you want to do that, Bruce," Rothfeld said, "you'll have to talk to Pete."

Pete was Peter Buchanan, the CEO of First Boston, with whom Wasserstein had a superficially cordial relationship. At a meeting with Buchanan, Wasserstein discussed the pros and cons of backing Campeau with First Boston's own capital, in a bridge loan that could be repaid later. A bridge loan itself was an old idea, but its use in a hostile transaction was uncommon; in fact, it had only been used once before on a smaller scale.

Ignoring any reservations they may have had about the recipient of the loan, Wasserstein and the M&A contingent touted it to Buchanan. Later, the finance group showed how the loan could be backed by a guarantee from Campeau Corp., how the value of the Allied stock itself was sufficient collateral to provide more than enough protection, and how the loan agreement could be written with plenty of covenants and restrictions on Campeau to protect First Boston's investment.

Without much hesitation, since this appeared to be a "no brainer," Buchanan concurred. First Boston now was officially prepared not only to represent Campeau, but to bankroll his aspirations out of its own pocket.

Meanwhile, with a rival bidder rumored to be entering the game, it was clear to First Boston that Campeau's $58 bid was too low. True, $58 was far beyond Paine Webber's initial $50 threshold, but to First Boston that only illustrated the unsophisticated nature of the Paine Webber number crunching. It was decided to bump the bid to $66, to try to cut off the phantom bidder preemptively, before whoever he was gained momentum. Campeau agreed to the bump, even though it added an estimated $400 million to the Allied purchase price.

As for the bridge loan, First Boston committed itself to putting up $455 million and the jilted Paine Webber, exhibiting saintly forgiveness, said it would put up $245 million, for a total of $700 million.

While First Boston had charged Campeau $1 million for the initial "highly confident" expression, Campeau hadn't yet paid that bill. And this latest bridge commitment was going to cost him $7 million more, $4.5 million of it going to First Boston and $2.5 million to Paine Webber.

Having noted Campeau's reluctance to pay what he already owed, Wasserstein asked "the real estate guy," as he often referred to Campeau, to send the funds by wire transfer. Normally, a check would have sufficed, but for Campeau, Wasserstein wanted to make sure the funds had cleared before the loan commitment was announced. Wasserstein's associates took this to mean while the firm was willing to lend Campeau $455 million, even Wasserstein had a gnawing doubt about his trustworthiness.

Wasserstein was sitting in his office, which was decorated in what could be called British Empire High-Tech—dark wood and faux bamboo, a rounded desk with brass fittings, two computer screens (one of which was reportedly dysfunctional), plus a Quotron, installed, say colleagues, to give the impression that Wasserstein was adept with numbers, although in fact he was terrible with numbers —when he received a message that Campeau's wire transfer had cleared. "Heh-heh," Wasserstein chortled. "We just made $7 million."

On September 29, Campeau announced he was bumping his offer to $66 for 40 million Allied shares, 80 percent of the total outstanding, the other 20 percent to be purchased later with cramdown paper. Then on October 7, DeBartolo surfaced. Having rejected all of Campeau's overtures, the Allied board immediately accepted DeBartolo's offer of $67 a share all cash, which included a nice $53 million breakup fee, plus expenses, to be paid to DeBartolo by the company if his bid failed.

Two rival bidders and a company in play; this was the latest contest in the most highly paid sport in America, the beginning of a three-week marathon of offers and counteroffers, offenses and defenses, suits and countersuits. There were First Boston and Citicorp, representing a stranger whom they thought capable of attacking a woman with earth-moving equipment, and Shearson and the ubiquitous Citicorp representing the octogenarian billionaire from Boardman, Ohio—although Citicorp's role in the DeBartolo bid still hadn't been made public.

The exhausting ritual of the deal, and the all-nighters that served to dramatize its importance, were both well established by the time Allied became a target. The M&A jocks proved their endurance and justified their salaries by hunkering in their offices for days on end, taking catnaps on couches, subsisting on Danish pastry and Chinese leftovers congealed in wax-paper cartons, returning home to Darien or Scarsdale only long enough to kiss their spouses and children, have a shower, change clothes, and return to the fray. Wasserstein, in keeping with his role as superstar, convened meetings after midnight in his apartment on Fifth Avenue, which First Boston people as well as Campeau people, Roddy in particular, felt obligated to attend. "The point of this," says one participant, "was to watch Bruce eat breadsticks on his couch."

In the heat of the contest, lawyers and bankers who normally worked ten-hour days could be reached by Campeau in their offices for strategy chats at hours he'd customarily have awakened them at home.

At First Boston, Shearson, and Citicorp, number crunchers and loan officers on both sides ran cash-flow scenarios through their computers, as lawyers for both sides filed charges and counter-charges in the Delaware and New York courts.

There was Campeau's original bid of $58 a share, rejected by the Allied board; Campeau's revised two-tiered counteroffer at $66; DeBartolo's $67 counter to Campeau's counter. Each successively higher bid raised the amount to be borrowed, which in turn raised the fees to the lenders, which sent the number crunchers scurrying back to their computers to prove that Allied's earnings could support the increased debt.

On the legal front, Allied's lawyers concocted a poison-pill defense, which in the event of attack, such as Campeau's, would trigger the automatic exchange of shares for $67 worth of bonds to every shareholder but the attacker, a financial self-mutilation that made the company an unattractive prize. Campeau's lawyers sued in district court to have the poison pill invalidated; Allied's lawyers sued to have the pill upheld and then to have Campeau's takeover bid invalidated; Campeau's lawyers accused Allied of not disclosing its negotiations with DeBartolo; Allied's lawyers accused Campeau of making an unlawful, coercive tender offer.

Campeau's lawyers condemned the "outrageous breakup fees" that Allied agreed to pay DeBartolo in the event his white-knight bid failed; they also claimed to have uncovered an ongoing "conspiracy to injure Campeau and deprive all Allied shareholders of material information." There were thrusts to each parry, parries to each thrust, and all across town the legal clocks were ticking at a merry pace of $150-plus an hour.

· · ·

Sitting in his office at Allied, Macioce was confident that Campeau's bid would fail. All his years of hobnobbing, serving on corporate boards, donating millions to Columbia University, had created widespread goodwill that could be cashed in here. Macioce had Shearson. Macioce had DeBartolo. Macioce had most of New York's large banks, including Chemical and Manufacturers Hanover. Citicorp was backing both bidders, but expected the white-knight to win. Observers in the New York courtroom detected pro-DeBartolo sympathies in the judge, who ruled consistently in Allied's favor. "You could tell by the tone of his voice," said one observer, "that he wasn't going to let this jerk steal the company."

From Park Avenue to Seventh Avenue, where even the garment workers were rooting for DeBartolo, Campeau's chances were rated near zero. But against the formidable resources lined up against him, not to mention the sympathetic resistance to a foreign real estate developer gobbling up an important U.S. retailer, Campeau had one extraordinary asset: Wasserstein.

"He is a brilliant, although misunderstood businessman," Wasserstein often told his colleagues at First Boston, referring to Campeau; but that didn't mean he gave Campeau his home phone number. More accustomed to working for large corporations, such as Conoco or DuPont, than for eccentric soloists, Wasserstein kept his distance from Campeau personally, but outdid himself with ingenious maneuvers on Campeau's behalf. To win with Conoco might be regarded as routine, but to win with Campeau against DeBartolo would be spectacular. Like a lawyer who's at his best when defending lost causes, Wasserstein gave what may have been his greatest performance here.

Already Wasserstein had broken new creative ground with the concept of the bridge loan to a hostile deal, which, beyond helping Campeau with his shaky financing, was an ingenious solution to the Drexel problem. With its highly confident letters and its control of the junk-bond market, Drexel had the advantage in M&A contests because it could make billion-dollar assurances overnight, whereas more traditional firms had to wait around for banks to approve the loans. But by investing its own money in a client's takeover offer with a bridge, First Boston could make a sizable extra profit from the bridge loan commitment fee and wipe out Drexel's advantage at the same time.

This was revolutionary. Up and down Wall Street, investment bankers had been looking for some way to get back at the odious, client-stealing Drexel, and the bridge loan was it.

As if the concept of the hostile bridge loan weren't enough creativity for one deal, in mid-October, just after DeBartolo raised his Allied bid, Wasserstein came up with the dividend ploy. On Wasserstein's advice, Campeau "raised" his bid by declaring a $3 dividend to all Allied shareholders, payable out of Allied funds as soon as Campeau took possession of the company.

"This dividend thing of Bruce's had two wonderful aspects," Finkelson recalls admiringly. "It enabled Campeau to sweeten his offer without actually adding any of his own money, which he didn't have. Moreover, by promising a dividend instead of raising his bid in a traditional way, Campeau might avoid having to revise his tender offer." This was important, because in revising the tender offer, Campeau had to give shareholders more time in which to respond, causing him to lose momentum in his contest with De-Bartolo.

In the end, the dividend ploy was disallowed by the Securities and Exchange Commission (SEC), but all sides agreed it was a fantastically imaginative try, just the sort of ingenious stroke that was attracting so many bright Ivy Leaguers to Wall Street. Among the many congratulatory messages received at the firm—as if Wasserstein had won a financial version of the Pultizer Prize—was one from Ivan Boesky, who was soon to plead guilty to his own, albeit criminal, improvisations.

But the dividend ploy was only a prelude to Wasserstein's strategic masterpiece, a maneuver far more daring than anything ever attempted in any of his takeover battles to date—the Street Sweep.

Wasserstein began plotting it on October 23, when things looked both bleak and promising in the Campeau camp. Bleak, because the odds of Campeau winning the company were reduced to almost nil. A federal district court in New York had just denied Campeau's application for an injunction against Allied's use of its poison-pill defense, which Campeau's lawyers had attempted to invalidate but the courts and the SEC had approved with certain modifications.

With the poison pill in place, ready to be triggered as soon as Campeau acquired 50 percent of Allied's stock, the acquisition would be senseless. That was the bleak part. When informed that the pill had been upheld in the courts, Campeau's chief financial officer, Roddy, started packing his bags to return to Toronto.

The promising part was that the Allied/DeBartolo forces were rumored to be preparing to offer Campeau a sizable going-away present in return for his agreeing not to make any further trouble for the company. A $60 million figure had been mentioned, which, along with the estimated $70 million profit that Campeau would have made from tendering his Allied shares to DeBartolo, would have more than covered the lawyers' fees, the bankers' fees, and the hotel bill at the Waldorf. This would have been quite a consolation prize.

Throughout the week, there'd been back-channel discussions between the Allied people, led by vice president Benjamin Frank, and the DeBartolo people (Paul Bilzerian in particular), leading to this possible severance agreement that many felt Campeau would be foolish not to accept. The takeover seemed a hopeless cause, so why not take the money and go home?

But no offer had actually been put on the table, and even if one had, from First Boston's point of view, bigger stakes were at risk here than the ownership of Allied. A DeBartolo victory meant that a major piece of business was lost to Shearson, and who could say what effect a defeat like this might have on First Boston's ability to attract the next client, and the client after that? In the M&A game, no self-respecting player could afford to throw in the towel before trying every conceivable last-minute ploy, and Wasserstein was the champion ploymaker.

This particular ploy, the Street Sweep, had been used once before by Hanson, a British conglomerate, in its acquisition of the SCM corporation. The idea was to bypass the tender-offer process and buy enough shares on the open market to gain immediate control. In Allied's case, Wasserstein figured, a Street Sweep was possible because of an interesting development his rivals had overlooked —a large percentage of the Allied shares had fallen into the hands of a single interested party named Boyd Jefferies,* a broker who was representing a group of arbitrageurs (arbs).

* Jefferies, like the aforementioned Boesky, would later plead guilty to securities fraud in an unrelated matter.

In the initial phase of the takeover game, when the Allied share price jumped from the mid-$40s to $58 and then beyond, millions of shares were retrieved from safety deposit boxes and sold by widows, orphans, individual investors, and institutional investors eager to cash in on the bonanza and delighted that their Allied stock was finally paying off. (There may be a correlation between how poorly a stock has done in the recent past and how quickly the shareholders cash in at the first uptick from the takeover rumor, but this is unproven.) The buyers of most of these shares were arbs.

The arbs had a fascinating symbiotic relationship with the dealmakers in the M&A departments. Their function was to scoop up as much stock as they could afford in companies already put into play or companies believed likely to be in play soon, on the theory that a bidding war was bound to drive prices even higher. If the owners of thoroughbreds hired an army of horseplayers and sent them to the track to make wagers, it would be similar to the investment firms' setting up elaborate offices full of arbs down the hall from the dealmakers, as was the custom in the 1980s. The arbs and the dealmakers were kept separate by more invisible Chinese walls, just like those that hid the Campeau team from the DeBartolo team at Citicorp.

It's not hard to imagine that if First Boston's arbs and its M&A people got together and compared notes—for instance, if the arbs bought Allied stock and related options after hearing of the Campeau takeover being hatched in Wasserstein's office—this would have become the most profitable financial operation since the Medicis opened their bank. Such collusion, however, was illegal, and arbs were not allowed to bet on their own in-house deals.

Nonetheless, everybody's arbs but those involved in the takeover were betting on Allied, to the extent that 32 million shares were accumulated by Jefferies and his colleagues in a span of two weeks. This was more than 50 percent of the stock. As public attention focused on the activities of Campeau, DeBartolo, and the Allied board of directors, the majority ownership of Allied stock was quietly passing into the arbs' control.

"Maximize shareholder value" was what the Allied board was legally required to do once the company was put into play; but as things developed, they were maximizing it not for widows and orphans but for Boyd Jefferies and a few of his arb friends. Wasserstein understood this; so did Tom Hill and Jim Stern at Shearson, the strategists for DeBartolo. Jefferies had been calling both sides, offering the huge arb block of shares to the highest bidder.

Thus far, neither side had dared buy the block, because with tender offers and merger offers still on the table, it was against the SEC regulations for them to acquire shares on the open market. A judge would surely nullify any purchase of Jefferies's shares, and perhaps invalidate the entire tender offer as well. But with Campeau flirting with capitulation, Wasserstein had a wild thought. What if Campeau withdrew his tender offer, then turned around and grabbed the Jefferies block a minute later? The combination of the Jefferies shares and the shares he already owned would give Campeau more than 51 percent. As Allied's new owner via this remarkable coup, Campeau could then force a second merger transaction in which he'd buy the remainder of the stock.

Would this be legal? Would the SEC approve it? What could Allied do about it? What could DeBartolo do about it? What was the worst-case scenario?

Finkelson was invited to First Boston to describe the possible ramifications, including a worst-case scenario that went as follows: Campeau buys the arb block for $1.8 billion. A disapproving judge refuses to let Campeau vote these shares, so even though Campeau technically owns a majority, he's barred from running the company. With Campeau's takeover threat now neutralized, DeBartolo pulls his offer from the table. The price of Allied stock plummets on the New York Stock Exchange; Campeau is stuck with millions of shares he can't unload except at a huge loss; the people who lent him the $1.8 billion in cash to do the Street Sweep want their money back; Campeau can only repay part of it; his Canadian real estate is liquidated and he's forced into bankruptcy. Other than that, everything is fine.

Finkelson didn't think the worst-case result was likely, and lawyers are paid to be pessimistic. But it was a possibility that had to be considered. A slightly less worst-case scenario had Campeau grabbing the Jefferies block, the judge barring him from voting the shares, and DeBartolo buying him out at a high enough price to enable him to pay back most of the money. The rest would come from the liquidation of Campeau real estate.

Another question was: Who would lend Campeau $1.8 billion

to engage in such a judicial crapshoot? Citicorp was a prospect, but First Boston had just found out that Citicorp was secretly backing the DeBartolo bid—an infuriating discovery.* Wasserstein's suggestion was that First Boston bypass Citicorp altogether and lend Campeau the money for the Street Sweep.

Earlier, and also at Wasserstein's suggestion, First Boston had committed itself to making Campeau the $455 million hostile bridge loan, a daring step in itself, but the Street Sweep bridge loan was much bigger and also riskier. Wasserstein was coaxing First Boston farther toward the edge of prudence, and the firm that wouldn't see Campeau the previous summer was now on the verge of investing in this uncertain ploy.†

Wasserstein himself was uncertain enough of the ramifications that he wavered Hamlet-like through dinner at Il Nido Restaurant the night of October 23. "Am I nuts?" he wondered out loud to himself and two dinner companions. "Does it make sense?"

Later that same evening, Wasserstein met with an old friend, lawyer Don Drapkin, and some other associates in Drapkin's office at Skadden, Arps to mull this over some more. (Drapkin would soon leave Skadden to become Ron Perelman's right-hand man at Revlon.) Wasserstein polled the room, everybody said "do it," and the papers were drawn up.

A final clearance came from First Boston's CEO, Buchanan, after he placed a conference call with the firm's executive committee on the morning of the twenty-fourth. There was no debate to speak of.

First Boston's management, including Buchanan, may have resented what they perceived to be Wasserstein's smart-ass attitude, but his M&A department made 90 percent of the profits, and if Wasserstein wanted to do a Street Sweep, he could do a Street Sweep. Also, the executive committee was convinced that Campeau had enough real estate assets to cover the downside. (A liquidation would be tough luck for Campeau, but not for the firm.) The upside was that First Boston would make over $100 million in extra fees,

---

* First Boston already suspected that Citicorp was dragging its feet on the Campeau negotiations, and now it figured it knew why.
† First Boston actually expected to put up $900 million for the Street Sweep, and to convince a commercial bank to offer the other $900 million in a "margin loan" secured by the Allied stock.

not to mention interest on the bridge loan, and would snatch Allied Stores from under the noses of Shearson. So it was that First Boston gave its official assent to betting 100 percent of its entire corporate capital on Campeau.

Over at his Waldorf suite, Campeau was trying to decide whether the Street Sweep was worth it to *him*. Should he bet everything he had, including his real estate, on Wasserstein's latest brainstorm? On October 23, he had taken a walk with Ron Tysoe and the two of them had ambled into Gucci, where Campeau faced his moment of truth. Trying on a pair of shoes, he turned to Tysoe and said: "I'm risking everything I've got. What do you think I should do?" "It's up to you to decide," Tysoe answered. Rarely had Tysoe seen Campeau acting so diffident.

That night, in the telephone meeting with his Campeau Corporation board, Campeau got the approval to go ahead with the Street Sweep. Some board members viewed it as very high risk, but they all agreed it was Bob's call.


At midnight on October 23, the phone rang in Ben Frank's bedroom. Frank, the Allied vice president who was trying to effect Campeau's going-away payment, had spent the day discussing it with Macioce and with DeBartolo. DeBartolo had wanted to think it over until the morning. But now an anxious-sounding emissary from First Boston was on the line, warning Frank that if Allied was serious about paying Campeau to withdraw from the takeover, then a formal offer would have to be extended immediately.

"Can't this wait until morning?" said a groggy Frank. "It's the middle of the night."

"No, it can't. Not really. No it can't. You have to do it now," said the First Boston emissary.

"How can we do it now? That's impossible. We've got to get approval from DeBartolo."

"We have to know now."

"I'm sorry," said Frank. "It will have to wait. Until 7:30 A.M. at least. DeBartolo wanted the night to think about it. I can't possibly call him now. What can happen between now and then?"

• • •

At 9 A.M., on October 24 a large crowd gathered in William Lambert's glassed-in office on First Boston's forty-second floor. Lambert was a managing director of the firm, also known as Wasserstein's "Rasputin." His office and Wasserstein's were connected by a small conference room.

Campeau was there, along with his staff, Finkelson, Wasserstein, and assorted First Bostonians. Having just put out the news on the financial wires that Campeau had dropped his tender offer for Allied Stores, they were staring anxiously at Lambert's telephone.

A few minutes later, the phone rang. It was Boyd Jefferies calling from Atlanta, where he happened to be traveling and saw the incredible story on the Dow Jones wire. He wondered if anybody at this number would be interested in buying 32 million shares of Allied Stores that he happened to have in his possession or could quickly obtain, for $67 a share.

"Just a minute," Jefferies was told by James Elliott, a First Boston arb who happened to be in Lambert's office and had picked up the telephone. Jefferies was put on hold as Don Carroll from Campeau's staff ambled over to the phone to say that yes, in fact, a certain Robert Campeau had been thinking about buying some Allied stock, but he'd only be interested in, say, 25.7 million shares, for which he'd be willing to pay $1.8 billion which he'd accumulated for just such a purpose.

Jefferies said that he'd be happy to accommodate Mr. Campeau for a nickel-a-share commission, and a tentative deal was struck. Jefferies then put his associate Frank Baxter on the phone, to work out the details. One problem was that Campeau had no account with Jefferies and Company, and anyone who has ever invested knows that you can't buy a share of stock without opening an account first.

"He'll open one," First Boston assured Jefferies, and Wasserstein was put on the line to vouch for Campeau's credibility. By 9:15 A.M. Campeau had bought Allied. The record of the trade, 25.7 million shares, $1.8 billion, etc., was sent to the client on the same sort of little slip that the brokerage firms send out to buyers of a single share.

Back at Allied headquarters, Ben Frank was on the phone with Paul Bilzerian, in Ohio. Since 7:30 that morning, Frank had been trying to get DeBartolo to agree to the Campeau severance, but DeBartolo had deferred to Bilzerian, and Bilzerian had balked.

Now, at 9 A.M., Bilzerian was commenting on the news that had just come over the financial wires—Campeau had dropped his tender offer. "Did you see this?" he yelled to Frank. "Campeau has given up. He's done. Finished. Withdrawn his tender offer. And you suckers at Allied wanted us to pay $60 million to get rid of him. What a waste of money that would have been. He's gone. History. Out of the picture. We didn't need to pay anything to get rid of him. He's . . . oh, my GOD."

Bilzerian had seen the second message on the financial wire. Campeau had bought 25-plus million shares of Allied stock from Boyd Jefferies. He was the majority shareholder.

From a legal point of view, the important question here was whether Jefferies just happened to call First Boston from Atlanta to find an officeful of bankers and a buyer for 25.7 million shares of Allied as a matter of lucky coincidence, or whether the call was prearranged.

The SEC was interested in this question, and so was the judge in the New York court who was ruling on Campeau's motions and DeBartolo's motions in the various court battles over Allied. If the Jefferies call had been prearranged, that meant Campeau would have agreed to buy the Jefferies block before dropping his tender offer, which was a violation of SEC rules. The judge, on deciding that such a thing had happened, could invalidate the Street Sweep, the worst-case scenario that Finkelson had described.

Campeau told the press that "we were just as surprised as anyone that Jefferies called," and his lawyers told the court that Campeau had no idea that Jefferies was going to offer the big block of shares on the morning of October 24. Neither Campeau nor his lawyers winked when they said this. On the other hand, what were all those people doing hanging around the telephone, and why would Wasserstein and First Boston have bothered to commit themselves to this giant bridge loan without any prior knowledge that Jefferies would be calling?

The SEC will only report that after a short investigation, it found no reason to take corrective action. However, the SEC couldn't have been too happy about the Street Sweep, because the agency moved quickly to close this latest loophole through which the brilliant Wasserstein had managed to squeeze Campeau, and disallowed all Street Sweeps thereafter. Campeau's was the last.

The judge in the case, Pierre Leval, issued a five-day temporary injunction against Campeau's buying the Street Sweep shares, but this was only mildly frightening to the Campeau team, since in any stock purchase, the buyer has five days to send in the money. On October 29, the fifth day, the judge lifted the restraining order and allowed Campeau to take possession of the shares. First Boston was relieved.

# Six

Jubilation at the Waldorf, astonishment at Allied headquarters: the flake from Canada had won. The judge had ruled in Campeau's favor; Campeau could vote his shares; congratulatory phone calls lit up the switchboard at First Boston. Wasserstein had outdone himself; he was calling this "the dawn of a new era of merchant banking" in which the unprecedented tactic of First Boston's loaning $900 million of its own capital to a deal-in-progress would revolutionize the M&A business, in much the same way that his "borrowing from the bank" had once revolutionized the Monopoly game in the Wasserstein household.

Citicorp, seeing a potential good thing, agreed to finance half of the Street Sweep bridge, putting up $900 million. "As soon as they heard we were doing it, they rushed back in to get in on the action," says a First Boston source.

Hill and Stern, Shearson's advisers to DeBartolo, who had assured their client and themselves that nobody would be so foolhardy as to pull a Street Sweep stunt—too risky, they thought—were nonetheless full of admiration for Wasserstein's brazen eleventh-hour coup. *The Wall Street Journal,* in its coverage of November 4, 1986, saw positive long-term implications:

"Campeau Corp.'s victory in the battle for Allied Stores Corp. signals major changes in takeover tactics. . . . By emerging victorious, Campeau has given a further boost to the controversial tactic of open-market stock accumulation, which bypasses a formal tender offer to all shareholders. And the willingness of major investment banking firms to bankroll large open-market purchases . . . is likely to make the tactic more prevalent."

In fact, it wasn't long at all before other investment banks followed First Boston's irresistible precedent and invested their firms' capital in deals-in-progress. And what a triumph this was for the recipient of the $900 million, who so recently would have been pleased to have a Brooks Brothers store installed in one of his malls and now was about to become the owner of Brooks Brothers, Ann Taylor, Bonwit, Jordan Marsh and 20 other Allied divisions, the retail mogul and overlord of 670 stores worldwide.

Allied's stunned executives received an "at your peril" letter, informing them that their services might no longer be required. Although the company's poison pill was technically still in effect, with Campeau the majority shareholder there wasn't much the leadership could do to stop him from getting it abolished eventually, and a drawn-out fight would be costly, damaging to the enterprise, and probably futile. In an atmosphere of dumbfounded resignation, Macioce opened talks with Campeau, and joined him for dinner at the Sky Club on the top of the Pan Am building. Pleasantries were exchanged, and there was superficial cordiality and no mention on Macioce's part of Campeau's flakiness or nervous breakdowns or thin-as-a-ham-sandwich financing or Macioce's having been "blindsided by a trainload of clowns" as he had privately observed. A negotiated settlement, calling for Campeau to buy up the remaining 49 percent of the shares for $69 each, was soon agreed to.

In this Phase II, more money would be required, of course, and Citicorp would have to put together another banking syndicate. (Since Campeau had accomplished Phase I with the Street Sweep and not the tender offer, the original Citicorp tender-offer syndicate never actually made its loans.)

Allied's front-office honchos had protected themselves with severance agreements that granted them large lump sums, including their entire salaries and bonuses they would have made until the end of their contracts, plus retirement money and deferred compensation. Several prepared to bail out to Florida in these golden parachutes. Macioce got the best deal of all: $15–20 million in direct benefits, including $5.2 million in retirement money, $2 million in salary, and his 112,000 Allied shares worth $7.7 million, plus options on another 35,000 shares.

But in his haste to settle with the conquering Canadian, Macioce neglected to consult his white knight, DeBartolo, who'd just spent two months fighting to save Allied for his old friend. It was only secondhand that DeBartolo learned that Allied had signed a formal truce with Campeau. DeBartolo was furious and never spoke to Macioce again.

At a movie theater on Broadway and Forty-fifth Street, rented for the occasion because it was large enough to hold hundreds of Allied employees, a smiling Macioce entered the front door with his arm around the shoulder of a smiling Campeau, and the two of them sort of wobbled along toward the podium, since Macioce was nearly a foot taller than his ebullient companion. This sight, Macioce arm-in-arm with an adversary whom he'd openly described as "nuts," was one that the Allied crowd had never expected to see.

But there they were in joyous reconciliation, Campeau taking the stage with the tamed Macioce beside him, telling the audience how much he loved America, how happy he was for Allied and for its employees, how everybody's job was safe for the moment, how he planned to reward them all with equity participation, how he was a tenderfoot when it came to retailing and therefore would rely for guidance on the man standing next to him, who had agreed to stay on as Allied's CEO. The crowd gasped in wonderment.

The Allied purchase was not yet formally closed, but already Campeau was borrowing the corporate Gulfstream jet, with its gold-handled bathroom fixtures and the gold-plated toilet seat, and the fourteen-passenger seating capacity, which during the takeover had been criticized as a symbol of Allied extravagance. Campeau at first requested the use of the Gulfstream from Macioce, but soon he was calling the pilot, Jerry Lamont, directly at home. "Let Tom know where we're going," he told Lamont. He flew to Cincinnati to see DeBartolo. He flew to Vail with Allen Finkelson, where they competed to see who could get down the slopes the fastest.

The glorious victor, who liked to intersperse periods of intense activity with frequent vacations, spent the next few weeks on the ski slopes or fishing at his thirty-square-mile Canadian retreat, or at his mansion in Toronto. His well-paid helpers at First Boston and Citicorp, meanwhile, were left to work out the details in New York.

Buying a company is like buying a house. First, there's the signing of a contract—as Campeau had just done with the Allied management—then there's a closing, when the new owner takes formal control. For complicated tax reasons, the Allied deal had to be closed by December 31, 1986, which gave Campeau's minions only six weeks to handle the complexities of a $4 billion transaction. "Let the bankers peddle their paper," Campeau often said, with the same tone one might have used for, "Let the yard men rake the leaves." But the bankers were having problems peddling Campeau's paper. The first problem was that Campeau couldn't make the down payment, the size of which had increased with the price of the deal.

The original story he'd told Citicorp and First Boston to prove his seriousness as a buyer, about the $300 million he was prepared to bring to the table, turned out to have been exaggerated. "He'd always indicated it was no problem, he would come up with it from his real estate assets," recalls a Citicorp source. But as of early November, Campeau hadn't come up with it. If the takeover itself was a fantasy become reality, Campeau's equity contribution was the reverse.

It was only after the Street Sweep that Campeau chose to inform his lenders there might be a shortfall in his equity obligation. "We were pissed," says the Citicorp source, "to find this out."

But here buying a company is different from buying a house. In buying a house, if you renege on the down payment, the bank will retract its offer of a mortgage. In the higher finance of the Campeau deal, there was a certain tolerance for such a failing, in spite of the bankers' bad feelings about it. Citicorp, for starters, agreed to solve part of Campeau's problem by *lending* him $150 million of his $300 million equity.

Again in our housing example, the bank that gives you a mortgage loan won't lend you the down payment on top of that, because then the bank would be putting up 100 percent of your investment —a great deal for you, perhaps, but precarious for the bank. But in the Allied example, Citicorp was volunteering to serve as both the principal lender and the lender of half the equity. Or perhaps "volunteering" is not the right word.

According to a Citicorp source, sometime after he'd gotten his original big commitment for the Allied financing from Citicorp in New York, Campeau had strolled into the offices of Citicorp in Toronto and asked for a $150 million loan, secured by real estate, for "general corporate purposes."

"General purposes? What do you think that is?" a banker at Citicorp remarked in New York when her Toronto colleagues described Campeau's loan request. "He probably wants it for his equity in Allied." Working in secrecy behind the Chinese wall, Campeau's Citicorp team had had no idea that Campeau was trying to use Citicorp Toronto as the source of his equity for a Citicorp New York takeover loan.

All the way up to the top of Citicorp's credit policy department, the bankers debated how they should respond to this clever but upsetting machination. But after assuring itself that the Toronto loan had already been approved and, moreover, was fully secured by Campeau's Canadian real estate assets, Citicorp approved the so-called "double-dip." After all, Campeau always had claimed that his equity would come from real estate, it's just that Citicorp hadn't realized that Citicorp itself would be the source for the actual cash.

The Citicorp equity loan was only one example of Campeau's imaginative and exhaustive approach to client-banker relations. "He called me all the time," says Jean Michel Gal, the lead banker for the Campeau team at Citicorp. "Sometimes at 4:30 A.M. He was rambling and asking all kinds of questions. There was one scheme after another, he wanted equity loans, he wanted to complain about fees, he wanted to change some terms—you never knew what was coming next."

And now, in addition to everything else, after Citicorp had agreed to loan Campeau $150 million to solve half of his equity problem, Campeau was telling the bank he couldn't produce the other half. He was relying on the bankers' forbearance and ingenuity to come up with that, too.

"Campeau understood," says one of his aides, "that Citicorp and First Boston, who together had invested $1.8 billion in the Street Sweep and who were going to make hundreds of millions in fees if this deal closed, were not about to let the deal fall apart because Campeau didn't pony up his equity. They had more of a vested interest in this deal than he did." Wasserstein's new era of merchant banking had brought with it this new and unanticipated situation.

Kim Fennebresque, a jocular, brassy young lawyer, and a managing director at First Boston, was put on the Campeau equity detail. Fennebresque, who shared Mike Rothfeld's lack of enthusiasm for the firm's most cantankerous client, was now receiving his share of predawn bedside briefings, as Campeau phoned from Toronto or from ski resorts.

First Boston had two possible solutions to the equity problem: advance Campeau the money in yet another bridge loan, or recruit an equity partner to make Campeau's contribution for him.

By the second week in November, Fennebresque had put together what Wasserstein's M&A department called the "dirtball list" —a Who's Who of financial daredevils who might be interested in taking a flyer on Campeau's down payment. Potential dirtballs included Ivan Boesky, felon-to-be, and Donald Trump of New York and Mel Simon of Texas, both real estate developers. In addition they considered the billionaire Reichmann brothers of Canada, who though not daredevils, were certainly deep pockets.

Most of the dirtballs said no immediately because they hadn't heard of Campeau. This left the Reichmanns, to whom Fennebresque devoted considerable attention. They seemed to be the most promising prospect. They knew Campeau from Toronto, where they'd made a much bigger fortune in real estate. Like Campeau, the Reichmanns existed outside the Toronto Establishment, but in their case, it was by choice. They kept to themselves, shunning cameras, avoiding interviews, and declining invitations to join social and civic clubs and committees. In fact, one of the unusual occasions on which the Reichmanns had participated in a well-publicized group effort was back in 1980, when they had bought stock in Royal Trustco, during the Establishment campaign to protect that company from Campeau's takeover raid. In the process, the Reichmanns ended up owning 20 percent of that Waspy insurance conglomerate, which bystanders took to mean that the Establishment's distaste for Campeau outweighed its long-standing reluctance to open up to Jews.

But the Reichmanns reportedly had purchased their shares only after it was apparent that Campeau had lost, and Paul Reichmann assured Campeau that their investment was not meant as a vote against him personally. Campeau said he appreciated the message.

Unaware of the Reichmanns' role in Royal Trustco, Fennebresque arranged a meeting between Campeau and Paul Reichmann in Toronto, and flew there to join them. Fennebresque observed that Campeau, who he knew could be gruff and short-tempered, acted solicitously, almost fawningly, toward the Lark-smoking billionaire with the rabbinical beard. The charm didn't work, however, and Reichmann politely but firmly declined the offer to put up Campeau's equity. He said he didn't invest in things he knew nothing about, such as retailing.

On the plane ride home, Fennebresque wondered whether First Boston was doing business with the wrong Canadian developer: "The Reichmanns were obviously much richer than Campeau, but the gulf between them was not just financial," Fennebresque recalls. "Compared to Paul Reichmann, Campeau was a supplicant, a lightweight, a parvenu."

By late November, with the deadline for the Allied closing fast approaching, Campeau's lack of equity was becoming a more desperate matter for the lenders. Citicorp and First Boston were playing an elaborate game of Alphonse and Gaston: "Why don't you put in the equity?" and "No, you put in the equity." First Boston had almost resigned itself to the "equity bridge solution," agreeing to loan Campeau the $150 million until a better source could be found, but it didn't tell Citicorp that. Even this unprecedented offer was swamped in niggles as Campeau tried to improve the terms.

Campeau was being creative on other fronts as well. With Citicorp banker Jean Michel Gal he brought up yet another possible side deal. He wanted to sell the Allied shopping centers back to himself.

These were the same shopping centers that a few weeks earlier Campeau was going to buy from Macioce instead of buying the company, but now that he had bought the company, he didn't see why he couldn't "take the centers out of Allied" and transfer them to his Canadian corporation, where they would do him more good. When Citicorp told him that he couldn't remove pieces from Allied without paying for them, he offered $300 million. This was the same price that Macioce had rejected as inadequate.

Soon after, Campeau proposed to use the shopping centers to

solve his down-payment problem. In this complicated scenario, he would buy the centers out of Allied for $300 million, then offer them as collateral for an additional loan from Citicorp, the proceeds of which would be applied to his missing $150 million equity. Even some of the bankers had a hard time following that one; they'd never encountered a more talented finagler, for whom no prior arrangement was exempt from further discussion, no angle safe from further exploration.

As the 1986 holiday season approached, the bankers and lawyers would normally look forward to a few days off. But all around Wall Street, nerves were afrazzle over the Allied deal. Potentially, it was the most lucrative in history for First Boston, from its growing list of Campeau fees: $1.5 million for the initial commitment, the $7 million "acquisition fee," the $1 million for issuing a "highly confident letter," the $7 million (shared with Paine Webber) for the original bridge-loan commitment, an additional $3.65 million for increasing the bridge commitment, $50 million for the Street Sweep loan, and more to come from the junk-bond financing and the selling off of Allied's parts. And these were just fees; there would also be the interest on the loans.

For Citibank, the Allied takeover was just as lucrative: the closing fee of one percent, the initial commitment fee of $3 million, the syndication fee of $8 million, an agency fee of $1 million payable on the first anniversary of the merger, the commitment fee of one percent per year of the unused portion of the loan, the bridge-loan fee for its half of the Street Sweep, and so on.

But the equity problem was not yet resolved, and Citicorp was having trouble putting together its new syndicate for Phase II. Syndication spreads the risk, and the additional $1.5 billion that Citicorp agreed to lend Campeau was more than it wanted to risk alone.

Normally, after a corporate raider wins majority control, the banks have an easy time selling the deal, but this one—the biggest takeover of any company other than an oil company in U.S. history —was failing to attract the crowd that regularly threw money at buyouts.

"You'd have thought," says a Citicorp banker, "that other banks would have jumped on our bandwagon as soon as he'd won the

Street Sweep victory. But it didn't happen. Even the Canadian banks, who we figured would be eager to get involved since they knew Campeau, declined to participate." So did Bankers Trust and Morgan Guaranty, both of whom had supported the DeBartolo bid. Citicorp expected those two large New York banks to switch sides as soon as DeBartolo capitulated, but neither did.

So with the end-of-year deadline in sight, Campeau's equity was still lacking, no dirtball had appeared, and Citicorp had not formed its syndicate. In desperation, that important bank was forced to swallow its pride and contemplate the unthinkable: cooperating with Manny Hanny.

Manny Hanny, Manufacturers Hanover Trust, was Citicorp's biggest rival in M&A lending. It had supported the DeBartolo bid, and Allied's Macioce sat on Manny Hanny's board. After the Street Sweep in late October, Manny Hanny *had* offered to join Citicorp's Campeau syndicate, but Citicorp, expecting a crowd of takers, had smugly rejected the overture. "We don't need you," was Citicorp's response. Now, Citicorp had to plead with Manny Hanny to come back.

"Get Citicorp to admit that the reason they returned to us is that they couldn't syndicate the deal without us," said a Manny Hanny M&A banker rather gleefully when he heard the news. In return for its last-minute rescue of the syndicate, Manny Hanny struck a hard bargain: equal status with Citicorp as co-manager, an increase in fees from $6 million to $9 million for both co-managers, and more restrictions on the borrower, Campeau.

Manny Hanny had had no direct involvement with Campeau prior to this point, but its leading M&A banker, Mark Solow, and others were aware of Macioce's first impressions, and wanted to toughen the terms. Citicorp went along. After the embarrassing return to Manny Hanny, Citicorp was finally able to form a lending group, but not until December 21.

At around the same time, Campeau had found his own "dirtball," to use First Boston's word. With his proven talent for making allies out of former adversaries (Firpo Taylor, the Toronto banker; Macioce; Clauda, after she found about Ilse; Ilse, after she found out about Clauda), Campeau forged an unlikely alliance with Ed DeBartolo.

Remarkably, Campeau, the enemy and rival bidder, was now on

good terms with DeBartolo, while Macioce, the old friend, was not. At a series of truce meetings arranged by the lawyers, Campeau was both charming and persuasive. He emphasized the possible synergy between Allied Stores and DeBartolo's malls. The two real estate developers spoke the same language; they discussed future joint ventures, such as DeBartolo's right of first refusal on certain Allied divisions if these were to be sold, and also Campeau's latest plan to solve his equity problem. Now, Campeau wanted to sell the Allied shopping centers to DeBartolo, who in turn would give Campeau the $150 million in missing equity.

DeBartolo was in a cooperative mood, having just signed a settlement agreement with Allied and with Campeau in which they jointly agreed to pay him $53 million as his going-away present, plus an estimated $50 million in expenses. This was essentially the same "break-up" deal that DeBartolo had made with Allied earlier, and which Campeau's lawyers had challenged in court as excessive. It was also rumored that DeBartolo and his partner Bilzerian had made an additional $50–$100 million from the Allied stock and stock options they'd bought.

In any event, DeBartolo wasn't putting his own money into Campeau's equity loan. For that, he got a commitment from the ubiquitous Citicorp, which in this newest twist was now prepared to provide 100 percent of Campeau's down payment, half of it via the Canadian loan and now the other half funneled through DeBartolo.

Four days before Christmas, all the potential beneficiaries of the upcoming Allied closing were resting easier. The equity problem was solved, the shopping-center disputes resolved, the Citicorp syndicate salvaged, Campeau was entertaining himself in Toronto, and Wasserstein was vacationing in Jamaica, at a resort surrounded by machine-gun-toting guards. This tranquillity, alas, was only temporary.

Small details are sometimes neglected in the course of taking over a company, which is a complicated procedure in any event. By the end of a deal, the participants often suffer from so-called "deal fatigue" after those weeks of sleeping on office couches and eating leftover Chinese takeout. The combination of long hours, MSG, screaming for fees, and staring at numbers may lead to lapses in judgment or even to memory loss, as they seemed to in this instance.

On December 23, John Weinberg of Goldman, Sachs called First Boston's CEO, Pete Buchanan. Weinberg said that Goldman would stop providing Allied with commercial paper as of December 26. As Allied's regular banker, Goldman had customarily "rolled over" the commercial paper every three months. Since Allied was a solid company with a strong balance sheet, these short-term loans were quite secure. But Weinberg said Goldman was unwilling to continue rolling over the paper for the new Campeau-owned Allied, about to be burdened with $3.5 billion of takeover debt. Allied depended on this regular source of working capital to meet such expenses as payrolls.

Citicorp, which was lending money in every other direction, had earlier volunteered to take over from Goldman as the provider of these important short-term loans. But Citicorp hadn't planned to make the actual disbursement until Campeau had formally acquired all of Allied.

Neither Citicorp, Cravath, Campeau's staff, nor Allied's own finance department had anticipated Allied's working-capital requirements in the interim. Weinberg warned Buchanan in their conversation on December 23 that Goldman would no longer participate in this uncertain situation, and would cease to take responsibility for selling Allied's paper in three days. And with no new commercial paper loans to pay off the old, Allied might well be forced into bankruptcy.

First Boston was aware that an Allied bankruptcy prior to the actual consummation of the Campeau purchase was the worst potential calamity in the history of M&A: a deal collapsing before the closing date and taking a perfectly solvent company down with it. Caught entirely off guard, Buchanan asked Mike Rothfeld if he could fix the problem.

Rothfeld called Citicorp and asked the bank to cooperate by rolling Allied's commercial paper right away. But Citicorp told Rothfeld it wouldn't cooperate unless Manny Hanny was also involved. When Rothfeld contacted Manny Hanny, he got more distressing news. Manny Hanny was on the verge of backing out of the Allied syndicate altogether. Manny Hanny's Mark Solow said he believed that Campeau had misled him during a recent meeting concerning the shopping-center sale, and he was angry at Citicorp for excluding his team from various discussions. He was no longer interested in acting as co-agent with Citicorp.

Now everything was mixed up together in a great confusion. The future of Allied depended on this commercial paper, the commercial paper depended on Citicorp, Citicorp depended on Manny Hanny, and Manny Hanny was in no mood to cooperate with either Citicorp or Campeau. Solow was convinced that Campeau was trying to pull a fast one by buying the shopping centers cheap from Allied and then selling them to his new pal, DeBartolo, for much more.

Rothfeld asked Solow what it would take to get Manny Hanny back in the deal. Solow said that Campeau would have to pay $450 million for the shopping centers, which he'd been trying to "steal" out of Allied for $300 million, then refinance and resell to DeBartolo.

With only six working days left before the Allied purchase had to close, or the deal would be subject to much higher taxes—a poison pill from the IRS—the exhausted principals were called back to yet another emergency meeting, this one on Christmas Eve day, in Solow's office at Manny Hanny.

One of Citicorp's young bankers, Carolyn Buck Luce, who had returned from maternity leave to take over as the head of that bank's Allied team, cut short a Florida vacation to take part in the discussion. Mike Rothfeld and Ken Colburn were there from First Boston along with two of Campeau's old guard, Don Carroll and David King, who'd distrusted this Allied adventure from the start but were going along with it. Wasserstein was still on the beach in Jamaica, oblivious to the maddening series of snags.

After hours of further negotiation, all sides agreed to new terms: The shopping centers would be sold for $400 million to DeBartolo, with Campeau reserving the right to repurchase a 50 percent interest later. DeBartolo would make his equity loan, Manny Hanny would return to the syndicate, and Citicorp and Manny Hanny would roll Allied's commercial paper.

But even *this* new agreement to supersede the previous agreement came undone as the afternoon turned to evening, and most New Yorkers had gone home to light their Chanukah candles or nail the children's Christmas stockings to their mantelpieces. Reversing itself yet again, the Campeau team demanded $450 million from DeBartolo for the shopping centers, rather than the agreed-upon $400 million. The DeBartolo people were on the phone with Campeau's team in Solow's office, getting madder by the minute.

Solow himself was about to walk out. His two children were waiting for him in the hall, and finally he put on his overcoat. Buck Luce was ashen-faced. She and Colburn and Rothfeld could see the entire takeover, six months, $4 billion, and the historic Street Sweep later, falling apart over a $50 million quibble. This was hauntingly reminiscent, on a larger scale, of that dispute over a lawn mower that had once held up the sale of a Campeau apartment complex in Ottawa.

"I've had it," Solow said, moving toward the reception area where the elevators were. Turning to the Campeau representatives, he said, "How could you be arguing that DeBartolo is paying too little for the shopping centers at $400 million, when earlier you tried to steal them for $300 million for yourselves?"

Rothfeld sprang into action. Realizing that if Solow disappeared for the Christmas holidays, the Allied deal would probably disappear right along with him, Rothfeld held back the Manny Hanny banker as he gave the Campeau team a lecture. "I'm going to say something that may be out of line, but you must understand how serious this situation is. If the commercial paper doesn't roll in two days, you easily could lose your investment in this deal and First Boston might have to move against Campeau Corporation on our guarantee. You are sitting here playing a high-stakes game of chicken with De-Bartolo and the banks, and there is no time left for that. You've got to get on the phone and make the deal with DeBartolo for the shopping centers."

"Do you think I'm stupid?" David King from Campeau's team asked.

"I will if you don't get on that phone," Rothfeld retorted. Rothfeld's speech had its desired effect; King got back on the phone. Ten minutes later, the Campeau team emerged from a final call with the DeBartolo people to announce an agreement, and Campeau himself, negotiating from Toronto, had reaffirmed the $400 million price on the shopping centers.

Campeau also agreed to put $50 million of his own money into

Allied at a later date, to make up for any possible shortfall in the shopping-center deal, and to satisfy Manny Hanny that he wasn't getting a $4 billion company for nothing. Leaving the bank in the darkness of early evening, Buck Luce turned to Rothfeld and wondered: "Do you realize what we've created here?" "I'm afraid so," Rothfeld replied.*

As Campeau's relationship manager at First Boston, Kim Fennebresque was getting more than his share of Campeau phone calls. Some had to do with Campeau's demand that First Boston provide him with an equity bridge. "Bruce Wasserstein promised me $200 million for equity," Campeau complained. "What happened to that?"

"Oh yeah," Fennebresque retorted. "What happened to the $300 million in equity that you promised to put in in the first place?"

The Campeau-Fennesbresque dialogue on who owed equity to whom was abruptly terminated on Christmas morning, after Fennebresque, at home with his family, already had been interrupted by one Campeau phone call and had managed to respond in a semicivil tone. A second call came through at the moment Fennebresque had begun to carve the Christmas turkey, and Fennebresque hung up on First Boston's most lucrative client. "Before I did that, I told him where to put the goose," Fennebresque recalls.

On Monday, December 29, a shareholders meeting was called by Allied's CEO, Macioce, to take a final vote on Campeau's $69 offer for the remaining shares. About fifty people showed up for this meeting, which was abruptly adjourned until Tuesday. On Tuesday, a smaller group of shareholders was told the meeting would be adjourned until Wednesday. Behind the scenes, yet another snag had developed between Campeau and DeBartolo.

"This is a very complex financing. We're dealing with eleven law firms and sixteen banks, it all takes time," an Allied attorney told the few shareholders who'd come back on Wednesday. But the lingering complication was the Campeau equity. If DeBartolo dropped out now, as he again threatened to do, then Campeau once again

---

* Thirty-six hours later, December 26, Citicorp refinanced the Allied commercial paper.

would be short $150 million. And, as it had before, First Boston considered giving Campeau the money with an emergency equity bridge. But the firm was reluctant to take this step.

Not until late Wednesday, hours away from New Year's Eve, did Campeau straighten things out with DeBartolo. The shareholders voted their approval, and Allied Stores was formally sold. A participant in the negotiations told Fairchild Publications' *Daily News Record,* "I haven't slept for four days. This was the hardest deal in the history of mankind."

# Seven

In the first week of January 1987, the conquering hero and his entourage entered Allied headquarters in the old W. R. Grace building at 1114 Avenue of the Americas in Manhattan, to inspect what they'd bought. Campeau was accompanied by his chief financial officer, Jim Roddy, who along with wunderkind Ron Tysoe had advanced to the forefront of the Campeau organization. Old-timers Don Carroll and David King, who'd thought of Campeau Corp. as a real estate company, were being phased out. Soon, both would resign.

Coming off the heady triumph of his $4.1 billion acquisition—for that was the final cost, including a whopping $612 million in fees, expenses, and financing charges—Campeau was at his energetic best. Associates said he'd never looked healthier or happier—and why not? Wall Street had given him a retail empire with almost no money down. Of course, he insisted he didn't plan to *run* the retail part. "I'm a tenderfoot," he'd said on several occasions. "I know nothing about the brassiere business." The management would be left to Macioce, Campeau's new buddy.

But by January 13, Macioce was gone. He'd stood arm-in-arm with Campeau on the stage of the rented theater only weeks earlier, but policy disagreements had arisen over the use of a limo and the

corporate jet, over which Campeau and Macioce had been squab-
bling for days.

Allied employees knew the end was near when Campeau ordered
Macioce to come to work on a Sunday. "That son of a bitch," Ma-
cioce complained to his pilot, "he agreed to let me run this place.
Then he violated my contract." Macioce resigned.

Campeau promptly took over Macioce's old office and hired an
architect to revamp it. He bought Macioce's Persian rug. He named
himself interim chief executive officer to Allied, and Howard Hassler, Macioce's second-in-command, the new president and chief
operating officer.

Macioce's exit was part of a general mass exodus out of Allied's
front office, and the company's four floors in the W. R. Grace Building were soon as devoid of human life as if they'd been hit by a
neutron bomb. On the executive floor, which had housed dozens of
employees across 25,000 square feet of space, there were now four
occupants: Campeau in Macioce's old office in one corner; his lieutenants Roddy and Tysoe in two more; and Howard Hassler in the
fourth. In between was a vast void of polyurethane.

The other Allied floors also began to vacate, and by the end of
1987, an estimated 3,500 employees, mostly from this central office,
the buying offices in the United States and in Europe, and the
division headquarters, would lose their jobs.

According to the theory and logic of the leveraged buyout, Campeau's takeover was beneficial, healthy, even virtuous. A sloppy inefficient company that muddled along under the uninspired
leadership of the dull, legalistic Macioce would be invigorated by
the flamboyant risk taker. Do-nothing bureaucrats would be given
the boot, flow charts redrawn, expenses reduced, all resulting in a
leaner and meaner Allied, more efficient, more profitable, more competitive, and more likely in the long run to survive.

The debt itself, the $4.1 billion borrowed from First Boston and
the commercial banks, was regarded in M&A circles as a puritanical
force, the whip under which the new Allied would be forced to shape
up. The Phase II Citicorp–Manny Hanny loan was syndicated and
complete, and First Boston had filed registration statements with the
SEC to get its bridge loan repaid by selling senior notes due in
1997, junk bonds maturing in 1999, and 10 million shares of a new

form of stock, "PIK preferred," which paid dividends not in money but in more paper.

The business plan for Allied Stores itself, developed by First Boston and by Roddy, was that Campeau would cut costs to add about $100 million to Allied's cash flow, and at the same time unload several unproductive divisions to pay back some of the debt.

Sixteen of the twenty-four divisions were put on the auction block—all the losers and the laggards that together had contributed only 12 percent of Allied's profits. Campeau would then be left with the eight divisions that generated 88 percent of the profits. He'd keep Ann Taylor, Brooks Brothers, Jordan Marsh in Boston and in Florida, Stern's in New Jersey, Maas Brothers in Florida, and the Bon Marché in Seattle. The Read's division in New England would be merged into Jordan Marsh.

In the alchemy of an LBO, a great fortune could be created out of nothing by making such simple realignments. Sell off losers to lower the debt and eliminate overhead, pay down the debt with cash flow from the retained divisions, and presto, the smaller, more efficient Allied would be worth billions, with Campeau owning 100 percent of it. These billions could be created without Allied having to increase its sales by a single dress or even a towel, or to expand into a single new mall.

It was all written down in First Boston and Roddy's plan that Campeau only had to follow, to let the financial magic do its work. The bankers were only slightly unsettled that Campeau had driven Macioce away and installed himself as CEO. The divisional managers seemed to be capable of directing the day-to-day operations. And after all, it was Campeau's company.


The ink had scarcely dried on the sale documents before Allied's new CEO announced: I want to have a party. I want to invite the most important corporate leaders of America. They will come to applaud my great victory. The First Boston people called this Campeau's Debutante Party. He asked Bruce Wasserstein to arrange it.

Party-planning is not one of the services that investment bankers normally provide, but Campeau was coming on strong about this, and besides, First Boston stood to make a total $200 million in fees, once the junk bonds and the sixteen divisions were sold, and it wasn't good business to alienate a client of the firm. "We weren't about to pay for it, though," says Kim Fennebresque, the man who had hung up on the client on Christmas Day, and to whom the unpopular assignment of planning the party was handed by Wasserstein. A proper site was chosen—the reconstructed Temple of Dendur at the Metropolitan Museum of Art.

Although First Boston didn't know it—First Boston being largely ignorant at this point about Campeau's colorful past—the applauding of great victories went back to the earliest Campeau subdivisions in Ottawa. Then, the catered homages were held in The Ottawa Auditorium, where as many as 7,000 people were invited to attend.

As Campeau got bigger, so also did the celebrations, which had culminated in the grand opening of his Harbour Castle Hotel in Toronto in 1976, with the Royal Regiment Guard of Honour in attendance and the miniskirted waitresses bearing plates of venison, plus the curious lecture by the guest of honor, previously described.

"Is he really serious?" Fennebresque rhetorically asked his colleagues. "Does he really think the leaders of government and industry care that he just took over Allied Stores?" But the party planning went forward.

Campeau and Ilse, who was known to First Boston only as the second wife and was rarely seen in the months Campeau was camped at the Waldorf, designed the invitations themselves. On the front was a reproduction of La Boulangère, a painting by Canadian artist Clarence Gagnon. The text inside explained the special meaning of this painting to the Campeaus: "During a live auction, Robert Campeau won his telephone bid for La Boulangère . . . Ilse Campeau saw this happy outcome as an omen of Campeau's successful entry into American commerce."

Fennebresque, the debutant coordinator, marveled at this self-glorifying artifact, but he nonetheless dutifully mailed it out to a wide selection of VIPs in New York. Responses were split evenly between "Who's Campeau?" and "So what?" As the big date, Thursday, January 15, approached, it was obvious to First Boston that the leaders of commerce and industry weren't tripping over themselves to reserve a table at the Temple of Dendur in order to honor Campeau. But nobody wanted to give the client this bad news.

As happened so often in this story, from the first meetings with the bankers in Toronto, Campeau's hirelings took the prudent course and declined to disabuse him of a fantasy—in this case, New York's applauding his victory. Invitations went out to employees at First Boston, Paine Webber, Cravath, and Citicorp, plus other vendors, bond salesmen and so forth, who stood to benefit from the deal. At First Boston, Fennebresque recalls, people were "strongly encouraged" to attend, and a contingent from the West Coast office was flown in to pad the crowd.

As for who would emcee this glorious event and toast the guest of honor, there was a noticeable lack of volunteers. It was one thing for First Boston to risk its entire capital for the sake of this client, but quite another to have to introduce him at a dinner party. Pete Buchanan didn't want to do it; Wasserstein didn't want to do it; Fennebresque didn't want to do it. But Fennebresque was pressured into it from higher-ups in the pecking order.

So much did Fennebresque despise the assignment of "eulogizing this jerk" that even after he'd agreed to take it, he feigned laryngitis and handed the job to Alvin Shoemaker, an old-timer who was First Boston's chairman.

Tables were set up on pallets on the stone floor, around the pool in front of the Temple. Strolling trumpeters passed through the pyramid; it was dramatically lit with floodlights. Campeau, resplendent in his tuxedo, was flanked by his wife, tall and pale as a Valkyrie and dressed in white; a Canadian Cardinal dressed in formal red; Pierre Trudeau, the ex–prime minister of Canada, whom Campeau had personally invited; actress Margo Kidder, Trudeau's companion; and a two-hundred-pound vocalist in a kaftan, whom Campeau had imported for entertainment.

Trudeau and Kidder were the only celebrities; the rest of the crowd was comprised of bankers and assistant bankers, attorneys, syndicators and number crunchers, and only five representatives from Allied Stores, Macioce of course not among them. It was a reunion of lenders and lawyers, sent out to applaud the lendee.

As the moment they'd all been waiting for arrived, Campeau took the microphone and congratulated America, congratulated free enterprise, thanked those who helped him win his wonderful victory, and then launched into an extemporaneous lecture on the state of the world currency markets. People in the audience were toying with coffee spoons and the remnants of their desserts, unsure of what to make of this.*

An enigmatic figure to his bankers, even after the months they'd spent with him, Campeau was now living nearly full-time at the Waldorf Towers and visiting Toronto on weekends. After an early-morning swim or a jog around Central Park, and then his usual breakfast of bran muffins, Evian water, and fresh-squeezed orange juice, he'd take a limousine downtown to his new office at Allied.

"It's the best deal I've ever done in my life. It's a terrific company, everything I want," Campeau told *Women's Wear Daily,* where his retailing opinions had begun to appear in print. "Buying at the right price, isn't that what it's all about?" he asked, in *Forbes.*

But buying at the right price, then sitting back and letting the LBO magic do its work were yesterday's objectives. Now that the deal had closed, Campeau's round-the-clock energy and relentless enthusiasm was loosed on Allied itself. He wanted it to be the show-piece of American retailing. Though he'd told the company's shell-shocked management more than once, "You guys take care of the retail side," he was personally involved from Day One. "Here," says a Jordan Marsh executive, "was a Steinbrenner in the making."

From Seattle to Boston, Campeau crisscrossed the country in the Gulfstream, on a combination victory tour and review of Allied operations. Often, he'd arrive late at the airport, chastising the pilot for having kept the engines running—"a waste of money," he said. Destinations and itineraries were subject to sudden change, sometimes in mid-flight. He traveled with several suitcases, which, with the pilot's assistance, he would open and rearrange on the tarmac: this pair of socks in that one—no, this shirt in this one. He carried no credit cards or money, expecting that someone in his entourage

* A later closing dinner for the financiers and lenders to the Allied deal was a more raucous occasion at which friendly insults were traded. Rothfeld of First Boston was awarded a whip to whip the junk-bond market into buying Campeau/Allied bonds, and everyone present was given a cowboy hat to which was stapled a card that proclaimed: "We Bet the Ranch."

would follow behind and pick up his tabs. At each stop, he'd be greeted by a division head, usually with one limousine but later sometimes with two—the first to take his numerous bags straight to the hotel and the second to carry him and the division head downtown to the flagship Allied store.

To these division heads, who remembered Macioce as a killjoy and a penny-pincher, tied to the New York office and thwarting their ambitions, Campeau was more than a pleasant surprise; he was a godsend. Macioce hadn't visited the Bon Marché in Seattle in five years; Campeau was there several times in two months. They found him to be attentive and full of questions about every aspect of retailing, down to the smallest detail. He was intelligent, charming, optimistic, and he listened to their ideas. Far from the tyrannical tightwad whom they were predisposed to dislike, the corporate raider come to cut the budget, here was a jolly fellow with a foreign accent, an open mind, and an open checkbook.

From the Bon Marché to Jordan Marsh, Campeau wowed them all. True, the division heads soon were aware of certain Campeau eccentricities—his constant need for pampering; his demand for fresh orange juice, special swimming goggles, and unchlorinated swimming pools; his never having money in his pocket and borrowing from everyone around him ("at restaurants, he'd eat and then just get up and leave," marveled one Allied executive); and his forgetting people's names—but these were understood as the prerogatives of a rich man and the absentmindedness of a visionary who was devoting his life to the betterment of Allied Stores. "I'm not breaking Allied into pieces to make money," Campeau told executives at Jordan Marsh headquarters in Miami. "I'm out to make an impact on the retail community."

In New England, he traveled like a presidential candidate, riding through Maine in a bus outfitted with phones and a TV to visit the farthest-flung Jordan Marsh outlets. At a Bon Marché store outside of Seattle, president William Fix happened to mention a pet project of his, remerchandising the store's lower level for $2 million. "I could hardly believe it," Fix recalled, "when Campeau said it would be no problem. Do it. Without a second thought. What about the paperwork? I asked. 'Just do it,' he answered, 'and send me a letter.' He did ask if the project would pay out. I assured him that it would.

"At dinner on his first visit," Fix continued, "Campeau told me that Allied was fat at the top and control-oriented, fat in the stores and mediocre in appearance, that the service was poor, that in retailing in America at large the service was poor. Most of these observations were right on target!

"We went to the downtown store, and Campeau was ecstatic about the old Art Deco building. He went on and on about restoring it. His idea was grandiose. He wanted it to be the kind of store I'd have liked to have, if I had the money. Marble. High ceilings. Fine wall coverings. Atriums. Skylights. The boutique idea. He said customers wanted boutiques.

"This was a big project, I told him. Probably not practical. Putting an atrium through the middle, adding skylights, balconies, boutiques, it was an unbelievable dream. But he wanted to pursue it. In the end, though, he agreed that the project was too costly, and we all settled on a more traditional remodel.

"We went to other stores. He wanted to open them up with atriums, too. At the initial meeting with the executive committee, he said upbeat things, dwelled a lot on marble, on atriums, on the boutiques. Where Macioce was negative, Campeau was positive. He was willing to spend money."

Same thing in Boston, atriums everywhere, Campeau had a fetish for atriums. There'd be increased sales at all the divisions. There'd be an instant replenishment system, so if a shelf emptied on Monday it would be full again on Tuesday. There'd be cost-cutting where it counted, in the overstaffed central office. There'd be a better computer network, commissions for salesclerks, stock options for executives, classier merchandise, renovated stores. The triumph of Allied would inspire the renaissance in retailing.

To his audiences, these were unrealistic expectations, but somewhat more believable coming from a man who had beaten the odds in the takeover, a man to whom the banks had lent billions. In early 1987, with the stock market moving to all-time highs, many things that sounded too good to be true were happening on Wall Street.

"One day," says an Allied source, "an Allied accountant noticed a strange request for a million-dollar-plus disbursement of Allied funds. Howard Hassler, Allied's newly appointed president, was notified. What was this? he must have wondered. It turned out that

Campeau was trying to make a down payment on an expensive apartment with a private swimming pool.

"Bob made no distinction between his own private money and the corporate treasure chest," the source continues. "He was used to that in his own company. He had his own accountant in Toronto, whose job it was to run behind him and to put his expenses in the proper columns in the ledger books. But at Allied we weren't used to this. Nobody had ever done anything like trying to buy an apartment with Allied funds. When we brought this up with his people, the disbursement was canceled."

This foiled purchase was only an example of Campeau's whimsical impulses and free-wheeling approach to money and projects to which Allied management, accustomed to careful study of even the smallest expenditure, was now subjected. If Ilse didn't like the bathroom at a Jordan Marsh store in Boston, Campeau wanted something done about it. At Brooks Brothers, he hounded the man in charge, Frank Riley, with his idea of introducing "Armani-type suits"—the kind that Campeau wore. Having taken a liking to Jordan Marsh, he decided it deserved to be a nationwide franchise. Having read about an innovative computer system in a magazine, he sent a team to Europe to study it.

"Not only did he create a project a minute, he thought he could clap his hands and things would be done immediately," says an Allied executive. "He thought it would be a good idea to merge Jordan Marsh with another New England division, Read's, which was part of the game plan. But Campeau's approach was to call and say, 'Tell me how much we can save with this and get back to me this afternoon.' He expected to merge the divisions immediately. He was oblivious to the politics."

In February, the top executives from all the Allied divisions were holed up in a New York office for three days in a snowstorm. Campeau didn't want them to leave until they came up with a five-year business plan for the company. "Our assignment," according to a member of the snowbound group, "was to figure out how Allied earnings, before interest and taxes, could be increased to 12 percent companywide. This was impossible. The best Jordan Marsh had ever done was 9–9½ percent, and some divisions had done much worse. The average was probably 6–7 percent.

"The 12 percent, we decided, was what Campeau needed to satisfy the banking syndicates so he could get his permanent financing. We tried to give it to him on paper, even though we knew it was ridiculous."

The winter and spring of 1987 was an exciting time to bump into Campeau. He was full of the Lotto winner's largess, and if caught on a good day, he might offer you a dream job with a remarkable salary, plus incentives such as stock options. Ben Riggs was a typical beneficiary. He was in the regional shopping mall business. Out of nowhere, he got a call from a headhunter and found himself sitting in the lobby of Allied Stores in New York, with an appointment to be interviewed by Campeau himself.

Riggs had settled into a chair in the waiting room and was reading a magazine when he saw a man in a funny hat run by him, muttering to himself about being late for an appointment. The Mad Hatter disappeared out the front door. "That wasn't Mr. Campeau by any chance, was it?" Riggs asked the secretary, sensing for some reason that it was. "He's the person I've just flown in to see."

The secretary apologized and went off to check with the inner office. She returned to say that Mr. Campeau had been called away unexpectedly, and wondered if Mr. Riggs would like to meet with Allied's president, Mr. Howard Hassler, as a substitute. Not knowing why he was being interviewed at Allied in the first place, Riggs answered, "Yes, why not?" and then met with Hassler. Riggs explained that he was involved in shopping-center management and before that had worked for the Sun Oil company. Hassler didn't have the slightest idea why Riggs had been invited to Allied, either.

The appointment was rescheduled. Once again, Riggs flew to New York, where he chatted briefly with Campeau and found him to be "dynamic and charming like Maurice Chevalier." "You'll do just fine," Campeau told him, after having asked a few questions. Riggs wondered, "Fine at what?" "Senior vice president of real estate," Campeau said. In addition to handling the real estate for the nine Allied divisions that Campeau said he was going to keep, Riggs would be planning ten new shopping centers that Campeau said he intended to build in the coming year.

Riggs was as impressed by this incredible job offer as he was dubious that anybody could build ten new shopping centers in a year. "That's ludicrous," he thought to himself. Out loud, he said, "It would be difficult to accomplish such a project in so short a time." "Don't be silly," scolded Campeau. "You're being too negative."

Hired at a generous salary, plus incentives, Riggs accepted the position of senior vice president of Campeau real estate. One of his functions was to accompany Campeau on trips, where he picked up the hotel and restaurant tabs that the boss never thought of paying. The ten shopping centers never materialized.

On Easter Sunday 1987, after a week or so on the job, Riggs was airborne with Campeau in the Gulfstream jet on a tour of the Allied stores. The boss, in another fine mood, offered Riggs another big promotion. "I want you to be the president of Campeau U.S.," Campeau blurted out matter-of-factly. This was a major post in the organization, as Campeau U.S. was the parent company of the department stores. From what Riggs could gather, Campeau had wanted his old friend David King, president of Campeau Canada, to take this new position as well, but he and King had had a falling out over the Allied purchase, with which King had disagreed.

By now accustomed to Campeau's unpredictability, Riggs was nonetheless unprepared for this elevation. In fact, he could hardly believe what he was hearing. He'd been on the job only a few days and was certainly no expert in retailing, so why should Campeau put him in charge of the most important U.S. holding company? Riggs decided to let the matter pass, and to wait for Campeau to bring it up a second time. Campeau did; and Riggs became president of Campeau U.S.

Later in 1987 Campeau and Riggs had a falling out. According to Riggs, this resulted from an argument Campeau was having with the owner of a shopping mall in Massachusetts. This owner wanted an Allied store to anchor his mall, but Campeau refused to cooperate unless he got a 50 percent equity interest in the mall as compensation. This demand was rejected by the owner as preposterous, but Campeau somehow got it into his head that the owner had agreed to the terms.

"When the imaginary 'deal' fell apart, for in truth there never was a deal, Campeau blamed me for screwing up the negotiations," says Riggs. "He blew up at me and called me stupid."

With Campeau flying around to create a renaissance in retailing, his lenders had a simpler task: getting their money back. First Boston was planning the junk-bond sale to repay its bridge loan. Citicorp and the banking syndicate were planning to retire more than $1 billion in Campeau debt with the proceeds from the sale of several Allied divisions. Another chunk of debt would be replaced with a giant mortgage on Allied's real estate. This was the textbook strategy for a leveraged buyout: substitute long-term financing, at lower interest rates, for the expensive short-term takeover loans.

In March, the first article revealing personal details about Campeau that Macioce had learned months earlier was published in Canada. Arthur Johnson's "The Best Revenge" appeared in Toronto's *Report on Business* magazine. In it, Johnson characterized Campeau as a "blood-sport enthusiast who is most alive when killing moose." He also described the two emotional breakdowns—the 1970 episode in which Campeau sold his entire company on a whim, fell apart, then put himself back together by swinging a hammer; and the 1980 episode that followed the thwarted attempt to take over Royal Trustco, about which Johnson wrote: "While he would dearly love to see his enemies burn in hell, the experience plunged Campeau back into his own mental purgatory . . . but this time, it was travel and contemplation that finally brought him around again."

*Report on Business* was not widely read in the United States, and the U.S. financial press didn't pick up the story. The math of the Campeau deal was far more important than any speculation about the owner's psychology, and it seemed there was considerable safety in Allied's numbers: the cash flow, the projected cost savings, and the company's valuable assets. Any slight concern on the part of First Boston that revelations about Campeau's moose-killing or prior emotional problems would disenchant the potential buyers of Allied junk bonds proved unfounded.

First Boston's junk-bond "road show" was a big hit with investors in ten cities. Campeau himself was isolated from the proceedings —"it's beneath you" and "a waste of your time" his advisers convinced him—and the presentations were made by Roddy and by Howard Hassler. First Boston sources say that Hassler was harboring some hostility to the new Allied owners, and he vented it here. At the meeting in New York, Hassler had to be warned to stop making snide comments, they were trying to sell junk! Still, the entire $1.15 billion issue sold out.

Insurance companies, pension funds, and many of the high-yield bond funds couldn't get enough of Allied. The Allied junk was so popular, that the yield was bid down to 11.5 percent—a record low for this sort of debt.

Buyers were impressed with Allied's cash-flow projections; with its famous divisions, Brooks Brothers, Ann Taylor, the Bon Marché, and Jordan Marsh; and with the explicit covenants in the lending agreements that restricted Campeau from diverting these assets for other purposes without compensating the bondholders.

Not only did the junk sell out, but First Boston was also able to peddle $250 million worth of pay-in-kind paper, the "PIK preferred." PIK preferred was riskier than a regular junk bond, since it ranked below junk in the lineup of claimants on the company's assets. In addition, instead of receiving dividends in cash for the first few years, the PIK holder was paid with more paper. This was a financier's dream—junk that was junkier than junk and paid off with junk, which for a long period of time amounted to an interest-free loan.

Customarily, when a corporate raider couldn't raise enough money to buy a company outright, as was often the case, he'd offer a package of cash and securities, a.k.a. cram-down paper. But cram-down paper, as previously noted, was very unpopular, especially with arbs who wanted cash for their shares. The solution was to sell the cram-down paper to third parties, repackaged and marketed as PIK preferred. The cash proceeds could then be applied to the takeover deal.

The successful sale of PIK preferred in Allied revolutionized the pricing of deals, just as the Street Sweep bridge loan revolutionized the funding of deals. Right away, other M&A departments started imitating First Boston, and investment bankers began to price their deals based on the amount of PIK paper they thought they could unload.

Inspired by Campeau, First Boston had now come up with two great innovations, the Street Sweep and PIK preferred, plus one good try, the dividend ploy.

The Campeau team was talking to Prudential, the insurance company, about giving Campeau the giant Allied mortgage. "We weren't going ahead with this until we'd met with the man personally," a Prudential source says. "Frankly, that was a unique experience. Our people asked Campeau a lot of specific questions about Allied that he didn't even bother to answer. He sort of flicked these questions off. He wanted to talk about real estate values worldwide. His attitude was 'I'm global.'

"We were also taken aback somewhat by his bullishness on retailing. In our back office, the experts were saying that retailing was due for a downturn, yet Campeau was being wildly positive. We asked him to explain why, but he didn't really have an explanation.

"On balance, though, we were favorably impressed. He came across as a big thinker, with a lot to say about Russia and such esoteric subjects as the effect of U.S.–Soviet relations on world oil prices.

"As for the mortgage deal itself, the Allied real estate seemed to us to be excellent collateral. We looked at Campeau's empire and saw a half billion in net worth there. We also saw that Brooks Brothers and Ann Taylor could be sold for emergency cash if a crisis ever developed.

"It took six months, from April to December, to work through all the paperwork—title searches, evaluation, hazardous waste reports, asbestos reports—but we ended up writing mortgages for three hundred Allied stores. All along the way, there were significant differences between what we thought these properties were worth and what Campeau thought they were worth. But in the end, we loaned him $462 million."

These were jolly times indeed for big borrowers, with government leading the way on its deficit binge, as banks, S&Ls, and insurance companies tripped over themselves to lend to the maximum of the giddy valuations attached to everything from condos to corporations to collectibles. The Debtor Barons became billionaires on paper almost overnight, not from steel or oil or railroads as was the case with their robber baron ancestors, but from takeover and real estate loans.

Along with the junk-bond road show, First Boston was also in charge of selling sixteen of Allied's least profitable divisions, hopefully at ridiculously high prices that would bring in another $1 billion or so to pay back Campeau's lenders. Among the minority of attractive franchises put on the block (Cain-Sloan of Nashville, Donaldson's in Minnesota), was a sorry conglomeration that had dragged down Allied profits for years. Who in his right mind would want to buy Block's, the number-three department store in Indianapolis and losing money; or worse, Herpolsheimer's in Grand Rapids, Michigan, with the unfortunate nickname "Herps"?

Indeed, who would want to buy the hapless Dey's of Syracuse; or Joske's of Texas, a major disappointment in a state suffering a recession; or Bonwit Teller, a big name but lately just as big a loser; or Garfinckel's, a women's store in Washington undone by the competition; or Plymouth Shops, which catered to secretaries on their lunch hour, a success in New York, but unproven elsewhere?

The task of marketing this unattractive merchandise, which First Boston, speaking the popular lingo, called "finding a synergistic fit," fell on the shoulders of Allan Ruchman and his thirty-year-old cohort, Jeff Branman. First Boston hired Branman away from the retailing business (he'd worked at the May Company in St. Louis) for just this sort of assignment. Branman, a good-natured chap with an appreciation for Campeau, knew Allied well. May Company had considered taking over Allied, before it decided to go after Associated Dry Goods instead.

Beginning in February, as Campeau was making his victory tour, Branman and Ruchman were racking their brains trying to think of prospective buyers, for the sixteen Allied divisions. "We got out our phone books and literally called the world," Branman says. Semiserious buyers were sent packets of information; serious buyers were invited to Allied headquarters to visit data rooms, about the size of fitting rooms, each of which contained a table and a couple of chairs and a book of financial and legal details on the division in question. Buyers who were still interested were then invited to interviews with division management. Whenever he could, Branman sat in on those interview sessions, trying to learn useful things that would help him coax them into making higher offers.

In theory, the information gathering would lead to an auction date, at which time Herps, Garfinckel's, etc., would be sold to the highest bidder. But the last thing First Boston wanted to do was rely entirely on auctions. In several cases where the interest was at best lukewarm, there was only one serious bidder, and in the case of Herps, there were no interested bidders at all.

Selling Cain-Sloan and Joske's proved not to be a problem, as Dillard Department Stores, a substantial franchise, offered a decent price for the pair. But with others, First Boston had discovered that the likely bids would be too low for Campeau to make the projected $1.1 billion in total proceeds from the asset sales that the banks were requiring. First Boston's solution to this dilemma was to induce the lukewarm bidders to raise their prices.

Where there was little apparent interest, Branman and Ruchman did their best to simulate it by creating the illusion of competition. The idea was to convince a likely buyer, aka "a live one," that other interested parties were ready to bid on whatever division he was thinking of buying, and then to scare him into making a generous preemptive offer. "Give us your best price now," Branman would advise, "and we'll shut down the auction process." When this ploy worked, First Boston was elated.

In one of the most spectacular examples of a live one overbidding for an Allied division, the Crown American company was panicked into making a ridiculously high preemptive bid for Miller's of Knoxville, a second-rate franchise for which First Boston expected to get $75–80 million at most. Crown American had wanted to buy Cain-Sloan, but when that franchise was awarded to Dillard, Crown American's management became desperate to buy Miller's. To Branman's amazement, Crown American shut down the auction process on Miller's with a bid of $95 million! "I was struggling to keep a straight face," Branman recalls, on receiving the news of this bid.

Another promising live one, whom First Boston could see coming from halfway across Manhattan Island, was George Herscu. Like Campeau, Herscu was a foreign real estate tycoon (Australian) who saw America as the land of opportunity for brilliant investors such as himself. Against good advice, Herscu was attracted to Block's, one of the most dismal of the Allied divisions, a chain of stores in Indianapolis where the cash flow was insufficient to support current operations. There were no other suitors for Block's; Herscu had the offbeat idea of opening a Block's in Denver.

But soon enough the Australian tycoon had fallen in love with a flashier loser: Bonwit Teller. Bonwit had a better name than balance sheet. Branman's analysis was: "struggling to get out of the hole," and "cheapening itself with downscale merchandise." At the right price, Bonwit might have been "turnaroundable," in Wall Street parlance, but First Boston's job was to insure that Herscu wouldn't pay the right price.

With only a slight push from the sidelines, the Australian was convinced to secure his ownership of Bonwit with a preemptive whopper of $95 million. The next highest offer—the only other offer, as it turned out—was in the $60 million range.

Herscu's own investment bankers at Shearson (you see how one deal could lead to many others) advised him that $95 million was a crazy price to pay for Bonwit. For an investment banker to poo-poo a potential deal was itself a rarity, and what's more unusual, Shearson volunteered to base its fee on a lower $70 million purchase price, just to prove that the firm had no vested interest in the client's overpayment.

Against his banker's advice, Herscu continued to stick to the $95 million offer, which Branman of First Boston was eager to formalize as quickly as possible. Expecting that Campeau himself would be overjoyed, Branman relayed the happy news to the Campeau staff in New York: "$95 million for Bonwit's. Can you believe it?"

But Campeau was neither overjoyed nor even satisfied. The word came back from wherever he was traveling that he was refusing Herscu's $95 million. He wanted more.

"Turning it down? Hey, guys, be reasonable," pleaded the incredulous Branman to Roddy and Tysoe. "Let's look at the risk/reward here. We've got ninety-five million dollars in the bag, and if this buyer drops out, the next highest bidder is in the sixties."

This argument meant nothing. The next highest bidder could have been in the twenties and it wouldn't have mattered. To Campeau's way of thinking, Bonwit Teller was worth more than $95 million and more was what he would get. He was adamant. Eventually, he got Herscu to increase his preemptive whopper from $95 million to an even more ridiculous $102 million. Campeau had risked losing the deal to squeeze an extra $7 million out of a buyer who didn't realize that he, and not Campeau, had the upper hand. "At negotiating, the guy was a genius," Branman says. "I still can't believe he pulled it off."

A similar thing happened with Crown American, after it was panicked into offering $95 million for Miller's of Knoxville. Campeau once again refused to accept the bid. He wanted $105 million. The incredulous Branman returned to Crown American and somehow managed to get its emissaries in New York to jack up the price to $102 million, and both sides shook hands on the revised deal.

At the same time and unbeknownst to Branman, Campeau had taken matters into his own hands and convinced his new pal and equity partner, Ed DeBartolo, to relay a message to Crown American's CEO, Frank Pascarella. Apparently on Campeau's word, DeBartolo informed Pascarella that there were other bidders for Miller's, and that in order to buy the division, Pascarella would have to raise his offer to $105 million. Pascarella did. He didn't realize that his investment bankers and advisers in New York had already made a deal with Campeau's advisers for $102 million, and in fact there were no other bidders willing to pay more than $75–80 million.

Riding the swell of these successes, which had proven to Campeau that he, and not First Boston, knew how much a retail franchise was really worth, Campeau nixed yet another sale: Donaldson's of Minneapolis. Donaldson's was the number-two chain in the area, and the most likely prospective buyer, Carson Pirie Scott of Chicago, flew a management team to New York to make the deal. Carson Pirie had been led to believe that both sides had come to terms, and that its winning bid was accepted.

Campeau ushered the Carson Pirie Scott team into his office. For twenty minutes or so, he lectured them about the U.S. economy, the importance of keeping interest rates low, and the negative impact of declining oil production. Had they taken a wrong turn, they wondered, and somehow ended up in a macroeconomics class? Finally, Campeau changed the subject to Donaldson's. He said he liked everything about the Carson Pirie offer except the price.

Campeau's own price was $35 million higher than the price that Carson Pirie thought both sides had agreed to, which was the basis for Carson Pirie's trip to New York. "Gee, I'm sorry to hear that," said Carson Pirie's CEO, Peter Willmott, as soon as Campeau had made his new demand. The Carson Pirie contingent got up, shook hands with Campeau, and left.

With no other bidders for Donaldson's, the division sat all summer without a buyer. Top executives quit, the stores deteriorated, and no counteroffers materialized. At the end of the summer, Campeau set up another meeting with Carson Pirie. This one was less cordial.

"He ranted and raved," said a participant in that meeting. "Then he issued us a threat. The gist of it was 'Buy Donaldson's if you know what's good for you, or else I might take *you* over.'" In September, Carson Pirie Scott bought Donaldson's for the price it had offered in the first place.

Within nine months, all of Allied's laggard divisions were sold to a variety of buyers, some of them live ones, for nearly $1.1 billion, within $100,000 of the amount needed to satisfy the banks. The extra $40–50 million Campeau had managed to wheedle out of Herscu and Crown American enabled First Boston to meet this goal. His investment bankers marveled at Campeau's steely bravado and his relentless pursuit of every iota of advantage.*

But if Campeau's successful last-minute interventions in three sales raised his stock in his bankers' eyes, it had the opposite effect on his opinion of them. After all, he told his own advisers, if he'd listened to First Boston and accepted those inadequate bids, he'd be out several million dollars, so what was the point of paying for all the high-priced advice?

* The sale of Allied divisions that was hailed as a great triumph for Campeau and his bankers, and a boon to the Allied balance sheet, had disastrous consequences for many of the buyers and their corporate balance sheets. Bonwit Teller, sold to Herscu at such a high price it couldn't possibly survive, fell into Chapter 11 with most of its outlets liquidated; Garfinckel's was sold to Raleigh's stores, which, thanks in part to the added burden, is also in Chapter 11; Miller & Rhoads, taken private in its own leveraged buyout, likewise has entered that familiar chapter; Plymouth Shops was sold to Tribeca, which struggled to restructure the excessive debt; Carson Pirie Scott, which bought Donaldson's, was yet another corporate casualty, having taken on excess debt as a defensive maneuver to avoid being acquired by the likes of Campeau.

In only a minority of cases, such as the purchases of Joske's and Cain-Sloan by the powerful and well-organized Dillard Department Stores, did the Allied divestitures add to anyone's prosperity except the bankruptcy lawyers'. Several became subsidiary fiascoes of the main fiasco, resulting in more shutdowns and more layoffs than usually are counted on the Campeau casualty list.

"You couldn't help noticing at meetings," says a source from Prudential, Campeau's mortgage lender, "how little respect he had for First Boston. I'd never in my life seen a client berate his bankers the way that Campeau did in mid-1987. One of them would ask Campeau a question, and he'd completely ignore it, shrug it off. Or else he'd say something like, 'Aren't you the people who said Bonwit's was only worth $95 million?' "

# Eight

For most of June and into July 1987, Campeau traveled around Europe in Allied's Gulfstream, on which he had spent $800,000 to redo the interior. He flew to Hannover, Germany, and to Venice, Italy, with a stop in Pisa, where, short on cash, he picked up $6,000 from an Allied representative. According to the pilot, he returned to Hannover to get more longevity injections. He went to London and Marseilles, and he briefly lent the plane to his new investors, the Reichmanns, their plane apparently having been disabled in Zurich.

(Although the Reichmanns had told Campeau they would not invest in a business they knew nothing about—i.e., retailing—Campeau had convinced them to buy a half interest in his new Toronto high rise, Scotia Plaza, for $50 million. He used the proceeds to add to his equity, thus satisfying a Manny Hanny requirement from the previous Christmas Eve.)

Returning to Toronto for the July annual meeting of the Campeau Corporation—the first since the Allied purchase—a calm and confident Campeau addressed the spillover crowd. The brunt of local jokes returned a hero, his many detractors forced to stew in his good fortune. He'd gone away a middling Canadian real estate developer and returned a major U.S. retailer, and a celebrity below the border. If Canada hadn't recognized the greatness in him, Wall Street obviously had. It loaned him $4 billion.

"I never doubted I could pull it off," Campeau told his assembled shareholders. "Clinching the deal required determination, some luck and hard work, and lots of eighteen- to twenty-hour days." In a slap at Canadian provincialism, he observed that his triumph was also a triumph of the "less controlled free market economy," in the United States.

The only bad news of the session was the continuing heavy losses from Texas real estate, with as many as three hundred Campeau condo units repossessed, but this was a minor nuisance as compared to the wonders of department stores, and underscored the wisdom of Campeau's having veered off in the unexpected direction. "At last year's annual meeting, I informed you that we were actively looking for additional shopping-center acquisitions," David King, still the president of Campeau Corp., observed. "Little did I know that our pursuit . . . would result in the purchase of one of the largest retailers in North America."

His earlier plan to go national with the Jordan Marsh chain apparently having been shelved, Campeau shared with the crowd the latest fantastic proposition, taking Brooks Brothers and Ann Taylor to Europe, and opening fifty stores of each, "side-by-side" in several countries, and also opening twelve to fifteen Brooks Brothers stores and twenty-five to thirty Ann Taylors in Canada.

The enthusiasm was infectious, as Allied's president, Howard Hassler, took the microphone and predicted that Ann Taylor, with $200 million in annual gross sales at the time, would be doing $500 million in five years and $1 billion in ten—why not? If Campeau could take over Allied Stores, anything was possible.

So much had gone better than expected—the sale of the divisions, the junk-bond financing, the dismantling of Allied's central office, the mortgage financing—Wall Street was admiring this deal as a slam dunk. By midsummer, Campeau had found a way to pay back DeBartolo for the equity loan. He'd bought a half interest in the Allied shopping centers from DeBartolo, finally getting a piece of that action—with money from his Canadian corporation.

"I have made many people who worked for me millionaires in my day," he told *Women's Wear Daily,* "and I'm going to make many more." "Jerry," he told his pilot, Jerry Lamont, echoing the sentiment, "you buy stock in my company and you will be very rich someday."

1

With the help of his cousin, Robert Campeau got into the housing business swinging his own hammer. The initial result, shown here, sold for a quick profit in the late 1940s and ultimately led to the building of the high rises and apartment complexes that gave Ottawa its Campeau-made skyline.

By the mid-1970s, the once-parochial developer had metamorphosed into a snazzy dresser with no fear of the microphone, as shown at a press conference here.

2

3

In 1976, Campeau opened his Harbour Castle Hotel with adjoining condominiums, built along a much-disparaged Toronto waterfront, where other developers had feared to tread. (Later they scrambled to follow his lead.)

4

5

Scotia Plaza, the second-tallest building in Canada, taller than the zoning codes would normally allow, which Campeau was able to squeeze into the middle of the Toronto banking district.

As construction on Scotia Plaza began in the mid-1980s, Campeau was turning his attention away from real estate, toward major corporate acquisitions.

6

Former Canadian prime minister Pierre Trudeau (shown here with Campeau in 1984) was a familiar face at Campeau's celebratory bashes, living proof of the developer's political clout. In the center is Ilse, Campeau's second wife and former mistress.

7

Campeau's Bridle Path mansion in Toronto, built over the remains of the more modest existing mansion he tore down. Parts of the new dwelling were hardly put up before they, too, were remodeled—the hole for the swimming pool with its special nonchlorinated water system was already dug when Campeau decided to move the pool to the other side of the property.

8

The billionaire Reichmann brothers, Paul *(left)*, Albert *(center)*, and Ralph *(right)*, who had parlayed an instinct for real estate into one of the world's great fortunes. As reclusive and understated as Campeau was gregarious and flamboyant, the Reichmanns ended up investing an ever-increasing sum in his new and ill-fated enterprises.

9

10

Austin Taylor, horse lover, gourmand about Toronto, and Campeau's longtime banker. Campeau engaged Taylor in 1984–85 to help him find a nice company to buy, preferably a bank or an S&L.

Edward Finkelstein, the chairman of R. H. Macy, whom Campeau tried unsuccessfully to meet in 1985. At the time, Campeau wanted to involve himself in Macy's own leveraged buyout, which he'd been reading about in the newspapers.

11

Macy's brush-off of the unknown Canadian inspired Campeau to pursue his own leveraged buyout of another major retailer, Allied Stores, a company that had only recently come to his attention.

12

Northgate, one of Allied's five shopping centers (this one located in Seattle) that Campeau's financial advisers thought he might want to buy. Instead, he decided he'd rather buy all of Allied and its twenty-four retail divisions, including Brooks Brothers, Ann Taylor, and Jordan Marsh.

13

Allen Finkelson of Cravath, Swaine & Moore, one of New York's most prestigious law firms, enlisted as Campeau's takeover strategist in the unlikely campaign for Allied, a company with ten times the market value of Campeau's own.

14

Ron Tysoe, the youngest member of Campeau's brain trust, suspended his disbelief in the Allied campaign to put in long hours on the takeover effort.

15

Jim Roddy and Carolyn Buck Luce, two of Campeau's closest advisers, who carried on a baffling and intricate fiscal rumba with a long list of skittish bankers, while trying to keep Campeau's stormy temperament from ruining the deal.

16

17

Peter Buchanan, then CEO of First Boston, the white-shoe investment bank that got itself more and more deeply involved with this contentious and eccentric client, pushed along by the prospect of bigger and bigger fees.

Bruce Wasserstein, First Boston's ingenious takeover strategist, whose eleventh-hour machinations resulted in Campeau's winning Allied Stores against all odds, largely thanks to the fact that First Boston invested its entire corporate capital in this unlikely cause.

18

19

Thomas Macioce, now-deceased head of Allied Stores, flew off on a golden parachute after losing his company to the Canadian real estate developer who six months earlier had never heard of it.

After several banks had declined to participate, Citicorp, America's largest bank, rushed in to become Campeau's lead commercial lender through two campaigns, lending him everything including Campeau's own equity contribution, or downpayment, in the Allied deal.

20

Having won Allied Stores with $4 billion in bank loans and essentially none of his own money down, Campeau had scarcely settled into his new office before he set his sights on an even bigger target, Federated Department Stores, whose Cincinnati headquarters is shown here.

21

Many of Federated's 130,000 employees expressed their feelings about being taken over by the acquisitive Canadian with their version of the "Just Say No" button.

It was on his visits to a Florida outlet of Bloomingdale's that Campeau reportedly fell in love with Federated's flashiest and best-known division.

Ed DeBartolo, America's most successful shopping-mall developer, was a frugal billionaire who kept the office hours of an overworked clerk. DeBartolo was Campeau's rival in the bidding war for Allied but then, in a remarkable switch, became his equity partner. DeBartolo later invested $480 million in Campeau's Federated deal.

Brooks Brothers, which Campeau vowed never to sell, was abruptly dumped for an astonishing price and some of the proceeds diverted to his Federated takeover.

24

25

Howard Goldfeder, Federated's combative CEO. At a hastily called board meeting, Goldfeder refused to sell his company to Campeau, who had telephoned him to discuss buyout terms from an Austrian restaurant where he had been eating dinner at the time.

At Bloomingdale's "Hooray for Hollywood!" party, the triumphant Campeau appeared with Ilse to steal the show from the regular celebrities. Thanks to $7 billion in Wall Street loans, Campeau was the new owner of Federated, having wrested the company from Macy's, his rival bidder, at a very high price.

26

28

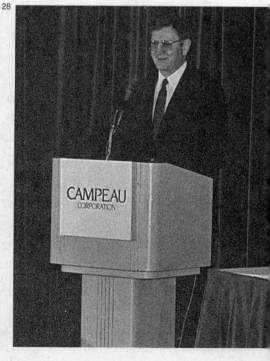

At a press conference after the Federated takeover, Campeau sits with his communications consultant, Davis Weinstock. Bob Morosky *(at podium),* Campeau's retailing expert, was introduced here as the new CEO of Federated. A week later, Morosky was gone.

27

Marvin Traub, known as Mr. Bloomingdale's for his devoted steward-
ship of the franchise, was pressed into service as tour guide and
party giver for his new boss. Once at a gathering in Chicago, Campeau announced: "Marvin, I'm going to teach you how to be more
profitable."

ROBERT CAMPEAU                       ALLEN FINKELSON

Campeau flew on a victory tour to Federated's divisions, including Rich's of Atlanta, shown here, which he continued to call "Rich." His slapdash management style and highly optimistic pronouncements made Rich's executives wonder if he was "crazy genius," or just "crazy crazy."

Campeau had picked up not one but two major U.S. retailers and planned to expand both in various combinations, such as the Jordan Marsh/Bloomingdale's project in Boston shown here. But $11 billion in takeover debt quickly proved fatal.

Campeau's domestic staff in Toronto expressing their enthusiasm for his takeover ventures. How could they have known that the mansion would soon be put up for sale?

CONGRATULATIONS MR. CAMPEAU

FROM STAFF

Campeau with his prized conversation piece, a twenty-three-hour clock from the French Revolution, which like the money to pay his takeover bills, regrettably came up short.

The dream house on Lake Attersee in Austria, built with bank loans from Canada. Following the bankruptcy filings of both Allied and Federated, Campeau spent much of his time here. The property is owned through a Liechtenstein foundation, which, Campeau's creditors have been saddened to discover, will likely protect it from them.

## 33

34

Campeau en route to a final meeting of his Campeau Corporation board of directors, where he was stripped of his chairmanship. Later, his own company sued him for unpaid loans.

In September, Campeau invited his entire executive staff—Campeau Canada plus Campeau/Allied—to a celebratory four-day retreat at the Homestead resort in Virginia. The corporate jet ferried key personnel back and forth between New York, Toronto, and Virginia.

This was the first chance for the old group from Canada, some of whom were still privately wary of the takeover, to meet the new group, including Allied's division heads, from the United States. The old group was amazed by the size of the Allied contingent and somewhat jealous of the new business family, on whom Campeau had been lavishing most of his attention. But it was a congenial gathering overall.

In the evenings, the Canadians sang songs in French with Campeau directing the chorus with his fork. Campeau, who loved to sing, had asked Richard Van Pelt, the president of Jordan Marsh, to initiate a sing-along to "break the ice." It was Campeau's idea to start the proceedings with a singing of the Canadian and the U.S. national anthems. That way, everyone would have to stand up.

In the afternoon there was a golf tournament. Campeau took golf very seriously. His golfing career, in fact, was a direct parallel to his business career: he was self-taught; he had improved his game by hitting hundreds of buckets of balls; he became an excellent player, but the best Canadian clubs had never offered him a membership. Among his friends, there was good-natured gossip about Campeau's kicking his ball back onto fairways or taking other emergency measures to improve his score, and about his punishing his golf clubs for their failure to perform by banging them against trees. That he couldn't stand losing was well known.

The tournament was for pairs of contestants, and Campeau was paired with Dick Van Pelt's wife, Joan. Mrs. Van Pelt wasn't much of a golfer, but nobody seemed to be taking this event very seriously.

The first time Mrs. Van Pelt flubbed a shot, Campeau took her by the shoulder and gently but firmly twisted her around to show her the proper swing. After eighteen holes of being pushed, pulled, exhorted, admonished, and reeducated by her husband's boss, Mrs. Van Pelt was an emotional and physical wreck. As for the scorekeeping, Ben Riggs, who was in a foursome with Campeau and Mrs. Van Pelt, recalls the following: "Campeau's secretary was my teammate. She was keeping score for the foursome, and didn't realize that

Campeau was keeping score himself. After the first nine holes, she announced something like, 'We've got a fifty-two and you've got a fifty-four,' which meant that Campeau and Mrs. Van Pelt were two strokes behind. Campeau quickly corrected her. 'No,' he said, 'you're wrong. We got a fifty-two and you got a fifty-six.' She wasn't going to argue with him. At the tenth tee, Campeau took over the official scorekeeping. He and Mrs. Van Pelt won the tournament."

Bob's winning was a tradition at Campeau outings, and the Allied people quickly caught on to the self-preserving efficacy of playing along. A year later at another retreat, this time in Bermuda, Campeau hit a shot that disappeared over a knoll, and a search for the lost ball ended when it was found mysteriously nestled in the cup for a hole-in-one. Campeau finished first in that tournament, too.

At an executive retreat at his fishing lodge in Canada—where, by the way, Campeau had scared off a couple of trespassing canoers with a rifle volley over the bow that overturned the canoe and caused them to swim frantically for safety—a friendly little wager developed: Who could catch the biggest fish? Campeau's son Bobby was in first place, until Campeau took a fish that he'd reeled in and stomped on it to make it longer. He confessed to this only after accepting the award for the biggest fish after dinner. Everybody had a laugh.

The amiable and easygoing mood of the Virginia retreat was abruptly altered on the last night after the sing-along, when the assembled revelers were treated to a highly emotional Campeau stream-of-consciousness, which began with the WASPs in Canada who'd never let him succeed, and then wandered off into the advantages of doing business in the United States, and ended up with Campeau's analysis of Jews.

This wouldn't be the last time Campeau would get in trouble for discussing Jews. Since his retail acquisition had surrounded him with Jewish businessmen for the first time in his career, Jewishness had become one of his favorite lecture topics, along with the improving prospects for U.S.–Soviet relations, etc. Although he was neither mean-spirited nor consciously prejudiced, Campeau's backwoods disingenuousness caused him to put his foot in his mouth with remarks such as "Finkelstein works hard, for a Jew" or with clinical treatises on the pros and cons of Hitler versus Napoleon. At staff meetings and elsewhere, his audiences squirmed.

The morning after his rambling oration, at 8 A.M., a note was shoved under the door of every Campeau guest at the retreat, summoning them to a mandatory session in the conference room. As they all sat wondering what this was about, Campeau appeared. He said that his wife Ilse had noted some displeasure with his remarks of the previous evening, and that he had meant no offense.

Since the departure of Macioce, the Campeau team had searched for a big-name retailer to give the operation stability and prestige, and to run Allied's remaining eight divisions and 275 stores. The search ended in October, when Robert Morosky agreed to become Allied's new CEO, a title that Campeau was willing to relinquish.

(Howard Hassler, Allied's number two, who'd been struggling to keep the remnants of the central office under control as Campeau bounced around the hinterlands making astounding predictions and stirring things up, had resigned in September.)

Morosky, the former number-two man from The Limited, a popular chain of women's clothing stores, was plucked from his yacht on the Atlantic coast of Florida. For several months, he'd been fishing and puttering around with plenty of money to pay for the bait and the gas, thanks to his having cashed in an estimated $40 million worth of Limited stock.

A lumbering redhead, six feet three, Morosky was an unlikely prospect for a career in the fashion world. He had played linebacker for Penn State. He was a passionate Catholic in the DeBartolo/ Macioce mold. He'd gotten a degree in accounting and a Harvard MBA, and in the late 1960s had gone to work in an Ohio accounting firm.

One of his clients was Leslie Wexner, the owner of The Limited, which then consisted of four stores in central Ohio. Soon there were ten Limiteds, then twenty, and Wexner hired Morosky full-time. Wexner was the design and marketing man; Morosky the operations and money man. This was a profitable combination.

By the 1970s, Wexner and Morosky had expanded The Limited to almost 1,000 outlets. There was a Limited in every important shopping mall in the United States, luring customers away from the less-imaginative department stores, such as those run by Allied. Specialty retailing was the trend, and Wexner understood it and took advantage. He also understood that the fashion market was now a national market—a sweater that sold in Cincinnati would probably sell in San Francisco or in Detroit. With the aid of snazzy theatrical backdrops, clever mass merchandising, and low-cost offshore manufacturing, The Limited outsold and outearned the competition and was the fastest-growing retailer in America.

Having survived a recession in 1978, The Limited entered its most highly profitable phase in the early 1980s. The entire operation was connected to a central computer and a huge warehouse in Columbus, Ohio. The latest designs were tested at a few locations, then produced in quantity overseas. This was Morosky's quick-response merchandise-distribution system. If a certain sweater was a hot item in a test market, it could be stocked on Limited shelves across the country in a matter of weeks. A traditional department store chain, with its hundreds of buyers and marketing experts, couldn't even reorder a sweater in that amount of time, let alone design and distribute a new line.

Wexner and Morosky, one the front man, the other behind-the-scenes, worked together, learned together, vacationed together, and got rich together. Although Wexner had an apartment in New York, he and Morosky maintained their principal residences in Columbus; Morosky's a mansion converted from a Catholic monastery. They kept in constant touch. "We were like brothers who could read each other's thoughts," Morosky says. In mid-1987, they had a spat.

As Morosky recalls it, the spat originated in—what else?—a difference of opinion about takeovers. Wexner, he says, was intent on taking over something—first Carter Hawley Hale and then, after two unsuccessful attempts at that, Henri Bendel. Morosky was opposed to these acquisitions—what did they need them for, especially at the prices that people were paying for "the ego trip of owning vanity stores that were losing money?"

"The purpose of business is profit, not a platform for your ego," Morosky told Wexner. He worried that an ill-conceived and overpriced acquisition would have an unpleasant side effect on the value of Limited stock, where his personal fortune lay.

Coincidentally, in its search for live ones to buy divisions from

Allied, First Boston had thought of Wexner, and Wexner and Morosky visited Campeau at the Waldorf before the Allied deal was even closed, in 1986. "Campeau seemed erratic," Morosky remembers. "He flitted from one subject to another and had a hard time staying on a topic. We didn't buy anything because the prices Campeau said he wanted for those divisions were astronomical." Wexner reportedly thought Campeau was nuts for demanding such prices.

Though Wexner bought nothing from Allied, he did buy Henri Bendel. This exacerbated his differences with Morosky, who reminded himself that Bendel had been losing money for several years. In the spring of 1987, Morosky told his old friend and partner he was quitting.

A few days later, Morosky returned to the office to clean out his desk. This was no longer possible—the desk had disappeared in rubble. Wexner had had the place bulldozed. Walls were demolished, wires dangled from the ceiling. As Morosky stood in the midst of the destruction it occurred to him that Wexner had been more upset than he'd anticipated. "He evidently felt I had divorced him," Morosky says. "But I didn't."

Wexner reportedly also terminated the lifetime discount at all Limited stores that had been extended to Morosky's wife. He and Morosky never spoke again, which makes the second time in this story that old friends had stopped speaking.

His office bulldozed and his wife's discount terminated, Morosky retired to the Gulf Stream in Florida, where he trolled for gamefish. Campeau immediately called and offered him a job. Morosky said he wasn't interested. Campeau called again. Again, he wasn't interested. With customary persistence, Campeau tried once more. By August, Morosky was bored with retirement. After all, he was only forty-six.

"This time, I admitted to Campeau I was getting bored," Morosky says. "Campeau said, 'I knew it!' and got very excited. He invited my wife and me to Toronto to meet Ilse. We got a tour of the house. Very prestigious neighborhood. Nouveau riche.

"I remember we went to a country club in the limo. My wife got in and Campeau said, 'Excuse me, that's Ilse's seat.' It seemed kind of pompous. Insecure. We had lunch at the country club. Talked about kids, his interest in the church. We had a commonality there, along with our interest in business. It was a nice discussion.

"He invited me to come to New York in September to meet his associate, Jim Roddy. Roddy asked me what I would do with Allied. I said I would first analyze the business by meeting the executives and visiting stores. I would analyze budgets. I would review corporate structure, before I took action. Retailing in general was softening, and I told Roddy that. He listened attentively. I said I'd take a store-by-store approach, an empirical approach.

"Roddy gave me the latest financial statements from Allied and I was floored. It was one of the most complicated messes I'd ever seen. They were so complex, I couldn't even understand them. I was surprised that Roddy was positive about these statements. How could he be?

"He told me the business had to be streamlined. That budgets had to be cut. I told him I admired Campeau's negotiating skills, and the fact that Campeau knew when to push a particular point. He knew how to cut through and deal with people face-to-face."

In October, the stock market crashed, diminishing Morosky's personal fortune, as well as that of everybody else who had invested in stocks. Campeau had extended Morosky an irresistible three-year contract at a salary of $1 million a year, plus one percent of the Allied stock, plus a $1 million interest-free loan to help him get settled in New York. Morosky accepted and was promptly named Allied's CEO. "I had to be in charge," he says. "That was an important part of it. Otherwise, I'm number two to a real estate guy."

Morosky's hiring was viewed as a promising development by the secured lenders, as well as by the owners of Allied's junk bonds. Although most of Wall Street's brain power had gone into figuring out how to win Allied for Campeau, as opposed to what he would do when he got it, bankers who worried that Campeau might declare himself CEO for life, as Baby Doc Duvalier had done in Haiti, were breathing easier. The landing of a recognized professional was powerful evidence that Campeau understood his limitations in the "brassiere business" despite any rumors to the contrary.

In November, a month ahead of schedule, Morosky set up shop at Allied headquarters and began to study Allied's books. He worried that the stock-market crash might lead to recession. "I told Campeau," Morosky says, "that we were at the end of the cycle in retailing. A downturn, and possibly a recession, was coming up next. Clearly the nation was overstored, with the same merchandise being offered everywhere. Many retailers, I expected, would fail."

Early in his investigations, Morosky uncovered one inefficiency after another in the wasteland of Allied's still-sizable bureaucracy. The various divisions, it seemed, made their own independent deals for basic merchandise, so that Jordan Marsh would pay a different price for Waterford crystal or Dan River pillowcases than Maas Brothers or the Bon Marché would pay. Even within a division, individual stores might handle their own purchases, so there might be twenty separate orders from twenty separate Allied buyers paying twenty separate amounts, and all for the same item.

Why not, Morosky argued, consolidate all the orders for Waterford crystal into one giant order, and get the best price at a volume discount? Why not do the same for dresses, for shoes, for basic merchandise in every department, put everything on a central computer, eliminate superfluous buyers, and consolidate systems? Why not distribute merchandise from a huge central warehouse, similar to The Limited's warehouse in Columbus, Ohio? Why not manufacture more clothing offshore under private label, the way The Limited did? Why not, in sum, make Allied more like The Limited in general?

Consolidation and cost saving were part of Campeau's plan, and an estimated $100 million had already been cut from Allied's budget. In Florida, the Maas Brothers headquarters was merged with Jordan Marsh, and in Boston, Jordan Marsh had absorbed Read's. But much remained to be done, and the surviving divisions had operated under somewhat contradictory priorities: (1) the lenders' mandate to cut costs, and (2) Campeau's momentary fascinations and expensive store renovations and other pet projects.

"Morosky was persuasive," says an observer, "and Campeau had a habit of running with the last idea that someone put in his ear." Efficiency and economy was the battle cry of November, as opposed to boutiques and atriums. The loose, decentralized regime favored by Allied's division heads, who felt they could manage Campeau's impetuosities and otherwise get what they wanted, was replaced with Morosky's rigorous central command.

Campeau himself had embraced the Morosky approach so enthusiastically that even Morosky was worried. "We'd visit the divisions, and Campeau would come on so strong about cutting costs, it was like he'd pulled out a sword and was swinging it over people's heads," says Morosky. "I worried how I could control the business and work with Campeau in view of his management style. How could I establish control when he was already directing everything because of his personal commitment to what I was supposed to be doing?"

Overall, Morosky was impressed with Campeau. He was impressed with the fact that Campeau was a strong family man and a good Catholic. He was impressed with Campeau's integrity. He was impressed with the fact that Campeau had thrown himself passionately into the task of making Allied Stores the best retail operation in America. He didn't think he'd ever seen such single-minded dedication. Inspired as he hadn't been since he'd left The Limited, Morosky began working overtime to devise a detailed, strategic plan. Graphs, spreadsheets, notes, and flip charts were stacked up around his desk.

# Nine

Campeau, who, as Jim Roddy had noted, "tends to do a deal and then lose interest," wasn't as passionately committed to Allied Stores as Morosky or Wall Street believed. Campeau, in fact, had discovered Bloomingdale's. During holiday trips to Florida, where he had another house, Campeau liked to visit the new Bloomingdale's at Boca Raton, with its fantastic atrium, shiny tile work, and wonderful displays.

He'd once invited Allied executives to this Florida Bloomingdale's to show them how a department store should look. Jordan Marsh, his former model for retail perfection, had been eclipsed. A tale told around South Florida, perhaps apocryphal, had Campeau raising his arms in the aisles of Bloomingdale's and shouting out to puzzled bystanders: "This is the store I should have bought."

Expressed or not, the sentiment was there. By late summer 1987, Campeau was quietly talking to Bruce Wasserstein about making another acquisition—in Campeau's spare time.

On flights to California to visit the Security Pacific bank (now angling for the chance to lend Campeau more money), along with the crates of oranges and mangoes and health food that Campeau kept on board, he'd brought along several large books, which he guarded as closely as a president would guard his nuclear war codes.

These books contained the top-secret research done at Campeau's behest by First Boston.

There was a book on the May Company, the powerful St. Louis chain, and another on Federated Department Stores, the company that owned Bloomingdale's—along with Bullock's in Los Angeles, Rich's in Atlanta, and Filene's and Filene's Basement in Boston.

Campeau's in-house advisers greeted this newly aroused passion for conquering a bigger retailer with about as much enthusiasm as they'd greeted his initial impulse to go after Allied Stores. Who in God's name needed it? They'd been camped out in New York for nearly eight months. They'd scarcely gotten over the Allied hassles —hirings, firings, syndicates breaking up, negotiations, renegotiations—and the constant chaos that appeared to have stabilized with the arrival of Morosky. Did they have to go through this again?

Wall Street analysts had begun to speculate that the payoff for Allied might be as high as $1 billion. That was the number being tossed around for the future value of the remaining Allied divisions, once the debt was paid down, and the alchemy had time to work. Presto, change-o, $1 billion created out of nothing, from a simple realigning of elements.

Campeau had only to sit back and wait to collect this fortune. A Campeau Corp. subsidiary owned 100 percent of Allied stock, and Campeau owned more than 50 percent of Campeau Corp. Theoretically, the Allied deal could make him $500 million. His brain trust could also see the dollar signs. Within a year or two, their Campeau Corp. stock would make them all multimillionaires.

On the ego front, Campeau already had pulled off one of the greatest and most unlikely triumphs of the modern corporate age. Only Perelman of Revlon and Peltz of National Can could rival him for out-of-nowhere conquests, and they were cronies of Drexel's Michael Milken. Besides, Allied was the biggest nonoil hostile takeover in history, and Campeau had done it freelance, berating and boggling his lenders in the process. He deserved a long vacation. He could go skiing, relax, rest on his laurels, as some of his advisers hoped he would. Why risk a sure $1 billion on another game he might not win?

Even if Federated was the fantastic franchise and Bloomingdale's the superior store that Campeau imagined it to be, where would he get the money to buy it? His Allied assets were tied up in restrictions, pledged to the lenders until the debts were further reduced. And Federated, being twice the size of Allied, might easily cost twice as much as Allied to acquire.

But Campeau wasn't interested in resting on his laurels, or in waiting for the alchemy to work. He wanted to do another deal. Acquaintances noticed in the post-Allied Campeau an expanded air of confidence, the result of highly stimulated ego molecules racing off in all directions. "He was always full of himself," says a Citicorp banker. "But now he was so full of himself, he was breaking out of his skin."

At First Boston, nobody was dissuading Campeau outright— although a few dissenters argued in-house that Campeau should at least let his new Allied run through one Christmas season before jumping into another complicated, costly fight. Rothfeld and Fennebresque, especially, felt that given Campeau's well-known erratic behavior, it was foolish for First Boston to risk a further alliance. All the previous unpleasant encounters and near-fiascoes left a nagging question: We got away with Allied, but do we really want to go through this again? But that was only on second thought. Of course they wanted to go through it again.

Wasserstein overruled the dissenters; if Campeau was foolish enough to make another acquisition, then First Boston was wise enough to represent him, and why not? Campeau was responsible for half the firm's total 1986–87 profit. Besides, the winning argument went, Bob would always be Bob, but Bob could be controlled. "Sedated" was actually the word most often used.

Like the would-be investors who pored over the records of the penultimate voyage of the *Pequod,* counting up the whale-blubber receipts while ignoring the ominous clunk of a peg leg on the deck, First Boston put aside all its collective intuition and concentrated instead on the initial computer runs, which showed Federated to be a promising undervalued situation.

Called into First Boston and sworn to secrecy, Morosky was shown the thick book that Campeau had been reading on the airplane. "This was the model," Morosky says, "a book full of numbers that showed how the acquisition could be justified at various purchase prices. I was shocked at the lack of operating input on how the acquisition could be managed."

"You can't take over Federated, it's not just a bunch of numbers,

it's a huge operation, like taking over the U.S. Navy," Morosky told
Campeau, which was more or less the same reaction he had had
when his previous boss, Wexner, had broached the subject of taking
over Federated in 1985. Morosky says he talked Wexner out of that
attempt with the parable of "The Limited minnow swallowing the
Federated whale."

"I was astounded by Campeau's interest in Federated," Morosky
continues, "because I thought it was a speculative investment at the
wrong time. But nobody was telling him the transaction was crazy."

As early as October, through a secret dummy corporation, Campeau was buying large blocks of Federated shares. Since Federated
headquarters was located in Cincinnati, home of a baseball player
famous for his Campeau-like grit, determination, and, as it turns out,
willingness to gamble, First Boston called this project Project Rose.


Citicorp, Campeau's lead commercial banker, learned something
was afoot when the client showed up in August, for the latest "let's
renegotiate" session. Campeau was particularly buoyant.

He was wondering if in light of his excellent performance to date,
Citicorp would be willing to lift a couple of bothersome requirements from his original agreement with the banks. The first was
that he put up an additional $70 million in equity (that damned
equity again!) to cover a slight shortfall in the proceeds from the sale
of Allied's parts. The second was the "protective covenant" which
prohibited him from borrowing money on his Allied stock for other
purposes. Campeau confided that he had another purpose already in
mind: buying Federated Department Stores.

Given the many troubles Citicorp has recently suffered, it would
be nice to be able to report that the bank scoffed at Campeau's latest
attempt to wheedle an advantage. But that wasn't exactly what happened. "We cautioned Campeau that it was too early to think about
another acquisition, before he'd been through even one season with
Allied Stores," says a Citicorp source. "We asked him to wait until
Christmas to judge the results, before he could expect us to alter
agreements and lift covenants."

However, when Campeau insisted he couldn't wait until Christmas, Citicorp agreed to consider altering the agreements and lifting

the covenants just as he had proposed. This was a near-saintly concession, given the trying relations that had preceded it.

It was Manny Hanny, Citicorp's co-manager in the lending syndicate, that refused to change the terms. Although a Citicorp representative had gone to Manny Hanny's Mark Solow and asked him to "give the guy a break, he sold the Allied divisions a year ahead of schedule," Solow was unimpressed. Manny Hanny hadn't trusted Campeau since the previous Christmas, when Campeau was short his equity and toyed around with DeBartolo over the shopping centers. Manny Hanny wasn't about to lengthen Campeau's leash now, and certainly not so he could borrow against Allied to make a run at Federated.

At Manny Hanny's headquarters on Park Avenue, nine months after the Christmas Eve blowup that had Solow on his way to the elevator, Campeau himself strode into the lobby. He was ushered into Solow's office, where loud voices could be heard through the closed door. "Waive the covenant!" Campeau shouted. "I don't have to take this from anybody!" Solow shouted back. Less flattering things were said, as well.

Although witnesses don't recall the exact words, the argument was followed from as far as several offices away by startled secretaries. They'd never known Solow to raise his voice like this. Before they could decide whether or not to call the police, Campeau sped by in a huff. Fed up with bankers who wouldn't modify agreements, he decided to fire them all.

How, you may wonder, could Campeau "fire" Citicorp/Manny Hanny while still owing their syndicate roughly $1.7 billion? His faith in ready cash was formed by thirty years of continuous borrowing for highly leveraged real estate projects. With the Wall Street lending spree in full swing, he had no reason to doubt that another commercial banker would volunteer to take the place of the last one. He was right. Enter Security Pacific.

Sec Pac, as it is popularly known, had taken a small piece of the Allied syndication and yearned to lend more. These West Coast bankers looked admiringly on the sophisticated M&A trade and dreamed of being on the tombstones as principal dealmakers and capturing the astronomical fees themselves. Sec Pac had been talking to Campeau about leading his campaign for Federated.

Sec Pac also was willing to forgive equity requirements, relax the covenants, and offer Campeau a break on interest rates in order to wrest the Allied loan away from the Citicorp syndicate—which thanks mainly to Manny Hanny—wasn't playing along. Carolyn Buck Luce, the former Citicorp banker, had been hired away by First Boston and was helping Campeau negotiate this change of lenders.

Switching to Sec Pac meant that Sec Pac had to pay off the Citicorp syndicate in full, then write up a new loan agreement with Campeau. This brought yet another shower of fees down on the Allied deal, a belated and unexpected dividend to the banking and legal professions. Once again, lawyers were ringing up the hours to prepare the required documents, once again a commercial bank was paid a sizable fee for its refinancing of the previous financing, and all so that Campeau could bend certain rules. The fee came out of Allied's till.

By December, Citicorp and Manny Hanny were paid back the entire balance of their Allied loans. They'd each made $20 million in fees alone for a twelve-month involvement in a single project, the best either bank had ever done in a transaction of this kind. They were free at last, free of last-minute surprises and phone calls before sunup, free of Campeau's haranguing and his temper tantrums. Mark Solow of Manny Hanny in particular was so eager to forget Campeau that in an interview with a European magazine about the bank's most lucrative deals, he didn't even mention Allied. Campeau was no less delighted to be rid of his spoilsport.

Campeau's fired bankers couldn't imagine why the new bankers from Sec Pac would give him everything he wanted. "We were shocked," says one of them, "when Sec Pac took us out, and especially at those bargain rates." That Sec Pac released Campeau from the covenants protecting the Allied assets for the remaining lenders didn't sit well with the Prudential, either. The Pru had invested $462 million in the package of Allied mortgages, and the last of these deals had recently closed. The Pru had assumed that Allied's covenants would remain in place. "We had," says a Prudential source somewhat wistfully, "been relying on the intelligence of the banks. The banks were stupider than we thought.

"As we were negotiating these mortgages with Campeau," the source continues, "it appalls me to think that he was sitting there

smiling, saying how important this was, trying to be nice and working along with us, when he was already thinking about Federated."

At the dinner held at First Boston to celebrate the closing of the
Allied mortgages, Campeau didn't bother to show up. He had more
important things to do.

On October 19, 1987, the Dow Jones industrial average fell 508
points, the scariest one-day decline in modern history, which added
some momentary sobriety to the ongoing pecuniary revels. Pessi-
mists, some of them bankers, worried that the financial system might
collapse. A few months earlier, famous stockpicker Ivan Boesky had
pled guilty to insider trading—was Wall Street being punished for
its sins?

Campeau wasn't worried. Where others saw distress, he saw a
distress sale. Witnessing the crash from his mansion in Toronto, he
couldn't believe that the Federated stock he'd been secretly buying
in the $45 range was knocked down to $34 a share. It was trading
at a three-year low.

Campeau was on the phone to Bruce Wasserstein, urging First
Boston to help him rush in and grab as many Federated shares as he
could get his hands on. "We ought to launch a bid for Federated
now," he contended. "Let's make an offer while the shareholders are
still desperate."

First Boston was too rattled by the 500-point drop to consider
such a thing. "We wanted to wait," says one of Wasserstein's colleagues, "to see if the world was coming to an end." Besides, Campeau had no financing, the junk-bond market was lousy, the
restructured Allied hadn't proven itself through the first holiday
season, and Campeau's board in Canada was yet to be informed of
another possible takeover. Nobody had decided how much to offer
for Federated, much less how Campeau could pay for it.

This momentary caution on First Boston's part should not be
mistaken for a reluctance to move ahead on Campeau's behalf, once
the target, Federated, had been chosen. Wasserstein, who'd kept his
distance since winning Allied for Campeau in the Street Sweep,
once again came to the forefront.

Privately, Wasserstein was saying he doubted that Campeau
could actually take over Federated, an attitude uncannily similar to

Peter Slusser's, Campeau's original adviser at Paine Webber, who had doubted that Campeau could take over Allied. Wasserstein viewed a Campeau bid as a way to put Federated in play, which at best might lead to Campeau's buying a couple of Federated divisions. Even Wasserstein didn't see how Campeau could get the financing and, in any event, such a huge undertaking could certainly wait at least until after the first of the year.

But Campeau couldn't stand waiting. He chafed through October and into November, frustrated that his advisers were bogged down in rigmarole when the Federated shares were sitting there, a bargain just asking to be snapped up. Financing he could always get and details he could always work out later. Hadn't he proved that enough times already?

In mid-November, a summit meeting was held at one of Wasserstein's favorite Chinese restaurants. Wasserstein and Campeau were both in attendance; as were Finkelson, Roddy, Tysoe, and Carolyn Buck Luce; and Morosky, who in addition to reorganizing Allied, now had to ponder what to do with Federated if Campeau got it.

The question of whether to launch or not to launch was discussed over dim sum. Except for Campeau himself, nobody was yet sure how seriously to take this latest fascination of his. An aura of indecisiveness, even surrealism, hung over the teapot. "The sense I got from that meeting," says Buck Luce, "was that Bob saw it as a choice between taking over Federated right now, or going skiing."

In late December 1987, Campeau used the holiday lull to negotiate a personal loan with the National Bank of Canada. "We were all tired," says Buck Luce, the latest addition to the Campeau retinue, "and had gone off to the beach somewhere, whereas he had gone off to another bank."

Campeau was working himself relentlessly, creating new wrinkles, groping for every possible advantage. His Christmas project was to borrow this money from the local bank, and to use the proceeds to buy back stock in his own Campeau Corp. for himself. Campeau Corp. shares, publicly traded in Toronto, had more than doubled in value from a $10.75 (Canadian dollars) low just prior to the Allied acquisition, to $26 a share before the 1987 Crash.

On his victory laps around the divisions, Campeau had tipped off

Allied's managers that his company's stock was destined for $50, perhaps as much as $100 a share. Why shouldn't he enjoy the bulk of the benefit, by putting a bank's money where his mouth was? What better time to increase his own holdings (already 76 percent of the voting shares) than with the price still in the post-Crash doldrums, and before the investing public discovered Project Rose and rushed to buy Campeau Corp. for itself? The offer that the National Bank financed was for 13 million shares.

At the outset of the Allied deal, several Canadian banks had wrinkled their brows and held on to their wallets, but the National Bank, along with the Bank of Montreal, had agreed to participate in the tender-offer financing. The string of astounding reports from Manhattan—that Paine Webber and Citicorp had taken Campeau seriously, that he'd enlisted the famous Bruce Wasserstein, outmaneuvered Ed DeBartolo, and forced a powerful U.S. corporation to capitulate—had caused other Canadian bankers to become less reticent.

"Up here," says Toronto securities analyst Ira Gluskin, who followed Campeau Corp. for years, "people were amazed by what had happened in New York. The prevailing viewpoint was that if Wall Street and all its geniuses would lend Campeau billions of dollars, there must be something to it. Wall Street, many Canadians decided, must know something about the guy that we didn't."

So in December 1987, Campeau had no trouble obtaining a $150 million personal loan to buy back his own stock, secured in part by real estate but mostly by the value of the stock itself. The National Bank of Canada, in effect, was taking a major gamble on Campeau's vision.

The Christmas season was a joyous one at the Bridle Path mansion, and no less so at First Boston, which gave out a record amount in year-end bonuses, thanks in large measure to the M&A department, which had outperformed all but one rival with $68.6 billion worth of successful slam dunks, according to IDD Information Services.

Campeau had done wonders for the white-collar GNP and the wealth of the upper-income brackets. Allied stockholders had traded in their shares for $3.5 billion, or twice what they'd have gotten before he arrived. First Boston was getting $125–150 million in fees, including bridge fees, junk-bond fees, divestiture fees, etc. Campeau's lawyers were getting an estimated $6 million; at least $40 million in fees would be paid to the Citicorp banking syndicate; another $53 million plus expenses in going-away money was paid to DeBartolo. There was $10 million paid to Citicorp for its support of the DeBartolo bid; $6-plus million to Paine Webber, in addition to the initial $6 million they were suing Campeau to get; golden parachutes to Allied's departed executives, beginning with Macioce's $15–20 million severance; fees to Prudential for writing the $462 million in mortgages; fees to the junk bond dealers and brokers; the syndicating banks; the lawyers and bankers involved in the sale of the sixteen Allied divisions. Some of this had trickled down to art dealers, Mercedes dealers, the sellers of Connecticut mansions and Park Avenue penthouses, and the maître d's of popular New York restaurants. All this from a single change in the ownership of one U.S. corporation.

The Christmas season was considerably less happy for the 3,500 Allied employees—including more than 400 formerly employed on five floors of the central office—recently given their pink slips in the accelerated cost-cutting campaign overseen by Morosky. At Jordan Marsh in Miami, there was a pink-slip party, at which the suddenly unemployed, dressed in pink slips, toasted their misfortune with pink champagne.

As good a year as it had been for M&A deals, retail sales for the 1987 holiday season were disappointing. Apparently, not enough of the beneficiaries of deals were spending their money in department stores. The Allied results were considerably below expectations. Three months of systematic layoffs and reductions in expenses, as demanded by the new regime, hadn't improved earnings in the remaining divisions. Costs were down, but customers were buying less, too. For example, the merger of Read's into Jordan Marsh may have saved the parent company millions in overhead, but it ruined Read's business. Jordan Marsh had to write off a hefty chunk of Read's unsold inventory.

That the new, efficient Campeau/Allied was having its problems did not dampen Campeau's enthusiasm for a takeover of Federated Department Stores. Campeau returned from vacation more determined than ever to pursue it. His advisors who'd taken a wait-and-see stance in November and December—in particular, Wasserstein and Finkelson—were more gung-ho by January. The stock market had rebounded and the world hadn't come to an end. It was time to put something big into play.

At a meeting in Toronto, the Campeau Corp. board of directors had approved the aptly named Project Rose without a dissenting vote. Morosky, who was there, describes what occurred:

"The economics, or models as they are called, were reviewed. First Boston had done these models to see if the transaction would make sense at various prices. I spoke out somewhat about my concerns. I thought it was a speculative investment at the wrong time. Retailing was going into a slump. It was very risky, because it depended on budget cuts in the company, and the mere submission of a lower budget didn't necessarily mean it would happen. There were broad discussions and we all voted to go ahead with it."

"I wasn't too proud of my vote, but I did it. If I'd voted no, it would have been irrelevant anyway because the majority clearly was in favor. Nobody dissented, as they were friends and supporters of Campeau. He'd won Allied in the first place, and had established his credibility. In the final analysis, I convinced myself the deal had a chance to work, given proper leadership and bold action to combine the operations of Allied and Federated."

In New York, two other factors added to First Boston's sense of urgency. An alarming antitakeover statute was rumored to be on the verge of passage in Delaware, a state in which Federated had its formal legal address. This horrible piece of legislation loomed as a possible wrecker of the very merger game itself, and by extension, the economies of the Upper East Side and southern Connecticut. Finkelson had speculated—incorrectly, as it turned out—that by launching a bid before the statute passed, Campeau might be "grandfathered" and exempt from the legislation.

The second important factor was that Donald Trump had filed with the SEC an intent to purchase up to $15 million worth of Federated's shares. Though Campeau strategists could only guess at Trump's intentions—Had he cracked the Project Rose code? Was he greenmailing?—they didn't want to be forced to play catch-up with this celebrated artist of the deal. By quickly attacking with a formal bid of his own, not only would Campeau get the jump on Trump, he might also sidestep the Delaware statute.

These two urgencies were far more compelling than any lingering reservations Finkelson or Wasserstein may have had about rushing into a second Campeau acquisition. That these same advisers who had tried to slow down Campeau in November, when Federated was selling in the low thirties, were by January urging him to speed up when the price had recovered to the high thirties, was duly noted by the frustrated client. It was another example of his knowing more than they did.

In a formal tender made public on January 25, 1988, Campeau, through his newly formed subsidiary, CRTF Corp. (Campeau, Roddy, Tysoe, Finkelson), offered $47 a share in cash for all 90 million shares outstanding, at an estimated total cost of $4.2 billion. This $47 was an arbitrary price that everyone involved knew was too low.

Campeau himself had chosen the lowball figure, which didn't matter to Wasserstein. Once again, Campeau's own backers—Wasserstein in particular—doubted that Campeau could ever take over Federated as a whole. The idea was to put the company in play and to be first in line when the parts were divvied up.

Anyway, what difference did it make what price Campeau chose, when not a penny in financing had yet been raised? This was the first formal $4 billion offer in recent takeover history in which there were no commitment letters, no highly confident letters, no equity of any kind. "Campeau has commenced discussions with major banking institutions regarding the formation of a banking syndicate . . . however, the terms of such financing have not been agreed upon and no commitment has been obtained," the offering documents admitted. The Campeau attitude—"let the bankers peddle their paper"—had become quite infectious.


Where the old Allied did $4 billion in annual sales, Federated did $10.5 billion. It had total assets of $6.2 billion. It had 22 divisions, 650 stores and 134,000 employees. It sold more merchandise than any other department-store retailer except for Sears and K Mart: more than Dayton Hudson, more than the May Company, more than Macy's and nearly three times as much as Allied.

Not only was Federated bigger than Allied, it was more glamorous. It had the number-one store, the dominant store, in Atlanta

(Rich's), Miami (Burdines), Boston (Filene's), Los Angeles (Bullock's), and Beverly Hills (Bullock's Wilshire). In New York, it had Bloomingdale's, the flashiest of all franchises, the most talked-about store in the 1980s, where theatrical backdrops gave customers the sensation of shopping onstage. The president of Bloomingdale's, Marvin Traub, was a subject for the social columns and appeared on the cover of *New York* magazine. Allied's most famous personality, Tom Macioce, had been a more likely subject for *Modern Retailer*.

Outside New York, several of Federated's department-store chains had created a loyal following that went back several generations. Certain downtown Federated stores were esteemed as benevolent public institutions. Shoppers in Atlanta talked of having "grown up" on Rich's and could recite the Rich's creed: "People are more important than things." Old-timers remembered the time in 1918 when Rich's accepted Liberty Bonds as payment from customers short on cash, the time when Rich's bought cotton at artificially high prices to help the farmers, the time during the Depression when Rich's accepted scrip from local teachers who hadn't received their paychecks.

Rich's had been a fixture in Atlanta since Morris Rich, a Hungarian immigrant, built the store from a pushcart in the late 1800s. Rich's installed the first plate-glass display window in town. Its Lighting of the Great Tree was Atlanta's most important Christmas ritual—the ceremony drew 120,000 people. For thousands of Atlantans who'd grown up on Rich's, the very path to adulthood was wound through the boys' and girls' departments—the first long pants, the first suit, prom dresses, Scout uniforms, baseball gloves, bras—were purchased there.*

---

* The central role of department stores in the way Americans celebrate national holidays is amply documented in *The Merchant Princes* by Leon Harris. According to that author, trimming the Christmas tree was popularized after department stores got into the business of selling ornaments; Santa Claus Americanus (derived from a fourth-century bishop in Lycia and later the patron saint of sailors, virgins, children, pawnbrokers, merchants, and even whores) was rescued from obscurity and elevated to national toygiver through department-store promotions; Mothering Day, established to honor the mother of God, was transformed into Mother's Day by John Wanamaker of Philadelphia's Wanamaker's store; and Fred Lazarus, Jr., of Lazarus stores in Cincinnati convinced President Franklin Roosevelt to change the date of Thanksgiving by presidential decree. The purpose was to make more shopping days between Thanksgiving and Christmas.

In 1929, a plan to organize a number of family-owned department stores into a nationwide federation similar to Allied's alliance was promoted by Fred Lazarus, Jr., the principal owner of the Lazarus stores in Ohio and a direct descendant of the founder, Simon Lazarus.

Simon Lazarus had emigrated from Germany to Columbus in 1851, choosing the mud streets of a frontier town over European cobblestones and anti-Semitism. There this hardworking shopkeeper founded what later became Ohio's "great one-price house" in Columbus, which later expanded to Cincinnati.

The Lazarus motto was "The customer is always right," and by all accounts, the store's founder practiced what he preached. Simon Lazarus was also a clever merchandiser. He introduced men's ready-to-wear suits to soldiers returning from the Civil War, on the theory that they were already accustomed to wearing uniforms. He gave away free suspenders with every suit he sold. He installed a live alligator in his store for pizzazz. He distributed consumer-protection brochures, warning clients against an inferior fabric known as shoddy—from which the modern meaning of the word derives. He installed a huge whistle on the rooftop, with a code system to signal changes in the weather to the outlying farms.

Around the turn of the century, Simon Lazarus's grandson, Fred Lazarus, Jr., took up where his imaginative grandfather had left off. He had been a small, sickly child whose bouts of scarlet fever and measles had left him with a permanent tremor in his hand. Fred Jr. got his start in the collar department. He tried college, but quit to return to the store. Soon he was running the place, and upsetting the status quo with his own shocking innovations. He put men's clothes on the second floor and installed a "stag" elevator. He merged men's accessories with women's accessories. He put in a soda fountain, making Lazarus the first store in Columbus other than a restaurant to serve food.

Fred Lazarus, Jr., is also credited with the invention of "accounts receivable," a bookkeeping wrinkle that enabled merchants to count as assets merchandise that was sold but not yet paid for. But his most ambitious project was the nationwide federation. In 1929, the year that one of his children was run over by a car and killed, the grieving Lazarus met with Louis Kirstein of Filene's, Samuel

Bloomingdale of Bloomingdale's, and Simon Rothschild of Abraham & Straus on Rothschild's yacht in Long Island Sound. Together, they discussed the benefits of forming a holding company.

As the prime mover behind the confederation, Fred Lazarus, Jr., was inspired by what John D. Rockefeller had accomplished with Standard Oil in his own state of Ohio; if the robber barons could consolidate, he argued, then why not the merchant princes of retailing?

Federated Department Stores was incorporated in November 1929, just a month after the Crash. During its first year of operation, in the midst of national Depression, its net income covered its interest expenses by more than three times, a prudent ratio soon to be radically altered by Robert Campeau.

The Federated Department Stores created in 1929 was hardly the Standard Oil of merchandising that Lazarus had envisioned. Throughout the Depression, it served as a glorified lobbying group for the four founding members. It wasn't until after World War II that Lazarus, then in his sixties, decided to devote himself to assembling a coordinated national enterprise through acquisitions. Burdines became affiliated with Federated in 1956, Rich's and Goldsmith's (against the wishes of some members of the Rich family) in 1976; I. Magnin of San Francisco and Bullock's of Los Angeles in 1964.

By the time Fred Lazarus, Jr., died in 1973, Federated had become the largest of the U.S. department-store conglomerates. The central office was located in Cincinnati, which was also the modern-day headquarters of Lazarus. The Federated Air Force, as it was called in-house, had four airplanes, eight pilots, and three assistants to transport VIPs back and forth from the divisions to Ohio.

The aging of the patriarchal Fred Lazarus, Jr., caused the business once again to be turned over to the offspring, the fourth generation of the Lazarus family to exercise control, and Federated was hardly the better for it. Fred Jr.'s son, Ralph, was reportedly more attracted to pomp than to profit margins, and Federated muddled through the 1970s in a secure but undistinguished way. It was run more like a men's club than a business. The divisions made money, but a sizable chunk of the proceeds was frittered away on the Air Force and other executive perks, and on splashy displays at Bloomingdale's and elsewhere. For example, on trips to California to visit Ralphs grocery stores, one of Federated's non-department-store divisions, Ralph Lazarus ordered Ralphs managers to supply him with large quantities of his favorite Pacific crabs, gratis, which he took back to Cincinnati to serve at his dinner parties.

Whereas under the penny-pinching Macioce, Allied was a cost-conscious company with drab earnings, Federated was known for spending more to make more. But the result was the same—Federated was a chronic underachiever, out of sync with Wall Street expectations. The earnings didn't grow fast enough to satisfy the institutions that owned the stock and fretted over immediate results. Federated had moderate debt and some valuable real estate assets, which made it a safe investment that paid a regular dividend. But it was a disappointment to the money pros.

Considerable pressure to boost profits was directed at Howard Goldfeder, the tall, churlish CEO who'd come up through the ranks to take over from the Lazarus clan in 1979. Goldfeder was a career department-store man, a workaholic, some said. He lived simply and ran a combative administration. His detractors accused him of having "terrible interpersonal skills."

Like Allied, Federated faced the challenge of the specialty retailers and the discounters by trying to play an expensive and somewhat belated game of catch-up. Goldfeder attempted to consolidate divisions. At his urging, Federated opened several new Filene's Basements, purchased a chain of specialty stores for children (The Children's Place), and opened a chain of moderately priced clothing stores in the Midwest (MainStreet). These attempts at diversification—"diworsification" as one Wall Street wag describes the process—got mediocre results.

Expanding Bloomingdale's into sixteen cities outside of New York was a disappointment also: Bloomie's didn't perform well on the road. Outside of a few of the department-store divisions, the only bright spot in Federated was Ralphs, the chain of California grocery stores.

For five years into the early 1980s, the company lagged behind its competitors in earnings per share, which were increasing at only 3 percent a year. Earnings at the better-organized May Company were increasing at 9 percent.

"Goldfeder," says an observer "had many tricks up his sleeve, but none of them fooled anybody. Under his leadership, the company never moved forward."

With its stock price depressed and Wall Street dissatisfied, Federated had known since the mid-1980s that it was a likely target for a hostile raid. In 1986, the company held off the greenmailing Hafts, a father-and-son team that Wall Street had nicknamed the Poodle and the Puppy Dog for their extravagant hairdos. The Hafts bought a large block of Federated stock, then reportedly sold it back to the company at a hefty premium in return for going away.

Early in 1986, the company adopted a poison-pill defense. It also engaged the services of Joseph Flom of Skadden, Arps, regarded as the Wasserstein of takeover lawyers, to ward off future attacks.


The news of Campeau's $47-a-share tender offer took Federated's directors by surprise, although by now they'd at least heard of him. Federated had been the winning bidder in the auction for one of Allied's castoff divisions, Block's. As a booby prize, Federated had won the unfortunate Herps.

Goldfeder was aware of how Campeau had appeared from nowhere to outmaneuver Macioce and wrest Allied from Ed De-Bartolo, but a quick analysis of the Campeau tender offer for Federated was more reassuring than worrisome. Not only was the price ridiculously low, but there was no mention of any commitment letters or highly confident letters. Campeau, it seemed, had launched his tender offer without a bank. How could the Federated board be expected to take a bid like this one seriously? Any schmo off the street could have made the same pitch.

The Federated board summarily rejected what it regarded as a frivolous overture, halfway between a joke and a nuisance. The reasons for its rejection were explained in a broadside that the board had planned to release to the newspapers, until cooler heads in the legal department advised against it. This letter to shareholders, under the headline "Why We Will Not Give Robert Campeau An Option on Federated" made the following four points:

"(1) Robert Campeau has been asked to demonstrate that he has the financing . . . to date he has not produced satisfactory evidence of the ability to finance. . . . Where is the money?

"(2) Campeau has stated that he wants four months to complete (the) transaction, even after it has been fully negotiated. Does this give you confidence that he has the financial capability? . . . In effect, Campeau is seeking an option to buy Federated.

"(3) If we were to give Campeau an option, Federated could be in a state of turmoil for an extended period of time. Our employees, customers, and suppliers are aware of Campeau's record:

"Campeau, despite his assurances that he did not 'intend to sell Allied's assets to pay for the transaction,' within months disposed of 16 of 24 divisions of Allied stores. . . . He also dismissed over 4,000 Allied employees.

"(4) How can we give him the option he wants when there is so much uncertainty as to his financing?"

# Ten

In this second gigantic takeover attempt in just over a year, Campeau's anything-is-possible attitude was abetted by his closest advisers and bankers, who in spite of everything were hankering to do another deal. The problem at First Boston was: Who could handle the client?

Fennebresque was taken off the case back in Allied, when he'd reached the limit of his tolerance and refused to have anything further to do with Campeau. Campeau, meanwhile, refused to work with Mike Rothfeld, to whom he'd taken a dislike since the first meetings at the Waldorf, when Rothfeld called him an unknown and contradicted him about his unworkable cram-down paper scheme. Also, Campeau didn't like the fact that Rothfeld had spoken rudely to his senior advisers during the Christmas Eve follies.

This was a tricky political problem, since Rothfeld had done a good job of defending First Boston against Campeau's Allied shenanigans, and Pete Buchanan wanted him involved. So did Jim Roddy, who'd just replaced David King as president of Campeau Corp./Canada.

After lunch one day in the managing director's dining room at First Boston, Buchanan told Rothfeld: "Protect me on this one (Federated), just like you did on Allied."

"I'll try, but I don't think anybody can on this deal, Pete," Rothfeld replied.

The solution was for First Boston to pretend to Campeau that Rothfeld was no longer involved. Ken Colburn, quieter and more malleable, was the Campeau relationship manager, and had the primary responsibility for "sedating" Bob.

During the regular conference calls between Campeau and his bankers, Campeau would call the roll, and everyone on the line was expected to answer "present" or "here" as they might have in grade school.

"Where's Bruce?" Campeau later demanded to know, when during the roll call he didn't hear Wasserstein respond.

"Well, uh, Bob, this is Mack Rossoff," one of Wasserstein's M&A cohorts would say. "Bruce had another engagement today and he couldn't come to the phone. But he wanted you to know he's aware of every aspect of this."

"I'm paying Bruce all this money, now where is he when he's supposed to be on the phone?" Campeau demanded, to no avail.

These relations were further complicated when Wasserstein quit the firm on February 2, a week after Campeau announced his $47 tender offer for Federated. Wasserstein took some key M&A partners with him, including his long-suffering sidekick, Joe Perella, who, colleagues say, had resigned himself to laboring in Wasserstein's lucrative shadow. Perhaps the only First Bostonian who had awed Campeau enough to win his unconditional respect ("Get me Bruce" was a constant Campeau refrain), Wasserstein was going into business for himself. Campeau was furious. "How could you do this to me at such a crucial moment?" he asked Wasserstein.

A rift between Wasserstein and his employer had been obvious for years, and some regarded the breakup as inevitable. Wasserstein made the most money of anybody in the firm, including Buchanan. "Arrogant" and "greedy" were two of the many uncomplimentary adjectives that followed First Boston's principal profitmaker down the hall and out the door. The success of the M&A department, which handled bigger and bigger transactions for bigger and bigger fees, contributed to the impression that Wasserstein and his M&A cohorts were, if not infallible, at least extremely gifted, and deserving of bigger and bigger bonuses beyond the millions they had already earned.

The reverential treatment that Wasserstein received in a succession of national magazines, the formal portrait of him and his children in *Fortune,* the equating of his deals with artistic masterworks, making his earliest effort, "Combustion Engineering's takeover of Vetco," sound as important as Fra Angelico's first triptych of the Adoration, only added to the envy harbored by Wasserstein's colleagues outside the M&A department, including Buchanan.

"It was apparent to all of us that Pete hated Bruce's guts," says an anonymous observer. Buchanan retired in 1989 to a Florida golf-course community and never commented publicly one way or the other, but others remember his sardonic asides: "an egomaniac and hard to live with as well," "an expert at belittling people and manipulating the press," "society is irrelevant, what's important is what's in the best interest of Bruce," "every time he opened his mouth it was long-winded," and "he never thought he made a mistake."

On one level, the Wasserstein-Buchanan feud was a personality conflict between the insufferable chutzpah of First Boston's biggest earner, and the countervailing arrogance of the firm's appointed head. But on another level, it was a political clash between the bond traders, the underwriters, and the corporate-finance people, who made a little money in the gentlemanly old-fashioned way, and the M&A upstarts, who made a lot of money in the ungentlemanly newfangled way.

As late as the Allied transaction, there were two separate chains of command at First Boston—the M&A people reported to Wasserstein, who reported to Buchanan, and the bridge-loan and junk-bond people reported to Tony Grassi, the head of corporate finance. This setup provided important checks and balances, and an occasional restraint on the M&A department's rushing into ill-conceived deals. In Allied, for instance, the guarantees and covenants that restricted Campeau were devised and then strengthened by the corporate-finance side. But Wasserstein itched for more control, and wanted M&A to capture the fees earned from bridge loans and junk bonds. By the end of 1986, he'd succeeded in dismantling corporate finance, and the bridge and junk people soon were reporting to him. Grassi was kicked upstairs.

By duplicating functions from other departments within the M&A area he controlled, Wasserstein was able to increase his autonomy. Basically, he was running his own independent show. These changes were approved by Buchanan, whose apparent dislike of Wasserstein didn't deter him from granting most of Wasserstein's wishes. Still, Wasserstein wasn't satisfied.

By midsummer 1987, when Federated was only a windmill on Campeau's horizon, Wasserstein made an offensive presentation to First Boston's management committee. Offensive, anyway, to Buchanan. In a speech in the board room, Wasserstein suggested that First Boston stop wasting money on the trading department, which was outmoded and unprofitable, and commit more if not all of its resources to mergers and acquisitions, which was the future of investment banking. Buchanan, who came out of the trading department, was unimpressed. "Their mini-debate boiled down to this," says an observer, "Bruce's position was 'trading, let's forget it.' Buchanan's position was 'Bruce, shut up.'"

Sometime after this meeting, Wasserstein presented Buchanan with a set of "personal goals." "In all my talks with Bruce," Buchanan reportedly told a confidant, "few had to do with strategy and most with his personal ambitions." One of these ambitions was that Wasserstein would be named CEO of First Boston as soon as Buchanan retired.

There was about as much chance of Buchanan's tagging Wasserstein his successor as there was of his doing chin-ups in the elevator shaft. But if Wasserstein couldn't get the top job, he sought a guarantee that when Buchanan retired, he'd be advanced to no less than number two. Buchanan wouldn't promise that either.

Matters came to a head at a dinner for the M&A department in January 1988, when there was a heated exchange between Wasserstein and Alvin Shoemaker, First Boston's chairman and second in command at the time. The next day, Wasserstein resigned. "The Shoemaker incident was only a pretext, anyway," a source says. "Wasserstein was already out looking for office space."

The new firm of Wasserstein Perella—Wasserella for short—began operations on an upper floor of a bank building less than two blocks from First Boston. Some of the most talented people from First Boston's M&A roster resigned en masse to take jobs with the superstar, in a place where the profits from their deals wouldn't have to be shared with an antiquated trading department. Wasserella got $100 million in seed money from the Japanese.

Wasserstein's exit put First Boston in a difficult position. In a more conservative era, when financiers stuck to their business and generally kept quiet, the departure of a well-known banker would have been an internal matter, of interest only to fellow bankers. But in the late 1980s, bankers had become public celebrities in a way they hadn't been since the 1920s, when the escapades of the Vanderbilts and Morgans were front-page news. The departure of Wasserstein and Perella was given almost as much attention, and reported in the same dire tones, as the later departure of Darryl Strawberry from the New York Mets. Wasserstein's exit had brought the firm's competence, its worthiness, its very masculinity into question.

"While First Boston's woes probably aren't fatal—the house's market value dropped by $127 million and could suffer more as competitors lure away other M&A experts," said *U.S. News & World Report.* "The engine suddenly fell out of one of the greatest money-making machines in Wall Street history," said *Business Week.*

"They took many of their top associates with them, leaving a gaping hole at First Boston and sending the price of its stock down 9 percent," said *Newsweek.* "Even people outside the financial industry had heard of Bruce Wasserstein, the top takeover guy. But who could name the chief executive officer at First Boston? For the record, the man's name is Peter Buchanan."

How that last line must have galled Buchanan. All along, Wasserstein had courted the press, and now it was paying off—the publicity about his exit was potentially more damaging than the exit itself. The hardest part of the M&A game was attracting the clients to do the takeovers—the easy part was finding the targets—and to attract the clients you needed a macho winner's reputation. Once you were tagged a rinky-dink, as Paine Webber had been, it was impossible to compete with Morgan Stanley or Shearson or First Boston. Even for a nobody like Campeau, Paine Webber had been muscled out.

References in magazines such as "gaping hole" and "the engine suddenly fell out" could have ruinous self-fulfilling consequences for First Boston. Unless the firm could prove quickly that without Wasserstein it wasn't rinky-dink and could still do billion-dollar megadeals, its chances of surviving as an M&A powerhouse were nil. And the only billion-dollar megadeal in progress was Campeau's proposed takeover of Federated Department Stores.

The fates had now tied the firm's fortunes, and the very future of the depleted M&A department, to the controversial client whom Pete Buchanan himself, colleagues say, had once called "a living water torture."

By the first week in February, First Boston found itself in the odd position of fighting with Wasserstein over who would get Campeau's business. While still with his old firm, Wasserstein somehow had overlooked getting Campeau to sign a formal engagement letter for the Federated deal, including the all-important fee schedules. Absent that contract, it was easier for Wasserstein's new firm to compete for the assignment.

Campeau himself, personally offended and let down by Wasserstein's leaving at such a critical moment, lobbied First Boston to split the fees with Wasserstein, and to bring him back into the deal. Of all the unusual requests Campeau had made of First Boston to date, the request to split the fee with Wasserstein was the first to be summarily rejected. Buchanan would have no part of it.

The night he left First Boston, Wasserstein met with Campeau at the Allied headquarters building. During a discussion of possible takeover maneuvers for Federated, Wasserstein noted that Campeau might face competition from Kohlberg Kravis Roberts (KKR)—"the top LBO firm," Wasserstein said, "that is, until today."

Unwilling to proceed without Wasserstein, Campeau decided to hire him as an outside consultant. So for an extra $10 million, Wasserstein was retained. "It paid for Bruce's first year's overhead in the new office," says a First Boston source. "He didn't have any furniture in there yet, but at least he had a client." Campeau was the biggest thing that First Boston and Wasserstein still had in common.

Over at Allied headquarters, Morosky was working on a master plan for Federated *and* Allied. His initial objections to Campeau's latest shopping spree had diminished with the realization that he might soon be named CEO of both enterprises, thus becoming the most powerful retailer in America and showing up his old boss, Les Wexner, all thanks to the dumb luck and fantastic timing that put him in the right place with the right corporate raider at the perfect moment.

Morosky's plan resembled a grand military campaign from the Civil War in which certain divisions would be combined in friendly shopping territory, then used to spearhead an assault on the malls of the Midwest, as follows:

"The strategy was to own department stores east of the Mississippi and to sell off all Federated businesses west of the Mississippi. The thinking was that these operations west of the Mississippi were only modestly successful and we could raise cash by selling them, and then concentrate more effectively east of the Mississippi, which had better demographics and good store locations. What we would do then, was to take what was left of Federated east of the Mississippi, and combine it with what was left of Allied.

"In Florida, we'd have a combination of Maas Brothers, Jordan Marsh, and Burdines, making us the dominant retailer in the state. In the future, with these divisions, we'd expand north out of Florida into Georgia, Alabama, and Mississippi. We would take Rich's in Atlanta, combine it with Goldsmith's in Memphis, and expand it from Memphis north and west into virgin territory like St. Louis, until we linked up with the Lazarus stores which we'd retained from Federated and which we planned to expand south and west from Ohio."

Morosky was particularly concerned about Bloomingdale's, which he correctly perceived had lost some of its allure. He was talking to Campeau's advisers one day about Bloomingdale's president, Marvin Traub, being over the hill when Carolyn Buck Luce, with a glint in her eye, suggested: "I'd love to run Bloomingdale's."

"You've got to be kidding," Morosky replied. "It seems that anybody who has been shopping these days is now a retailer."


As Morosky was busily conceiving his campaign, Campeau's own harried coterie was once again engaged in the challenging task of raising equity money that Campeau didn't have. In the Federated model produced by the number crunchers at First Boston, $1 billion would be required, more than triple the amount that had given everybody so many headaches in Allied. "Bob thought with a billion in equity, he wouldn't have to use junk bonds," said Tysoe. "It was the rates that mattered most. Though he'd gotten a good deal with Allied junk, with Federated he expected to have to pay higher interest."

As usual, Campeau proposed a novel solution to the equity requirement: Security Pacific, that charming West Coast bank, would lend him the money. Campeau already had hinted he wanted Sec Pac to be his lead commercial banker in the Federated acquisition, and in return for this huge bit of business thrown Sec Pac's way, he expected Sec Pac to accommodate him on the down payment as well. Thus far, Sec Pac had given him everything he asked in refinancing the Allied debt, including a reduction in the interest rate, so why not this?

For the umpteenth time, Campeau's staff saw a potential reality problem here. Carolyn Buck Luce, who had been intimately involved in the Allied deliberations from behind the Chinese Wall, was certain that Sec Pac wouldn't lend Campeau $1 billion on the value of his Allied stock, which is what Campeau planned to offer as collateral. At this point, the value of the Allied stock was still uncertain, and that company was still encumbered with more than $1 billion in junk debt and $1.7 billion in commercial bank debt, to which Allied assets were pledged. "Bob was so confident it wouldn't be a problem," Buck Luce recalls. "But of course it was."

During January, Campeau and his team had several discussions with Sec Pac about the equity proposition. Campeau's brain trust, especially Buck Luce, was hoping for a firm "no" answer from Sec Pac, so that the message from the marketplace would convince Campeau to develop a more realistic approach. But according to her, "Sec Pac never really said no, they were afraid to say no to Bob, so they just dragged their feet and analyzed his proposal to death."

"It was dangerous to be politic with Bob," recalls Tysoe. "He would think he had a perfect understanding, which would turn out later to be miles apart. He'd propose something, and if somebody didn't say 'that's ridiculous,' then he'd think there was an agreement. Some people couldn't stand up to his forceful personality. This was true of Sec Pac."

Meanwhile, Campeau was also talking to Citicorp about a $1 billion equity loan. After having been bought out of the Allied syndicate and divorced from Campeau for no more than a month, Citi-corp was lobbying for another chance to play a role in another Campeau acquisition. "They didn't throw us out," said Tysoe, in amazement.

But by early February, even Campeau had given up on Citicorp or Sec Pac ever committing themselves to the Federated equity loan. He'd turned his attention to a couple of familiar deep pockets who weren't bankers: Ed DeBartolo and Paul Reichmann.

Bystanders who observed Campeau with DeBartolo at lunches in New York report that Campeau was unusually gracious and charming, smiling and never raising his voice, inquiring about DeBartolo's bad back, bringing him gifts, and inviting him to Europe for health treatments.

Whether the buttering up had any influence on the cantankerous billionaire or not, DeBartolo agreed to provide Campeau with $400 million in equity for Federated, so long as the Federated takeover was friendly and the board of directors approved it. DeBartolo was the landlord in too many malls in which Federated stores were prominent tenants to risk antagonizing the company by supporting a hostile Campeau bid.

The new and more amiable DeBartolo-Campeau relationship took a brief turn for the worse during a four-way conference call among DeBartolo; Citicorp's Larry Small; a group of lawyers and bankers on a speaker phone at the Allied offices; and Campeau himself, who was on his plane, waiting to take off for the winter Olympics in Calgary.

In the middle of the conversation, Campeau broke in to exclaim: "The Yugoslav ambassador just arrived, I have to take off!" He slammed down the telephone. After a brief silence, DeBartolo said: "What is this? I'm about to surface as a backer in a major takeover action against one of the biggest tenants in my malls, Federated, and the guy I'm supporting is running off to the Olympics? Get him back, now." Somebody did.

Campeau made a similar pitch to the Reichmann brothers, who had turned him down for an initial equity loan during Allied, but later bought half interest in his Scotia Plaza building in Toronto. Campeau, reportedly, was just as solicitous and charming with Paul Reichmann as he had been with Reichmann's equal in net worth, DeBartolo.

Meeting with Campeau in Toronto, Reichmann reiterated that he and his brother Albert hadn't changed their minds about investing directly in retailing, which they still knew nothing about. Nonetheless, Reichmann said, they were willing to invest further in Campeau real estate, which they did know something about.

The agreement that followed was for the Reichmanns to buy convertible debentures in Campeau Corp., the proceeds from which could be used by Campeau as equity for Federated. From the Reichmanns' point of view, this seemed like a no-lose proposition. If Campeau's retailing experiment succeeded, then the value of Campeau Corp. stock surely would increase as Campeau predicted, and the Reichmanns would make a sizable profit by converting their debentures into common shares. If Campeau's retailing experiment failed, the Reichmanns' debentures were protected by Campeau Corp. properties, which the Reichmanns regarded as solid collateral.

Not to leave any possibility unexplored, Campeau also talked First Boston into agreeing to make an equity bridge loan, if such became necessary, which he would repay by selling Canadian real estate. Some First Bostonians opposed such a loan, but Wasserstein's replacement, James Maher, and Bill Mayer, who was expected to follow Buchanan as CEO, ordered it approved.

On February 11, Campeau Corp. announced that DeBartolo and the Reichmanns had together agreed to provide $660 million in loans ($400 million from DeBartolo, $260 million from the Reichmanns) in support of a Campeau sweetened bid for Federated.

Donald Trump turned out to be a false alarm. That renowned dealmaker hadn't parlayed his investment in Federated into a full-scale takeover attempt, so a Bloomingtrump's would never join the Trump Tower, the Trump Plaza, the Tour de Trump, the Trump Princess, and the Trump Taj Mahal as part of the ongoing Trumpty Trumping of America. But the Campeau bid, launched in part out of fear of a Trump bid, brought other players into the game. By late January, not only was Henry Kravis of Kohlberg Kravis Roberts looking at Federated, but so were the Pritzker Brothers and Mel Simon and the Dillards from Arkansas.

Campeau had brought another windfall to Wall Street. Time clocks were whizzing merrily at law firms across town, and banks were stumbling over each other to sign commitment letters with one or more potential Federated bidders, of which there were rumored to be six. At one point, Citicorp was in on all six possible Federated transactions, as well as the company's own restructuring plan. There were so many Chinese walls inside the bank's New York headquarters that wags were calling the building "Peking."

As the news spread that Federated was soon to be sold off, a side game grew up around the big game. In the side game, would-be buyers of Federated divisions made tentative deals with the various would-be buyers of the whole company. If the May Company, for instance, wanted to buy Bullock's department stores, it would negotiate separately with Campeau, with KKR, with the Simons, with the Pritzkers, etc. The most desirable Federated divisions were presold numerous times to the different contenders. "It was like a national convention of baseball card traders," says a First Boston source. "You take this one. I'll take that one."

Between the main game and the side game, plus the shifting alliances among the potential bidders (DeBartolo, for instance, was working with KKR as well as with Campeau) and with so many bankers angling for fees, the situation became more frenzied and confused than any other that the players could recall.

What happened to William Dillard II, a straight-talking Arkansan and an owner of Dillard Department Stores, was typical. He'd come to New York to work with the Simon and the Pritzker factions and possibly to bid for some of the Federated parts from Campeau, whom he'd met during Allied:

"In Allied, Campeau had called us in Arkansas, told us to fly to New York right away, he wanted to sell us one of those divisions, it would be mutually beneficial; he sounded so excited that we left immediately, got rooms at the Waldorf, and met with Campeau, who said, 'Oh, you didn't need to come. The deal is off.' In Federated, we met with the Campeau people and made what we thought was a deal for one of its divisions on Sunday night, with all the major points decided. But by Monday morning Campeau had changed the terms; he wanted to keep a couple of key stores from the division we were buying. After this retrading on his part, we went away."

Dillard then turned his attention to supporting Simon and Pritzker in their bids for Federated. For hours, he was trapped in bankers' offices where the M&A types tried to convince him and his collaborators to pay huge up-front commitment fees. "They wanted $10 million and we got it down to $8 million," says Dillard, "and then we told them we wouldn't spend that kind of money without anything to show for it." He went out for dinner, and then returned, and the bankers were still clamoring for fees and other advantages until well after midnight. "This is unbearable," Dillard finally said. "Where I come from, people don't ask to get paid until *after* they've done something." He left for Arkansas the next morning.

"Are we in play? Are we in play?" Federated's CEO, Howard Goldfeder, asked his financial advisers from Shearson, in the same anxious tone with which passengers of the *Titanic* might have asked: "Are we sinking? Are we sinking?" Sure enough, they were.

On February 5, the Federated board rejected Campeau's original $47-a-share tender offer, citing the lack of financing. On February 11, Campeau was back, with the announcement that DeBartolo and the Reichmanns were contributing the equity money. He bumped his bid to $61 a share (which he told the wire services would be his final price). Federated was beginning to realize it might be in serious trouble.

In Cincinnati, a Federated vice president, Boris Auerbach, sought out a former neighbor of his, the chairman of the Ohio Senate finance committee. Emergency legislation was drafted, one bill to revise the state's antitakeover law so it would apply more directly to Federated, and another to give the state power to review hostile acquisitions by foreigners. This was a political version of whistling past the graveyard. Even Federated's lawyers said that these proposed measures were almost certain to be declared unconstitutional.

The two bills reached the Ohio House on February 10, just at the time the DeBartolo involvement with Campeau was announced. This put a further damper on the sponsors' enthusiasm. DeBartolo had long been active in Ohio Democratic politics, and the Democrats controlled the House and the governor's mansion at the time.

As a symbolic gesture, the second bill involving takeovers by foreigners was passed and hastily signed into law by the governor. Four hours after that, Federal Judge Carl Rubin blocked its enforcement, and ten days later he ruled it unconstitutional.

U.S. Representative Thomas Luken (D-Ohio), the father of Cincinnati's mayor at the time, held hearings in Washington on the evils of this takeover, and Senator Howard Metzenbaum held a news conference outside Federated headquarters, where employees wore Say No to Campeau buttons—a maple leaf crossed with a red slash.

Campeau's lawyers were making simultaneous appearances in the Delaware, Florida, South Carolina, and Nebraska courts, where they sought to strike down other potential legal obstacles to the takeover. There were antitrust implications, since in Miami, for instance, Campeau would own both major retailers, Burdines and Jordan Marsh. In a New York district court, Campeau's lawyers asked the judge for a temporary restraining order against Federated's poison pill. Federated's lawyers sought to uphold the pill, and filed counter-suits to the various Campeau suits. It was all very bullish for the legal business.

On February 12, believing that a competing offer from Kohlberg Kravis Roberts was imminent, Campeau fired off a letter to the Federated board, warning it not to agree to anything before giving him a chance to compete. He fired off a nastier letter to KKR, threatening legal action if KKR attempted to lock up a favorable backroom deal with the company. This began an almost daily barrage of letters and press releases that continued for several weeks.

Campeau was passionately involved in the press campaign, and his communications consultant, Davis Weinstock, was getting his share of 6 A.M. phone calls. Campeau's advisers tried to keep the boss from releasing his own broadsides and from giving his own impromptu interviews, which invariably made people mad. Regularly, Campeau would fire Weinstock in the morning for not complying with instructions, and Campeau's staff would rehire Weinstock in the afternoon.

Responding to the rumors of competing bids, Campeau had been urged by Wasserstein and by First Boston's new M&A team to raise his offer from the low ball $47 to $61. They then urged a second increase to $65. Campeau readily agreed to these recommendations. Each $1 bump added nearly $100 million to the purchase price, which was beginning to make the other potential bidders nervous.

William Dillard II, who'd been in on several possible combinations with KKR, the Pritzker Brothers, and Mel Simon says, "The price was too rich at $65—we tried to see a way to stretch a bid to $66.50 and couldn't do it. The numbers didn't work." Henry Kravis of KKR, the same Kravis who later shocked the world by paying $25 billion for RJR Nabisco, folded in the low $60s; Federated's own board, in its restructuring plan, concluded it couldn't compete beyond $65 a share. "In our minds, a deal simply wasn't doable above that level," says a Federated board member.

Campeau's latest raise was putting him alone, beyond the range of his professional competitors, beyond the initial calculations of what he ought to pay. His retailer Morosky recalls that "early on First Boston's numbers showed very clearly that beyond $60 or so the transaction wasn't going to work. At $60, to make ends meet we'd have to increase sales every year by 5 percent compounded; we couldn't build any new stores; and we had to cut $300 million out of Federated's expense structure.

"I remember a chat I had with Campeau himself about $60 being the drop-dead price. Above that, I doubted we could make it work."

Back in November, after the stock-market crash, Campeau had told Jim Roddy that $55 would be his limit. But now he'd exceeded that limit by $10 a share, or nearly one billion dollars. The number crunchers proved on paper that with more cost-cutting and more selling of Federated divisions, and with Campeau putting up more equity, the purchase would still make sense.

On February 16, Campeau raised his price once again, to $66, to put more pressure on the board. An official press release listing Campeau's new, improved lineup of equity partners was put out on February 16. DeBartolo now was in for $480 million; the Reichmanns for $260 million; two Canadian banks, the Bank of Montreal and Banque Paribas, for $500 million; Campeau had managed to round up $1.2 billion in equity—who could quibble with that?

The fact that most of this was borrowed money, and therefore not "true equity" was bothersome to Ron Tysoe, who could see the danger of loans piled on loans. "I told him that although from Federated's point of view, this might be equity, that it was borrowed, and that long-term we could have a problem. Bob said, 'Don't worry.' Bob was a true entrepreneurial dealmaker, thriving on leverage. If somebody lends a dollar, you take it. The ramifications can be handled later. There's always some way out."

In addition to the equity, Campeau had wangled a "prepared to commit" statement out of First Boston, for another $1 billion in bridge loans, to be repaid with proceeds from another junk-bond sale. "Prepared to commit" was something sort of like "highly confident," and had the virtue of enabling him to use First Boston's name without actually having to pay for it.

The February 16 press release announcing Campeau's equity lineup caused the Federated board to begin to prepare for the worst. With no hope of doing a defensive restructuring to compete with Campeau's $66 offer, with other more acceptable bidders getting nervous at the price, with legal maneuvers in the Ohio courts and elsewhere having for the most part failed, with no white knight having come to the rescue, with only an untested poison pill and a new Delaware statute protecting it from a hostile Campeau takeover, the company sent out a signal that it might be prepared to capitulate.

Having been advised by their lawyer, Joe Flom, that their sole responsibility at this point was to get top dollar for the shareholders, Federated's board members tried one last time to raise the ante by intimating that the company might give itself up for $68 a share.

Additionally, the board had asked for the chance to meet the prospective owner in person just once, so it could at least see what he looked like and chat with him about his plans, which were certain to affect the lives of 134,000 Federated employees. Such a meeting, the board was told, was an impossibility.


With Federated on the verge of surrendering for $7.5 billion even without meeting the new owner, Campeau's bid still lacked a critical element: a commercial bank. This was no trivial omission, since the plan called for a commercial bank to provide at least $3 billion in secured loans, and perhaps more.

Whereas in the Allied deal Campeau had lined up his commercial bank, Citicorp, long before he lined up his equity, here he'd lined up his equity and the question of a commercial bank was left hanging.

Actually, there were two commercial banks competing for the opportunity to provide financing. One was Security Pacific, which recently had refinanced Allied on such favorable terms to Campeau. Since that time, Campeau and Sec Pac had traded compliments and other expressions of affection in what some described as the "Campeau–Sec Pac extended honeymoon." In spite of the bank's refusal to advance him the Federated equity, Campeau still wanted to use Sec Pac as his lead lender for the major secured portion of the Federated loan.

Sec Pac's David Risdon worked on the details with Campeau in a series of get-togethers in California and New York. Jointly they devised a strategy of combining Allied and Federated into a single package deal. By merging the companies, Risdon theorized, the Federated acquisition could be financed without the junk bonds that Campeau so despised. Most important, Campeau could borrow more money on the combined assets than on Federated alone, and he'd be free to sell more Allied divisions to raise cash. In the massive re-refinancing of a previous refinancing that Sec Pac envisioned, Allied's pesky bondholders would be paid off.

"We felt Allied still had a lot of value," says Risdon. "We saw the price that Campeau had gotten for Brooks Brothers and thought he could get close to the same value with Ann Taylor. If he had sold these specialty-store divisions and merged what was left of Allied with Federated, he could have substantially reduced the junk debt from Day One."

Campeau's initial preference for using Sec Pac met with strong opposition from First Boston, especially after First Boston heard the terms and witnessed one too many screaming matches during the negotiations. First Boston worried that Sec Pac would never be able to syndicate its "naive" structure to other banks. Sec Pac had never completed a major hostile takeover, and with Federated being the largest nonoil company ever put into play, First Boston figured that this was no time for Sec Pac to practice. "These were a bunch of amateurs," says a First Boston source, "in over their heads."

(Sec Pac's position is that First Boston had a substantial vested interest in keeping junk in the deal, because of the fees it would make on bridge loans and the subsequent sale of the junk bonds. "No wonder," says a Sec Pac source, "they were pushing so hard for Campeau to dump us.")

But where the dealmakers had convinced Campeau to switch from amateurish Paine Webber to First Boston during Allied, here he was asserting himself, continuing to tout Sec Pac in spite of First Boston's objections, because he'd taken a fancy to the bank.

Sec Pac's competitor for the bank portion of Campeau's Allied bid was none other than Citicorp—who else?

Back in November, Citicorp had been "taken out" of its Campeau Allied loans and was free of one of its biggest, albeit most profitable, headaches; but by January it was sidling up to Campeau once again. Everybody, it seemed, who'd had troublesome dealings with Campeau was sidling up to him again, including Paine Webber. Demoted in Allied and forced to sue Campeau for nonpayment, with one of its top executives later characterizing Campeau as a "financial Hitler," for his relentless attempts to conquer companies, Paine Webber was now fighting hard for the privilege of investing $500 million of its own money in a Campeau Federated bridge loan. Politics could not have made stranger bedfellows than a Wall Street LBO.

Sec Pac, meanwhile, was growing worried at the escalations in price beyond $66 a share. It had occurred to Sec Pac, as it had to Campeau's rival bidders, that the deal might not make sense at these levels. According to Buck Luce, the way Sec Pac expressed these reservations was by abruptly dropping out of sight. "One day we were in constant contact with Sec Pac," says Buck Luce, "and the next they weren't returning our phone calls. And this after we'd paid them a $5 million fee." Risdon at Sec Pac suggests that this apparent snub might have been the bank's way of saying no to Bob. The result, in any event, was that a few days before the scheduled board meeting at which Federated was expected to capitulate and sell the company, Campeau still didn't have a commercial bank to help him pay for it. He hadn't made a deal with either Sec Pac or Citicorp.

Over at First Boston, which naturally was rooting for the sale of Federated, one of the managing directors joked to Finkelson: "Now I guess you'll want a highly confident letter from us on the banking financing." First Boston, after all, already had been paid to be highly confident about numerous other deficiencies in the Campeau funding, and had promised him bridge loans for almost all occasions.

The following morning, the joke became reality when Jim Roddy called First Boston requesting just such a letter. Although the in-house nay sayers objected to First Boston's lending its good name to a declaration of faith in Campeau's coming to terms with a bank, given the history of his relations with banks thus far, for yet another $5 million fee the higher-ups suspended their disbelief. First Boston produced the highly confident letter on February 16. One stipulation of this agreement was that First Boston be directly involved in all pertinent negotiations on the subject of Campeau and commercial banks.

But that very afternoon, Buck Luce had a bank meeting and neglected to invite First Boston to attend. First Boston complained about this to Roddy, but Roddy had a complaint of his own. He demanded a renegotiation of the agreed-upon $5 million fee, which seemed to him an excessive reward for First Boston's simply writing a letter expressing its confidence in Campeau's already proven ability to find willing lenders. (It also seemed to Roddy that every time the Campeau people turned around they were stuck with another bill from First Boston.) First Boston dutifully reduced the fee to $1.85 million.

In spite of First Boston's opinion, offered at the renegotiated discount, that Campeau would have no trouble getting a commitment from a bank, by Wednesday, February 24—a day before the Campeau team was scheduled to address the Federated board, no such commitment existed. This created a tremendous new challenge for Campeau's advisers—convincing the board to sell the company not only to a stranger whom they'd never met but also one who at this point lacked the wherewithal to pay the price. Again, this was the kind of foolishness that no house seller would tolerate from a buyer on the eve of the closing date when the keys are handed over.

In a typical what-are-we-going-to-do-this-time? session in Allen Finkelson's office, the lawyer proposed an ingenious who-needs-a-bank? approach. "It was Finkelson's idea," says Buck Luce, "to go in to the meeting with Federated with a positive attitude. We decided to take the tack that there were plenty of banks around and we could always find one when we needed it, especially after we got formal approval from the board to sell us the company. Our not having lined up a bank beforehand, we decided to tell them, was an attempt on our part to save on unnecessary fees in case we couldn't reach an agreement. We wanted to present it as a thought-out, cost-conscious policy."

All day Thursday behind the scenes, First Boston pressured the Campeau people to abandon this who-needs-a-bank stance and actually sign up with a bank—preferably Citicorp—but to no avail. To maintain momentum with the Federated board, the Campeau team continued to exhibit confidence that their unfunded offer would soon enough be funded.

Campeau, meanwhile, had flown off to London to sell Brooks Brothers. When last we checked, Brooks Brothers was Campeau's favorite division, the untouchable franchise, the key to Allied's future, and soon to be expanded by fifty or more outlets in Europe and ten to twenty in Canada. In speeches and interviews, Campeau had vowed never to sell Brooks Brothers, a vow that reassured the debt holders of Allied.

But a more important priority had arisen: Campeau's need for more equity. Equity had been the constant preoccupation of the previous eighteen months. Such a fuss was made over the shortage in Allied that Campeau seemed determined to raise more than enough for Federated—not out-of-pocket, of course. The selling of properties in Canada, so often alluded to as the best way to raise equity, was something Campeau could never bring himself to do. Instead, he had the Reichmann loan as equity—secured by his property—and the DeBartolo loan as equity, and to add to these, the latest brainstorm, Brooks Brothers as equity. A live one was waiting to buy it.

The live one, Lord Rayner of Marks & Spencer, the British retailer, had long admired Brooks Brothers as the closest thing in America to a classic British men's store, and as a sensible way to get involved in the U.S. market. Rayner had twice approached Campeau about making a deal. In late January 1988, with the Federated takeover already planned, Campeau met with Lord Rayner in Toronto and insisted that Brooks Brothers wasn't for sale. While giving the British aristocrat a tour of his real estate, Campeau had a better idea—that Lord Rayner buy a share in Campeau Corp. instead. His lordship turned this down.

In mid-February, Campeau changed his mind. Brooks Brothers, it seemed, was for sale after all. A First Boston executive, Allan Ruchman, flew to London to open the discussions, and Campeau followed to close the sale personally.

Campeau's estimate of the value of Brooks Brothers far exceeded what anybody on his staff or at First Boston imagined it was worth. "When we heard that Bob was flying to London to meet with Lord Rayner and sell Brooks Brothers for $750 million, our immediate reaction was 'Sure, Bob,' " says Jim Roddy. "Nobody around here thought he'd get more than $450 million. When he called two days later to say he had a definite deal at $750 million, we all said several more 'Sure, Bobs.' When we found out he wasn't exaggerating, we couldn't believe it."

Campeau with Lord Rayner was Campeau at his best—in a face-to-face negotiation with an eager buyer he never blinked first, gave no hint of compromise, stuck to his price with such passionate conviction that to his adversary it began to seem reasonable, or if not, there seemed to be no choice but to accept Campeau's price or walk away empty-handed. Lord Rayner had the same foreigner's inflated conception of the worth of U.S. businesses that Campeau did, but otherwise he was no match for the Canadian. Not only did his lordship pay the sucker's price, but Campeau also sold him an option to run the food concessions in all his stores, if and when those stores got around to serving food, which they never did.

"The lord got Herscued," says a First Boston source, referring to Australian George Herscu and his disastrously dumb purchase of Bonwit Teller out of Allied. "But you know, Campeau didn't think of this as a con job. He really thought Brooks Brothers was worth the $750 million. This was the key to his persuasion."

First Boston's Ruchman, assigned to handle the details, took the Concorde back to New York and arrived at the same hour he left. In an all-night session at the Cravath law firm, Ruchman prepared the sale papers. He and Ron Tysoe slept on couches in the office.

Back in London, Campeau had dialed up DeBartolo in Ohio, using his car phone. DeBartolo, who'd agreed to invest in Campeau's equity only as long as the deal was friendly, was upset at a recent public announcement that implied that his support was uncondi- tional. Campeau asked him to *make* his support unconditional by consenting to help to finance a hostile bid. For this, DeBartolo wanted some concessions—more leeway to put Allied stores in his shopping centers, his primary interest all along.

A snag developed over a minor detail, which escalated into a shouting match across continents, and Campeau hung up on his backer. Informed of this newest spat back in New York, Ron Tysoe tried to play mediator, but he couldn't reach Campeau on the car phone. He called one of DeBartolo's lieutenants, and the conflict was resolved.

All this accomplished in a few days, Campeau headed to Ger- many and Austria for more sheep treatments and to work on the plans for his new villa in the foothills around Salzburg. His original conception had been a 180 by 90-foot house, but when he learned that the property he'd acquired was located in protected wilderness where space for a 16,200-square-footer couldn't be cleared, he re- duced the dimensions to a more modest 60 by 60 feet, or roughly the size of the mansion he had torn down. Work on this building project was competing with Federated for his passionate attention.

Campeau's trio of advisers—Roddy, Tysoe, and Buck Luce, had encouraged this hiatus in Europe, fearing that if the boss stayed in New York, he might further antagonize the Federated board or potential lenders, since there was never any telling whose door he might slam next or what indiscreet remark he might blurt out to the nearest reporter. Campeau's absence also made it possible for his own executives to avoid his frequent harangues by not answering the phone or by taking it off the hook, which they sometimes did.

Late on the afternoon of February 25, a large and diverse crowd assembled in a conference room at Federated's law firm, Skadden, Arps. A half-dozen Federated board members, including Howard Goldfeder and G. William Miller, former Secretary of the Treasury, had arrived from Cincinnati. Goldfeder was in a grumpy mood.

Wasserstein was there as Campeau's private adviser and tacti- cian, along with Mike Rothfeld and Jim Maher from First Boston (Maher was Wasserstein's replacement as head of investment banking), and Finkelson from Cravath. Finkelson's boss, Sam Butler, was brought along to add credibility. This was as impressive a lineup as had ever been assembled to present the case for an absentee buyer.

During an early stage of the meeting, Tom Hill, the Shearson investment banker who'd represented DeBartolo in Allied and now represented him here at Federated (investment banking was a small world, as well as lucrative) left the room to make a telephone call and then returned. A member of the Campeau team went out to make a phone call, and noticed a yellow legal pad that either Hill or one of his associates had left near the telephone. There was a list of familiar names: "Pritzker," "KKR," and others, alongside some familiar numbers, "$62," "$64," and so on, on the pad.

Analyzing this data in a huddle in the hallway, the Campeau contingent deduced the numbers were prices that rival bidders had offered for Federated. Since the highest numbers were in the $65 area, it seemed a certainty that Campeau would win the company at $68. Why else would the board have invited them here?

There was the bank problem, of course, but Finkelson gave a rousing "Who needs a bank?" lecture to the board, and Wasserstein gave a version of his "dare to be great" speech for good measure. This appeared to satisfy the sellers, and a deal satisfactory to all parties at $68 all-cash seemed imminent.

At that moment, around 4 P.M. New York time, it occurred to the Campeau people that they didn't know where Campeau was. The last they'd heard, he'd left London for Austria. But at the critical moment in the sale when they had to reach him, they couldn't. He'd been out of touch for more than a day. "It was an odd time for Bob to be incommunicado," says Buck Luce. "He almost always left a number where he could be reached." Buck Luce and Roddy couldn't very well buy him Federated at the $68 price without his consent. What would they say: "Bob, we couldn't resist picking up Federated for you yesterday while you were busy and we went shopping"?

That being the case, the largest takeover of any company other than an oil company in U.S. history was stalled in a conference room as bankers and lawyers who stood to make millions frantically searched their Rolodexes for Campeau phone numbers and speculated as to his whereabouts. It was the first time that so many had been so desperate to reach *him*.

The Campeau team went to Wasserstein's new office to look for Campeau phone numbers. The place was still decorated with Christmas ornaments left by the previous occupants from E. F. Hutton, who'd abandoned it quickly after agreeing to a bailout merger with Shearson Lehman. Back at Skadden, Arps, Federated board members wandered the halls or played cards and read magazines. Someone had called out for a paralegal who spoke German.

It wasn't until 7 P.M. that the German-speaking paralegal finally reached someone in Campeau's chalet who said he was eating at a local restaurant. It was on the restaurant phone, after midnight in Austria, that Campeau was briefed by Wasserstein (who had returned to Skadden) and agreed to pay $68 a share, or nearly $7 billion, for Federated. He hung up and returned to his meal.

The news of Campeau's transatlantic OK traveled quickly down the hallways at Skadden, and the various factions returned to the conference room. Wasserstein began to press the Federated board to draw up the contract immediately and sign it that very night. All major points had been agreed to, Wasserstein argued, so why wait? His do-it-now stance was supported by Tom Hill, Federated's investment banker, and the board appeared ready to go along with it.

But Howard Goldfeder, a man who preferred to make calm and careful decisions, a man who was tired of flying back and forth from Cincinnati, a man who didn't appreciate being pressured like a sales prospect at a time-share resort, resisted.

Motioning Hill into the hallway, Goldfeder said in a loud voice, "I won't be stampeded into this. This isn't going to be a surrender like Pearl Harbor." Though Wasserstein continued to push for a quick signing—otherwise, who knew what snag might develop?— Goldfeder stood his ground. There were details to be worked out, Goldfeder said, clauses to be written. What was the hurry? Couldn't it wait until Monday?

# Eleven

•

For some forty-eight hours over the weekend, parties to the proposed transaction could ponder the implications of selling a major company to a stranger in a pay phone at a German restaurant after midnight. Campeau's bankers and lawyers had more meetings with the lawyers from the Federated board to work out the small print.

Reviewing the positives and the negatives from the board's point of view, the positives were that Campeau had amassed $1.4 billion in equity from some impressive sources, including DeBartolo and the Reichmanns; he had Wasserstein on his side; and his investment bankers at First Boston were willing to lend him more than $1 billion from their own corporate funds to tide him over if any of the above failed to materialize. Also, Campeau had gotten a great price for Brooks Brothers, which had made the board take him more seriously. He'd proven in Allied he was not a greenmailer; his lawyer was Allen Finkelson of Cravath; and he was agreeing to pay $68 a share all cash.

The negatives were that Campeau hadn't engaged a commercial bank, and that he was a real estate developer with less than a year's experience in retailing. Also, certain disquieting anecdotes about his behavior had come to the board's attention. But Federated's lawyer had many times instructed the board on what it could and could not do. It could not, for instance, refuse to sell the company to a nincompoop. Nor could it reject an offer because a buyer knew nothing about the business or had borrowed too much money for his or the company's own good.

In other words, the scrutiny to which any applicant for a routine job at Federated would be subjected could not be applied to the ownership position here. The board's task, as mandated by civil law, was to accept the best and the highest offer for the shareholders. The only important issue to consider was the buyer's ability to come up with the cash.

On Monday morning, Campeau was still in Austria, waiting to hear from his aides in New York that Federated had been won. By mid-afternoon everything was resolved, with the Federated board ready to ratify the sale of the company. But not to Campeau. It was to R. H. Macy. Over the weekend, Macy's had surfaced as a secret rival bidder, and Goldfeder and his retinue promptly shelved the Campeau contract they had almost signed on Friday in favor of a Macy's contract that the board had received. The Campeau team learned of the Federated sale to Macy's over the financial wires.

In the confusing couple of weeks that had preceded this surprise, Macy's had been maneuvering behind the scenes, seeking to make side deals for at least two of Federated's better-known divisions, Bullock's of Los Angeles and Bloomingdale's. Macy's had yearned for an outlet on the West Coast. Macy's also had conferred with the KKR group and the Pritzker group about joining in their bids for the company at large, but these alliances were scuttled when KKR and the Pritzkers dropped out of the competition. Then on the final weekend, Macy's had entered the bidding directly on its own.

A First Boston representative present at the final Campeau negotiating session at Skadden, Arps the previous Friday recalls seeing one of Macy's investment bankers from Kidder, Peabody in a conference room and wondering what he was doing there. "My guess is," the source says, "that Federated was meeting with the Macy's bankers at the same time it was meeting with the Campeau group. These parallel meetings must have continued over the weekend, with the Federated lawyers jumping from one conference room to another like busy orthodontists, tightening the wires on both prospective deals."

Neither Macy's nor Federated's lawyers will confirm that these weekend meetings took place, but it makes sense that they would have. Ed Finkelstein, the CEO of Macy's, was an old friend of Gold-feder's. Goldfeder would have preferred to gargle with Drano rather than turn over his company to Campeau. At last there was an alternative, and Federated took it. Anyway, a complex definitive agreement, such as the one Federated and Macy's signed on Monday, couldn't have been produced on Monday morning.

Campeau was furious to learn over the telephone of Macy's sneaky late-hour interference and Federated's treacherous acceptance of its offer. This sort of thing had happened to him before. In fact, the Macy's weekend was almost an exact rerun of a depressing episode in Canada, when Campeau thought he'd won control of a real estate outfit called Markborough Properties on a Friday, celebrated the victory on a Saturday, and discovered on the following Monday that he'd been betrayed.

Wasserstein and First Boston had been right in pushing for a signed contract immediately, and in urging Campeau to make his financing credible by signing up with a commercial bank.

The Macy's announcement made it imperative that Campeau get a commercial bank, and quickly. With a serious rival bidder in the picture, First Boston reminded Campeau's aides, they'd have to have all their financing in place or else the Federated board wouldn't give them a second thought. Sec Pac, for one, was once again ready and willing to cooperate. Sec Pac, which had disappeared before the weekend, had resurfaced by Monday, angling to lend Campeau the required billions to buy Federated, in spite of the fact that the scary price was getting scarier.

At this point, however, Campeau wasn't sure he wanted Sec Pac. He was still in Germany, vacillating on the subject of whether to sign up with Citicorp—favored by First Boston—which wanted to add more junk bonds to his deal, or Sec Pac, which wanted him to combine Federated with Allied and avoid the junk bonds.

"One minute Bob would be mad at Citicorp for telling him there had to be junk bonds," says Carolyn Buck Luce. "And the next he would be mad at Sec Pac for telling him he had to sell his precious assets out of Allied. He really wanted to hold out for a deal where he didn't have to sell assets and there were no junk bonds either. But such a deal didn't exist."

Back in New York, the Sec Pac contingent, led by David Risdon, assumed it was about to be chosen as the lead bank. "Everything seemed OK when I was out with my wife one afternoon buying furniture," recalls Risdon. "But I came back to our apartment and there were six messages on the answering machine about the Campeau deal. An emergency meeting was set for that evening at First Boston."

"Our people went over, and Roddy, Tysoe, and Buck Luce were the Campeau people there.

"Buck Luce has a lovely personality, but she can chat breezily with you as she takes a machete right up your back, and basically she sat down and calmly explained that Campeau had decided to use Citicorp for the Federated acquisition but wanted us to come along as a partner in Citicorp's deal."

The Sec Pac contingent did not react well to this news. One of Risdon's associates stood up and asked, "Are we going to put up with this bullshit?" and Risdon answered with an emphatic, "No, I'm with you," at which time the Sec Pac bankers stood up, left the room, and booked a flight to California to review these events with senior management.

That left Campeau with Citicorp, the bank that First Boston had favored all along. In theory, Citicorp was willing to fund Campeau's Federated bid but a snag had developed over a $10 million fee that Citicorp had demanded and that Campeau had instructed his people not to pay. When he finally relented and sent a check, Citicorp waited for the funds to clear before it began discussing the particulars of the financial structure it would accept. That structure was profoundly disturbing to the Campeau team. "We'd been led to believe that there would be $750 million worth of junk in Citicorp's plan," says Buck Luce. "But after they cashed our fee check, they told us there would be $1.4 billion in junk." Campeau was furious. This was more junk than he'd ever imagined. He was later able to get the amount reduced a certain extent by adding more equity. He felt betrayed, but at this late date, what could he do?

The Finkelstein of Macy's with whom Campeau was now competing for the prize of Federated was the same person with whom he hadn't been able to get an interview eighteen months earlier, when he was an obscure real estate developer trying to participate in the Macy's LBO. Thanks to Campeau's pluck, luck, and debt financing, the two of them were now fellow retailers, competing as equals.

Macy's was, as one investment banker put it, "borrowed up the wazoo from taking itself private" but some of its debt was paid off by the time the Federated chance came along. On Macy's own board there was heated debate over whether to proceed, with Laurence Tisch of CBS, among others, vehemently opposed. Finkelstein argued that Federated had terrific locations and great expansion opportunities. Also, there was some thought that if the takeover were structured correctly, Macy's could turn around and go public again, at considerable profit to the owners.

Finkelstein's opinions prevailed, and Macy's made what appeared to be a fantastic offer of $73.50 a share. This was nearly $500 million more than Campeau's $68 overture, which had been bumped to $69 during the supposedly final negotiations with the Federated board. On closer inspection, the Macy's offer was only 80 percent cash, with the rest made up of stock, or cram-down paper, of the kind that Campeau once proposed in one of his Allied bids. Analysts on the sidelines were doubting that the $73.50 in cash and paper actually measured up to Campeau's $69 pure cash. Nonetheless, the Federated board favored Macy's.

Lambasting the Macy's approach as "highly speculative, two-tiered, and not competitive," the Campeau team prepared to nudge its $69 all-cash bid another fifty cents to $69.50. Campeau himself was flying back from Germany.

The deal was gathering its own momentum, the participants punchy from a lack of sleep, from the continuous posturing and bargaining, and from the relentless pressure to win. Campeau wasn't backing down. The word from his advisers was that he was more determined than ever to wrest Federated from the clutches of Ed Finkelstein. "You could see it in his eyes when he got back," says a Campeau insider. "He wasn't going to capitulate."

First Boston couldn't afford for Campeau to lose the Federated game, because if he did, Wall Street would wonder if First Boston could still do deals without Wasserstein. Wasserstein couldn't afford for Campeau to lose, either, because then Wall Street would wonder if Wasserstein could still do deals without First Boston.

As to whether Campeau could afford to win, each higher bid

sent the First Boston number crunchers scrambling back to their computers to produce yet another scenario in which more Federated divisions could be sold, or other measures could be taken to enable the company's cash flow to cover the additional debt. "We kept hearing higher and higher prices for the Federated assets," Mack Rossoff, a Wasserstein cohort, told the Los Angeles *Times*. "That gave us a different view of the value. Another thing is that the banks were coming out of their shell and were willing to lend more."

The bidding war with Macy's had gone on for three weeks. On March 22, Campeau jumped his offer to $73 all cash, an extraordinary escalation that his advisers believed might "blow Macy's away." But it didn't. There was a barrage of offers and counteroffers— Macy's amended tender; Campeau's revised single-tiered tender and later his amended two-tiered tender; Macy's raise to $74.50; Campeau's raise of the Macy's raise to $75—each more lucrative for the shareholders than the last.

As the price went higher, the Campeau team, Wasserstein and First Boston assured one another that the Macy's team knew what it was doing. The faithful assumption that Macy's wouldn't have bid so much unless Federated was worth every borrowed penny gave the Campeau people confidence that their bids were also reasonable. Thus was a seemingly nonsensical price tag made to appear sensible.

Joe Flom was working hard to keep the bidding open. As one investment banker puts it, "Flom was trying to goose Macy's into raising its price even more."

Lawyers for both sides were having a busy time in the various courtrooms. In New York, the validity of Federated's poison pill was being argued in U.S. District Court. Stuart Shapiro from Skadden, Arps represented Federated, and Frederick A. O. Schwarz, Jr., the grandson of the founder of the toy business and the former corporation counsel (chief attorney) for New York City, represented Campeau from Cravath.

Shapiro, according to news accounts, had fortified himself with a nap and a glass of Bordeaux before heading to the packed courtroom on March 14. There, Judge Leonard B. Sand was hearing arguments on whether to let the poison pill stand, thus protecting the company while the auction continued, or to invalidate the pill, in which case nothing could stop Campeau from gaining control without the consent of Federated's board. "You could tell he rather liked playing the role of the auctioneer," said one of Campeau's bankers. "You could also tell that he was doing everything possible to avert a Campeau victory."

Unfortunately for Schwarz, Stu Shapiro had shown the judge a copy of a news release in which Campeau was quoted as saying that he didn't plan to raise his offer anymore at all. This spontaneous remark was uttered to a reporter when Campeau's baby-sitting public relations managers were out of earshot. It undercut his own lawyer's argument that removing the pill would allow the bidding to progress.

(Another of Campeau's famous bons mots, uttered during a break in a deposition he gave to Federated's lawyers, was that if he had had a Jewish name, maybe he'd have a better chance with a Jewish judge. This remark was highly offensive to Campeau's own Jewish lawyers and bankers, and Schwarz apologized to Shapiro for Campeau's having said it.)

A surprised Schwarz, making a valiant attempt at a comeback, admitted that while Campeau didn't plan to raise his bid if the pill were removed, he might raise it if the pill were retained. This was just what Federated's lawyer wanted to hear. "We're still squeezing the bidders," Shapiro reportedly told the judge. "Don't stop the auction." The pill was upheld.

As this legal wrangling proceeded, Macy's and Campeau were both making side deals for a growing number of Federated divisions that the winner would have to sell in order to pay for the company. There was a brisk traffic in potential divestitures. The May Company was talking to both Macy's and Campeau about buying Foley's and Filene's of Boston. Dillard was talking to Campeau and to Macy's about buying I. Magnin of San Francisco, etc.

This was the most enervating takeover battle on record. Campeau's PR people were answering four hundred calls a day, and were generally lost in a bedlam of news releases and requests for information. Lawyers and bankers were roused from their beds to attend emergency late-night meetings, and some were forced to cancel their vacations. Marvin Traub, Bloomingdale's CEO and a member of Federated's board, cut short a ski trip and later missed the Paris kickoff of the new Dior collection in order to take a conference call.

Board members from Cincinnati flew to and from New York via the Federated Air Force. They groaned in dismay at the daily delivery of formal letters from Campeau's lawyers.

At least one spouse threatened her husband with divorce because he hadn't been home in so long. Another bought a vacation home sight unseen by her husband, who was too busy to visit it. The wife of Ken Colburn, Campeau's relationship manager at First Boston, brought the children to the office one day to remind them what their father looked like. Finkelson was called away from his parents' wedding anniversary party in Palm Beach, and spent the next twenty-four hours on the phone. He was also getting a daily 7 A.M. phone call from Campeau, whether he liked it or not.

Early in the deal, Finkelson and Campeau went skiing together at Vail, where they planned to compete for who could carve the best turns, but their "Campeau Cup" final was postponed so many times to allow Campeau to talk to his bankers that they decided to cancel it altogether. "You don't want to be on a chairlift with your client at a critical time of the deal," Finkelson told the *Los Angeles Times*.

The bidding continued apace, with a Campeau bump to $77, and a Macy's bump to $77.50 and again to $79 with a new combination of cash and cram-down paper. Neither Campeau nor Macy's Finkelstein showed any sign of backing down. At each higher level, the number crunchers dutifully produced another computer simulation to prove the deal made sense—would there ever be an end to this? Buck Luce was sent out to search for more money so that Campeau could afford these ever-higher prices.

The Federated board was playing the auction for all it was worth, accepting a Macy's "final bid" and informing Campeau he'd lost, then turning around and allowing Campeau "one last chance" to top the Macy's final bid with his own, then going back to Macy's to invite yet another final bid. Joe Flom was a principal orchestrator of these latter escalations, continuing to goose Macy's to bid more on the one hand, while encouraging Campeau not to drop out on the other.

But having just squeezed another fifty cents ($50 million for the shareholders) out of Macy's, Flom and the Federated board began to worry that the rival bidders might soon come to their senses.

After all, what was to prevent Campeau and Macy's from calling an independent truce?

It was clear already that the price had gone so high that the winning bidder could only afford to keep a few of Federated's divisions, and would be forced to sell the rest to pay off part of the debt. The Federated board knew that both Campeau and Macy's had presold several divisions, including Bullock's and I. Magnin, and there were rumors of back-channel discussions between the two sides. If allowed to join forces voluntarily, Campeau and Macy's could sit down together, divvy up Federated between themselves, retract their $75-plus bids, and approach the board with a take-it-or-leave-it offer in the more reasonable $60-plus range.

Such a result might have been healthier for the future of the enterprise, but shareholders would have lost the $1 billion windfall that the Macy's-Campeau bidding war produced, and the board's mandate was to maximize shareholder value.

So on March 29, leaving nothing to chance, the clever Flom decided to shut down the auction by negotiating a truce between Campeau and Macy's before the two parties discovered that they could do the same thing for $1 billion less on their own. The terms of Flom's truce called for Campeau to acquire Federated at large for $73.50 a share all cash, which was lower than his last and highest bid, a discount proffered as a goodwill gesture by Flom and the board. Macy's would be allowed to buy three Federated divisions (Bullock's, Bullock's/Wilshire, and I. Magnin) from Campeau for $1.1 billion, thus getting the West Coast outlets that it craved. Additionally, Macy's would get a $60 million cash settlement with which to pay its bankers and lawyers, the very same arrangement that it had made earlier with Federated, and that Campeau's lawyers had opposed in court as unfair.

Campeau had returned home to Toronto from Germany, reportedly demoralized by Macy's continuous bidding and concerned about the resulting high price of his competing offers. First Boston dispatched its retail expert, Jeff Branman, to ride with Campeau on the corporate jet from Toronto back to New York to review the settlement with Finkelstein and also, according to a First Boston source, to lift his spirits. The last thing the investment bankers wanted was for Campeau to drop out.

But Campeau didn't drop out, and now he and Ed Finkelstein were on the verge of meeting to discuss Flom's truce. Even this did not go smoothly, as a snag developed around the critical issue of *where* to meet. Finkelstein proposed that the conference be held in his office, the same office to which Campeau couldn't get a simple invitation back in 1986, and if he'd been allowed to participate in the Macy's LBO, none of this would have happened. Campeau rejected Finkelstein's proposal on the grounds that his going to Finkelstein's office might be interpreted as a sign of weakness, such as the Holy Roman Emperor Henry IV showed when he went to petition Pope Gregory VII at Canossa.

Finkelstein, meanwhile, declined the invitation to meet in Campeau's Waldorf apartment, so once again the two sides were at an impasse over issues with no apparent resolution. It was the ingenious Flom who once again came up with a compromise within a compromise. He got Finkelstein to invite Campeau to his New York townhouse, and then convinced Campeau that this townhouse was not Finkelstein's principal residence, which made it more or less a neutral site. That the two men met there on April Fool's night does not lack in future significance.

Campeau had brought along Allen Finkelson, and Finkelstein had his lawyer, Ira Millstein, so between Millstein and Finkelstein and Finkelson there was ample room for confusion. Campeau had his team huddled in the kitchen, while Finkelstein's team huddled in the downstairs rec room, with the two principals sitting in armchairs in the living room. Initiatives were shuttled back and forth from the rec room and the kitchen and brought to the principals' attention.

Both sides reached quick agreement on the basic points: Campeau would win Federated for $73.50 all cash and would pay Macy's its $60 million going-away fee; Macy's would buy the Bullock's, Bullock's/Wilshire, and I. Magnin divisions for $1.1 billion.

By ten-thirty or so, when everything appeared to be settled, the lawyers in the kitchen heard raised voices coming from the living room, and Campeau's throaty "The hell I will" carried all the way to the third-floor bedroom, where Mrs. Finkelstein wondered what was going on.

Racing up from his post in the basement, Finkelson arrived at the armchairs in time to calm his client and rescue the takeover from a final disagreement over a couple of million dollars' worth of expense reimbursements.

Campeau had bought Federated, and was now the largest retailer in America. He and Finkelstein drank a perfunctory toast of half a glass of champagne. Project Rose had come to a successful end.

The next morning, the Campeau group met at Skadden, Arps's Third Avenue offices to sign the papers. As Roddy and Tysoe stood at a window, Roddy noticed Bloomingdale's famous flagship store a few stories below them and a few blocks to the north. "Gee," Roddy admired, "it's the whole block."

# Twelve

•

Just because he'd removed himself to Austria during the battle with Macy's didn't mean that Campeau was any less involved in Federated than he had been in Allied. If anything, he was more involved, for in a subtle way the balance of power had shifted.

In Allied, he may have complained on occasion and second-guessed his advisers, but in the end, he could be counted on to follow Wasserstein's advice or Finkelson's advice, as he did on the day of the Street Sweep. In Federated, things were different, the takeover process no longer mysterious. Campeau had seen how Wall Street worked and more than once he had shown his high-priced bankers that their thinking was inferior to his own. If Allied was a Wall Street production, Federated was a Campeau production, on Campeau's terms.

In the souk of Federated, where dozens of elaborate bargains had to be struck, Campeau was once again doing what he seemed to love best, haggling. He involved himself personally in so many haggles that people marveled at how he could possibly keep them all straight. As his interest in Federated waxed, his enthusiasm for last year's project, Allied Stores, appeared to have waned.

The news from what was left of Allied—Stern's in New Jersey, Jordan Marsh of Boston, Jordan Marsh and Maas Brothers of Florida, the Bon Marché in Seattle, and Ann Taylor nationwide—was not very good. A general slump in retailing, blamed in part on the attempt of fashion experts to impose short skirts on American women, who in turn rebelled by wearing their old clothes, had resulted in lower profits everywhere.

At Allied, recent quarterly results were particularly soft. The price of Allied bonds had fallen about 10 percent from what the original buyers had paid, as a result in part of a general retreat in the junk market to less euphoric valuations. The goal of the 12 percent EBIT (earnings before interest and taxes) to which Campeau had gotten his weary executives to pledge during a New York snowstorm was farther from sight than before Campeau had ordered the budget cuts and other, more imaginative, reforms. And in spite of the sales of Allied divisions, Campeau was left with $1.65 billion in Allied debt, and a 1987 net loss of $187 million.

"He seemed to think that all those things he talked about on the store tours—upgrading the merchandise, consolidating back offices, motivating the salespeople—would be done with a snap of his finger," says an Allied vice president. But Allied's leadership, at first impressed by Campeau's gung-ho attitude, had learned that today's urgent mission was likely to be forgotten tomorrow, and by humoring the boss to maintain good relations, they could carry on with business as usual.

Allied had, nonetheless, begun to achieve the cost savings in the original takeover plan. In fact, one of the reasons that bankers in the Federated deal accepted the Campeau cash-flow projections for Federated was that most of the promised budget cuts were delivered in Allied.


In March, in the midst of the Federated haggle, and with Allied having reported slow sales, Campeau was at a party where Allen Finkelson's wife said she didn't like the Ann Taylor catalogue. The entire Ann Taylor division was failing to live up to Campeau's great expectations that had caused him to want to sprinkle Ann Taylor stores around Canada and Europe. He called in Morris Saffer, a Canadian advertising executive whom he'd never met but who was a friend of Jim Roddy's, to anaylze the Ann Taylor problem.

Saffer arrived at the Waldorf for the 6 A.M. appointment, only to find himself in a crowd of security guards pounding on the door of Campeau's suite. The door opened, and Campeau appeared, dripping wet and naked except for the towel around his waist, demanding to know the cause of this intrusion. After the guards explained that Campeau hadn't answered his wake-up call—which had aroused concern at the front desk—and Saffer explained that he wasn't one of the guards, Campeau invited Saffer into his suite.

There, they had an amiable discussion about who Saffer was, and about Ann Taylor and the catalogue, which Saffer had spent the prior day evaluating.

At six-thirty or so, Campeau's jogging buddy and Allied vice president, Harold Leppo; Ann Taylor's president, Michelle Fortune; Morosky; Saffer; and a couple of other interested parties sat down to breakfast in Campeau's dining room. They'd hardly unrolled their napkins before Campeau started in on the catalogue, and what a disaster it was, what a disaster Ann Taylor was, and what a disaster the president of Ann Taylor was. Fortune sat, mesmerized, as Campeau berated her.

When Saffer finally got a word in, he praised Fortune and tried to downplay the problem of the catalogue, in an effort to head off Campeau's tirade. Granted, there was room for improvement, Saffer said, but Ann Taylor had good management and a sensible plan. Its biggest problem was the bad market. This speech only made Campeau madder, as Morosky recalls:

"Hearing that the problem with Ann Taylor was not as simple as revising the catalogue sent Campeau into a rage. He picked up his fork and stabbed the table. The fork penetrated the table and was vibrating back and forth, and I'll never forget it, looking at that fork vibrating there and the guy's eyes bulging wide and his hands shaking, and I looked at this poor woman, Michelle Fortune, and thought she was going to have a heart attack and then I saw the looks on the other faces and I wondered who was going to have the first heart attack in the room.

"Campeau ran around in a circle, circled the table, once, then twice. Then he stopped and sat down, took a couple of deep breaths, and apologized.

"We all tried to remain calm, to pretend we hadn't noticed this outburst, that nothing had happened, and we went back to eating our breakfast and having a rational, low-key discussion of the problems of Ann Taylor. But Michelle seemed to be in shock, and the rest of us were amazed at what we had witnessed."

In closing, Campeau said he wanted a full report on the Ann Taylor situation at a forthcoming meeting. Fortune wasn't sure what sort of report to produce, so she decided to wait for further instructions. But there were no further instructions; there was no forthcoming meeting; Campeau never called back.


Campeau had won Bloomingdale's just five days before the Hooray for Hollywood! Party held at the Bloomingdale's flagship store on Lexington Avenue. This glamorous benefit for the victims of AIDS was planned long before the takeover, but in a lucky coincidence was perfectly timed for Campeau's second Coming Out.

Hosted jointly by Revlon, *People* magazine, and Bloomingdale's, Hooray for Hollywood! was a synergistic bash in which celebrities could mingle at the sales counters with the products they promoted —Brooke Shields and her Calvins, Calvin and his Obsession, de la Renta and his de la Rentas, Lauren and his Chaps. Previews of upcoming movies were shown on TV monitors deployed above the jewelry displays and the garment racks.

The main entrance at Fifty-ninth and Lexington was flanked with floodlights, and in a scene from what might as well have been opening night at the Academy Awards, a crowd of onlookers, cordoned off from the red carpet, ogled the familiar faces emerging from limousines: Cher, Lynn von Furstenberg, Frank Gifford, Fawn Hall, Jane Powell, Judd Nelson, Douglas Fairbanks Jr., Jaclyn Smith, Jane Seymour, and Lauren Hutton. In the midst of the hoopla, a radiant Campeau, dressed in a tuxedo, arrived with the beautiful Ilse.

As soon as Campeau entered the store, he was surrounded by well-wishers and reporters; movie stars ambled over to introduce themselves; and a majority of the cameras focused on him. Escorted by Marvin Traub, the well-known Mr. Bloomingdale's and soon-to-be Campeau employee, and accompanied by Bob Morosky, Campeau inspected the first-floor displays, including the homage to Cher and *People* magazine's gallery of stars, with the same jaunty aplomb with which he once inspected the Royal Guards at the grand opening of the Harbour Castle Hotel in Toronto.

What better proof of the power of debt and the glory of the debtor than this scene at Bloomingdale's, where the borrower of $11 billion (if you count both Allied and Federated) stole the show from designers, actors, actresses, athletes, and the many career retailers who'd devoted their lives to building this business? Thanks to the banks and the lawyers, Campeau had upstaged them all, and Hooray for Hollywood! had turned into the great celebration that the Temple of Dendur party never was. "It's a fantastic acquisition for us," Campeau told the press. Who could doubt it?

There was Mr. Bloomingdale's himself, Traub, sixty-three, a man so devoted to his store that no detail escaped his curiosity, who had joined Bloomingdale's in 1950 and worked his way up from the basement to become CEO in 1978, who held business meetings in his car (the Traubmobile) so as not to waste valuable time, who had discovered Ralph Lauren, brought the Japanese designer Kenzo to America, pioneered the boutique concept, the department store as theater, the China promotion, the Africa promotion, and otherwise would have been the toast of the evening and a center of attention, instead reduced to tour guide, standing in the shadow of his effervescent new boss.

"I think I was the first to call and congratulate him," Traub said graciously, and also, "I have great respect for Mr. Campeau. He accomplished a great deal." But as Traub toured the upper floors with Campeau and Morosky (who paid special attention to the furniture displays to get some ideas for his new living room), a reporter described him as ill at ease. Traub's wife, Lee, was heard to remark: "They don't belong here. It's our store."

Soon the upstaged Traub would have as one of his regular duties the planning and hosting of Campeau parties, including a birthday celebration for Ilse at Bloomingdale's restaurant, Le Train Bleu, at which Campeau sang along with the musicians. Traub began getting phone calls very early in the morning, and once was pulled out of a meeting in Paris to answer Campeau's urgent request for fashion-show tickets.

•   •   •

On April 5, four days after the takeover and two days after the Hooray for Hollywood! party, there was a press conference at the Waldorf-Astoria. More than two hundred journalists, financial analysts, and other interested parties packed the large conference room.

Campeau had told First Boston he wanted a "victory press conference." From First Boston's point of view, this was an opportunity to further expose financial analysts to Bob Morosky, who already had been billed to the bond market as the cost-conscious operator who would cut the Federated budget and teach its free-spending retailers how to run a business more profitably. Morosky was seen by the bank strategists as the key to the upcoming sale of Federated junk bonds, and a solid counterbalance to the dynamic but flighty Campeau. Morosky, after all, had written the strategic plan for how to run Federated.

It was no accident that the only people sitting at the head table on the makeshift stage were Campeau, Morosky, Finkelson, and Campeau's communications consultant, Davis Weinstock, who was there to introduce the others.

Campeau had just flown in from Florida, where he'd spent a couple of days playing golf. Looking tanned and fit, he strode to the head table to confront his audience, many of whom were carrying copies of the April 4 edition of *The Wall Street Journal,* with its long front-page sidebar, "Betting the Store." The article, by Jacquie McNish, was the first detailed personal history of Campeau ever published in the U.S. There was nothing about his marriages in this article, but it did include a reference to the "deep depression" he'd suffered in 1980 after the failure of Royal Trustco.

The story repeated the information that had appeared a year earlier in Toronto's *Report on Business,* corroborated by Campeau himself, who in an interview with McNish in Toronto, had let down his guard and discussed these episodes. Campeau's wife, Ilse, who was present at the interview, worried about how some of this would sound, and convinced her husband to call Weinstock, and get him to dissuade McNish from printing the personal parts of the story.

But Weinstock had had no luck with the reporter, and when the article appeared April 4, it infuriated Campeau. Early that morning, he demanded a meeting with the editors of *The Wall Street Journal* and also called McNish and threatened her with a lawsuit. (Neither the meeting nor the lawsuit ever materialized.)

Brushing the article aside, Campeau gave an upbeat presentation. "The fact is," he told the crowd, "we bought Federated at an even better cost than Allied." Instead of spreading Brooks Brothers stores around the world, now he was spreading Bloomingdale's.

"We're going to expand to our fullest ability," Campeau said, announcing that he and DeBartolo were planning to build fifty to one hundred new regional malls anchored by Federated stores. He also said that the cost of the Federated acquisition, $10.9 billion, would be reduced by at least $5 billion from the sale of eight divisions. He predicted that the company would have no trouble paying its debts from the "great cash flow." He estimated that earnings before interest and taxes would be $675–700 million on an annualized basis.

He said that the job cuts at Federated headquarters would be modest, that the Ann Taylor franchise wasn't for sale in spite of what had just happened to Brooks Brothers, and that Morosky would be CEO of Federated as well as Allied.

But after Campeau finished his speech, which he'd given while seated at the table, Morosky got up and walked to a podium to make his remarks, and remained there to answer questions. "What's that guy doing?" Campeau was overheard muttering to Weinstock, sitting at his side, as Morosky lingered at the center of attention, discussing how the nineties would be a great decade for department stores. It occurred to those within earshot of Campeau that Morosky's tenure as CEO of Federated as well as Allied might be short.

By the time questions finally were redirected Campeau's way, his mood had darkened. He responded testily to several analysts who seemed to doubt his projections. When asked about the Federated junk bonds, he stunned the crowd by denying their existence. "I will not have junk bonds," he sneered. Nobody quite knew what to make of this remark, which contradicted everything the analysts had read in the newspapers, in the press releases, and in the filings with the SEC about the more than $1 billion of junk bonds in the deal— not to mention the same requirement in Citicorp's commitment letter that Campeau recently had signed.

The press conference that was supposed to reassure the financial markets and make it easier for First Boston to sell Federated junk had just the opposite effect. How could First Boston sell junk bonds with the owner of the company insisting publicly that there weren't any? For days afterward, financial analysts were calling First Boston for clarification. "In explaining what Bob meant," a First Boston source says, "we took the approach that in Bob's mind, there were no junk bonds, whereas in the deal itself, there were."

Meanwhile, Morosky, introduced to the financial markets as Campeau's "maven," had returned to his office to work on the Federated/Allied master plan that would eliminate featherbedding and duplication of effort, cut costs, and increase profits. He'd just put the finishing touches on a report that showed how to consolidate Federated's computer system when Campeau called to say he was traveling to Cincinnati to meet with the Federated division heads, whom Morosky had nicknamed "the Magnificent Seven," for the golden parachute they'd received after the takeover.

"One of our biggest concerns," said Morosky, "was that the Magnificent Seven were the likely enemies of what we were trying to do and would have to be somehow controlled until they left the company. But now Campeau was going off to consult with them.

"I had to make an important career decision whether to accompany Campeau and insulate him from these guys, who I knew would politic him and undermine his success, or stay in New York and sequester myself in my room and lay out the master plan as best I could.

"I said a prayer and decided to trust my contract with Campeau, and the fact that he'd made me chairman. So I stayed in New York."

As Morosky had feared, in a matter of hours, the Magnificent Seven (including Howard Goldfeder, who had stayed on for a few days to aid Campeau in his transition) were advising the new owner that Federated should be run by a merchant, which Morosky wasn't. Campeau, who tended to act on the last strong opinion that he heard, and who was displeased by Morosky's grandstanding at the Waldorf press conference anyway, was listening.

Many of Federated's top executives were about to bail out on $28 million worth of golden parachutes crafted by Goldfeder for himself and his senior executives in 1985 ("grossly excessive and wholly unjustifiable," Campeau's team had called the parachutes during the takeover battle, only to acquiesce to them after Campeau had won). But the fleeing executives were having a surprising influence on the person from whom they were fleeing.

By the time Morosky flew in for the celebration dinner held in Cincinnati, in the banquet room of the Cincinnatian Hotel, he realized what he was up against. "Campeau was making his usual inane remarks," says a Federated executive, "and Morosky was saying nothing. Morosky was keeping a low profile, which was hard to do, since the guy is about six feet two, and standing next to us retail types, who tend to be small, he looked like Paul Bunyan without the ox.

"Meanwhile, the Federated people were all whispering to each other how much they hated Morosky. They'd just met him and they hated his supercilious attitude. They snickered about his wearing a red toupee. They hated that he resembled a football coach. They hated that he had the savoir faire of a crane operator. They hated that he wasn't saying anything. When he did say something, they hated that. Soon it was more than hatred. It was revulsion. Jim Zimmerman, the number one at Rich's, got so upset just watching Morosky that he went to the bathroom several times."

When Campeau and Morosky returned to New York, less than two weeks after Campeau announced to the crowd at the Waldorf that Morosky was Federated's new CEO, Campeau announced to Morosky that he wasn't the new Federated CEO. "I called my attorney," Morosky says, "and we got together with Campeau's attorney, Finkelson, in New York. I told Finkelson that I didn't want to confront Campeau, but that Finkelson ought to have a little discussion with him about the fact that I had a signed contract that said I would be chairman.

"The next day, Campeau called me into his office and said, 'I know you have a contract to be CEO, and I know I made you CEO, but maybe we ought to get a Federated merchant in here. Will you stay on, also, and help us out?' "

"I said, 'You could probably get a merchant in here, Bob. There are several people out there you could talk to, but how many of them have ever made bold strategical moves or innovative changes? Federated's management is weak and caused the problems that led to your successful acquisition. We need somebody strong, a retail operator who can make the changes. He should be an outsider. We have a plan and you know the wisdom of this plan and to carry out the plan I must be primarily responsible.' Bob said, 'I can't accept that. I want to be involved myself as well. But I'll honor our agreement.'

"I went back to my office and cleaned out my desk, went back to my apartment, packed my belongings, and booked the next flight out of New York."

Campeau paid Morosky the balance of his contract, $3 million for six months' work. Morosky also cashed in an estimated $200,000 worth of options in Campeau Corporation stock, then selling—thanks in part to Morosky's being touted as CEO of Federated—for more than $20.

"Morosky's exit," says a banker who worked on the Federated deal, "coupled with Campeau's having overpaid for Federated, was a fatal double blow. The merchants and mandarins at Federated had no conception of how to operate a leveraged business."

Whereas the Allied financing plan was a Wall Street concoction, the Federated financing plan was more a Campeau concoction. This was because the equity portion was much larger—$1.4 billion for Federated—and Campeau had raised it himself, on his own terms. In fact, the word "equity" does no justice to the work of immense complexity that Campeau had engineered. The equity package was actually a collection of intricate and overlapping microdeals, the details of which were negotiated by Roddy and Buck Luce.

The closing for the Federated tender offer, in all its complexity, was held on May 3, 1988, on the second floor of the New York offices of Shearman & Sterling, Citicorp's lawyers. Since no one room, or small group of rooms, could have accommodated this crowd, this law firm had made almost its entire center available to Campeau. Whether this was an omen or not, the only space not allocated to Campeau's Federated closing was at the far end of the floor, nicknamed the "Brazil Area," where bankers were meeting to work out their defaulted loans to Latin America. Nervous lenders were scurrying around at that end, and occasionally wandered into the Federated area to lament their problems.

Within the Federated area, a large open space was surrounded on three sides by small offices, like a monastery courtyard ringed

with monks' cubicles. In the middle of the open space was a reception area, where Roddy, Buck Luce and Tysoe directed traffic. The
cubicle nearest the reception area was converted to a food room,
where as a First Boston participant noted, "you'd know it was morning because the Danishes would be out, and you'd know it was
evening because the sweet-and-sour pork would be out, and you'd
know it was midnight because the pork fat had congealed on the
inside of the Chinese takeout boxes. Otherwise, how could we tell?
Many of us hadn't been exposed to natural light for forty-eight
hours. Prior to coming here, we'd been working around the clock
on Campeau details for two straight days."

Around the open space, First Boston was in one cubicle, the
Reichmann team in another; there were cubicles for the DeBartolo
team, the Citicorp team, the Marks & Spencer team that had come
to complete the sale of Brooks Brothers, the Bank of Montreal
(Beemo) team, and the Banque Paribas team. Roddy and Buck
Luce, and/or Tysoe and Buck Luce moved from room to room with
a horde of lawyers from Cravath, trying to settle the hundreds of
interrelated fine points that were yet to be resolved.

The last-minute trades and retrades, typical of a Campeau negotiation, here had multiplied exponentially. There were pecking-
order problems. The two Canadian banks, committed to an initial
$200 million equity loan that was increased to $500 million, had
earlier agreed that their loan would be subordinate to First Boston's
bridge but ahead of DeBartolo's equity loan in the lineup for some
of Campeau's assets in case of a default. Now these banks wanted to
move ahead of First Boston in the lineup and also to reduce the term
of their loan from three years to one. This came up at 2 A.M.

This late-hour stance of the Canadian banks had alarmed the
Citicorp and First Boston teams. It meant that the whole of Federated could be brought down by these two equity lenders if Campeau
didn't repay them on time. The resulting domino effect might collapse the rest of the financing, by accelerating several hundred million in tax deferrals that depended on the deal's success. Why, First
Boston wanted to know, hadn't the two banks brought this up
earlier?

The Bank of Montreal and Banque Paribas claimed that Campeau had been aware of the new demands for some time, but nobody
had done anything about them. Buck Luce ran frantically back and

forth between cubicles trying to produce a compromise, but this shuttle diplomacy failed. Finally, the other parties gave in to the Beemo-Paribas demands, if only because (1) they were too tired to resist; (2) if they hadn't, then the Federated purchase would have collapsed, causing shareholders to sue everybody in sight for their lost profits.

"Many things like this were left hanging to this last minute," recalls a banker. "In fact, the closing was delayed a couple of times already. It went on and on."

There were two dummy corporations and several subsidiary holding companies through which Campeau orchestrated his complex arrangements. There was DeBartolo's $480 million long-term equity loan, secured by Allied and by one of the holding companies. There was Ralphs, the Federated grocery-store division that Campeau had decided to spin off in a separate leveraged buyout. There was the $500 million loan from the two Canadian banks, secured by Campeau real estate and by second liens on both Federated and Allied stock. There was the $260 million Reichmann equity loan, secured by Campeau Corp. stock.

There was the Brooks Brothers sale, with $200 million of the proceeds to be used as Campeau equity in Federated, and the rest to be returned to Allied to repay part of Allied's secured loan from Sec Pac. There was the $2.1 billion bridge loan advanced by First Boston, Dillon Read, and Paine Webber, the latter having joined the Campeau venture in spite of its unfortunate earlier experiences. This bridge loan was supposed to be paid back later from the sale of junk bonds and from the permanent bank financing. Speaking of that, there was $4 billion in secured loans from a syndicate led by Citicorp, and co-managed by the giant Japanese bank Sumitomo, which had chosen the Campeau deal for its first involvement in a hostile, junk-bond-financed buyout. This was the first time any Japanese bank had co-managed such an LBO.

Citicorp had brought along eighteen other banks; Sumitomo, thirteen other banks; and the Bank of America, five other banks. "You'd go to the bathroom," says John Garnet of Sumitomo, "and you'd see friends and acquaintances you didn't even know were in the deal. 'Where did you come from?' you'd ask, and it turned out they were in a nearby cubicle, signing papers like everybody else."

Also to be resolved were the sales of I. Magnin's, Bullock's, and

Bullock's/Wilshire to Macy's, plus Foley's and Filene's to the May Company. All of these had special tax angles—for instance, in the Brooks Brothers sale to Marks & Spencer, the price was paid part in cash and part in a so-called monetized note.

This rococo of finance, with all its pecuniary flourish and intricate legal detail and its harmonious fusion of separate understandings, was Campeau's masterpiece to creative indebtedness, with not a penny's worth of outlay from his own pocket. And he wasn't even here to appreciate it. He was vacationing in Austria.

In early May, Campeau took formal control of Federated, or rather, what was left of it. The three presold major divisions (Bullock's, Bullock's Wilshire, and I. Magnin) to Macy's, and two others (Foley's and Filene's) to the May Company altogether netted Campeau $2.6 billion. What he'd really acquired were the six remaining major divisions (Bloomingdale's, Abraham & Straus, Rich's, Lazarus, Burdines, and Goldsmith's) plus several minor enterprises that he planned to sell off.

In effect, he'd bought a piece of Federated for $4.2 billion. Was it worth the price he paid—$73.50 per share? At a celebration dinner at the swanky Le Cygne restaurant in New York, his triumphant bankers and lawyers had whooped it up and pounded on the tables like hungry Visigoths, chanting "May, May, May," which referred to the next department-store company they wanted Campeau to attack. In the midst of the jovial repartee, Campeau pointed to Joe Perella, who was standing in for Wasserstein, who arrived late. "Bruce cost me an extra $500 million," Campeau said.

Campeau was referring to the difference between the $68 per share price that the Federated board had apparently agreed to over that fateful—or perhaps, fatal—weekend, and the $73.50 that Campeau finally paid.*

To blame the $500 million on Wasserstein was to miss the point; Wasserstein had pushed for an immediate signing of the $68 deal, and if anything, it was Campeau's refusal to commit to a commercial

---

* At another celebration dinner for the bank financing in Federated, cowboy hats were once again given out to the dealmakers, just as they had been in Allied. Stapled to the brims was the message: "We Bet the Ranch—Again."

bank that encouraged Federated's board to wait to hear from Macy's. The more pertinent issue was: Was Campeau the biggest live one of all? There was some doubt that Macy's had been a serious bidder after all.

The rumor on the Street was that Macy's had never secured its financing from Kidder, Peabody and from Drexel Burnham Lambert, in spite of Drexel's famous ability to raise instant billions for almost any sort of deal. If so, then in the latter and most costly stage of the bidding, Campeau may have been bidding against himself, with Macy's serving only as a stalking horse for the Federated board.

A source from the Macy's side, whom we'll call Deep Pockets, says this Stalking Horse theory may be partly true and partly false. False, because from the outset Ed Finkelstein "had fallen in love with Federated, the retail giant, and wanted desperately to have it." True, because a faction on the Macy's board, led by Larry Tisch of CBS, didn't want to bid for Federated.

"A dollar for a dollar was Tisch's attitude," says Deep Pockets. "And he didn't see that Macy's was going to get a dollar for a dollar from buying Federated at these prices. But in the end, the Tisch faction wasn't too worried, because they believed that Campeau wanted the company so badly that he could be counted on to make a higher bid. They also knew that Macy's could always back out due to its lack of financing.

"As one of the bankers involved, I never felt there was a reasonable chance for Macy's to own Federated. But Campeau could be taken to the wall and forced to give Macy's some valuable concessions."

If Campeau was chasing phantoms and bidding against himself, with the Federated board playing the auction for all its worth, with bankers cheering for the transaction to proceed, whose rule was it to tell Campeau not to overpay? Campeau on his own wasn't going to stop bidding—he was full of hubris from his Allied success. The bankers sensed that. "In the end, it was him against Ed Finkelstein," a Campeau aide says. "This wasn't about money. It was about victory at any cost."

Wasserstein had implied it wasn't his role to advise Campeau on numbers; he was a strategy man; the numbers were coming from his old firm, First Boston, with whom he had very little contact. First Boston admits that it was advising Campeau on numbers, but says that the numbers made sense. Each bump in the bidding was preceded by a computer run ("iteration" as it was called) that proved that the numbers made sense. "It was an amazing thing in these LBO transactions," recalls Bill Dillard of Dillard Department Stores, who had dropped out of the Federated bidding early, "whatever the price was, the bankers could prove it would work."

"Did the Federated board think Campeau paid too much?"

"We thought he had the financing."

"But did you think, with this much debt, the company would survive?"

"We thought he had the financing."

"Yes, but could Federated survive this transaction?"

"The board clearly understood that everything had to work perfectly for Federated to survive the transaction. There was no cushion."

"Does everything ever work perfectly?"

"We thought he had the financing."

In this coy exchange, one of the Federated investment bankers indicated to me that some of the sellers suspected that Campeau was doomed at $73.50, but as the lawyers advised, the board's role was to get top dollar for the shareholders.

A closer inspection of Federated's numbers shows the following: During 1987, the year prior to the deal, the Federated divisions that Campeau planned to keep had generated $543 million in operating cash flow, before taxes. Campeau's estimated interest charges for the acquisition were about $450 million a year to begin with, which would decline as his loans were repaid. Thus, he had a $93 million cushion, which didn't leave much room to cover a sharp decline in the retailing business, or to pay for expanding and renovating stores.

An important part of the equation was the cost savings, as laid out in some detail by Jim Roddy and by Bob Morosky, prior to Morosky's departure. According to the plan, the new Federated would save $240 million from budget cuts, and another $25 million from Federated/Allied synergies in 1989. Thus, the new Federated could produce nearly $800 million in operating cash flow, without any increase in sales in the stores, In fact, the working assumption was that Federated's 1989 sales under Campeau would be 5 percent higher than the 1987 sales.

The number crunchers also figured that the Campeau/DeBartolo shopping center partnership would build and finance new stores and lease them to Federated, a less costly way to expand than Federated's building new stores on its own. And with Federated already planning to open eighteen new stores during 1989–92, including a new Blooomie's in Chicago and the mammoth Abraham & Straus across from Macy's flagship store on New York's Herald Square, the modest projections in sales growth seemed reasonable.

As per the scenario above, in 1989, Federated would generate an *excess* cash flow of $165 million, which could be used either for working capital or to repay debt ahead of schedule.

Moreover, Campeau had sold the superfluous Allied divisions at the higher end of the First Boston value range, and already had presold several Federated divisions for what were believed to be very high prices. His bankers expected that the sales of other Federated divisions, such as Filene's Basement, the Gold Circle, The Children's Place, and MainStreet, as well as the spinning off of Ralphs, would bring in enough cash to repay Citicorp for one of its loans— a $1.65 billion asset sale bridge. It was also expected that by taking out mortgages on his new Federated properties, Campeau could pay Citicorp for its $800 million mortgage loan bridge. Citicorp was already talking about doing the mortgage takeout itself, thus paying back its own loan with more of its own money.

Such was the Federated deal, as it appeared on paper. All would be well, the number crunchers predicted, provided of course that the divisions on the block sold for the expected high prices, that Campeau would take out the Federated mortgages, the Federated budget would be cut on schedule, etc. Interestingly enough, Citicorp, which had put the financing package together, wasn't taking this bet.

As it worked to syndicate the Federated deal and to form a permanent bank group, Citicorp was also assiduously laying off its own part of the Campeau loans so that it would end up with practically no ongoing exposure to Federated after it booked its big fees.

Meanwhile, the First Boston bridge-loan syndicate, which included Dillon, Read and Paine Webber, was confident that as long as Bob could be controlled, its $2.1 billion investment from its own capital—soon to be reduced to $1.1 billion via yet another Citicorp refinancing—would be paid back completely from the sale of junk bonds, scheduled for late July or early August.

And who could resist the wonderful procession of fees: $1.5 million for being the "dealer-manager"; another $1 million for the "highly confident" junk bond letter; another $1.85 million, reduced from $5 million, for the "highly confident" bank letter; $4.5 million for a "willingness to commit" letter (Wall Street having brought back the art of letter-writing in a most profitable fashion); $2 million for the equity bridge commitment; $15 million for the junk bridge commitment; $20 million for the funding of the junk bridge; $10.5 million for M&A advisory work; $38 million for the interest on the bridge loan; $17.6 million in profits from the spread on the junk-bond deal; $15 million in divestiture fees, including $12 million for selling the Ralphs grocery stores junk bonds; plus a few other fees and interest charges, producing a grand total of $130 million, plus expenses, and all this for First Boston alone.

Add to that the Citicorp commitment fees; the 3-plus percent fee for Citicorp's providing more than $3 billion in secured loans; the fees to Paine Webber and Dillon, Read for backing up First Boston; the fees to Shearson for representing Federated; and the fees to Drexel and Kidder, Peabody for representing Macy's; all of which were paid by Campeau for the privilege of acquiring Federated. The result exceeded $200 million—more in fees and charges than the entire Federated, with all its stores nationwide, earned in a year.

# Thirteen

•

Wall Street's dual assumptions that Campeau would be controlled and that Federated's operating budget would be tamed by the new ownership were shaken at once by the startling announcement of May 8, 1988: Morosky was gone. A week after Campeau formally took control of Federated, he changed his mind and declared himself the CEO, exactly as he'd done in Allied.

This reversal undid several months of strategic planning, as well as First Boston's public relations campaign to sell Morosky to the bond market.

It might not have mattered so much to First Boston who ran Federated, except that Campeau's investment bankers, along with Dillon, Read and the forgiving Paine Webber, were now sitting on a $1.1 billion loan that was supposed to be paid back with proceeds from the sale of the junk bonds. Campeau's remark about there being no junk bonds in Federated hadn't helped either.

Wall Street could only hope that Campeau would quickly hire Alan Questrom, a respected merchant in Federated's executive ranks who had run Bullock's in Los Angeles and was being groomed as Goldfeder's replacement as the CEO. But Questrom had fled to Neiman Marcus after the takeover, and had told the press: "I have been sitting shiva over this [Campeau's acquisition] . . . and have no good feelings about it. It is very difficult to find one positive thing about the change."

With Questrom refusing to come back, and with First Boston, Cravath, and Citicorp pressuring Campeau to hire somebody fast, on May 31, he turned to John Burden III, a Federated vice president who had bailed out on a $3 million golden parachute earlier that month. Burden, who was nearing retirement age, anyway, was in the process of making a leisurely landing on the beach in Sanibel Island, Florida.

With plenty of fuck-you money in the bank, and the powerful leverage of indifference, Burden got a lucrative new $1 million a year contract, plus a living allowance of $250,000, to return. Leaving and returning was worth considerably more to Burden than if he'd stayed on with the new Campeau regime in the first place.

Campeau also agreed to let Burden live on Sanibel Island, Florida and commute to New York (where Burden maintained a nice apartment) to run Federated from there, as opposed to requiring him to move to Cincinnati, where the headquarters is actually located.

Along with Burden, the new chairman and CEO, Campeau on the same day hired Jim Zimmerman to be Federated's president. Zimmerman, who ran Rich's in Atlanta, was in Boston visiting Jordan Marsh, which Campeau wanted to use as a "streamlining model," when he heard the news. "Congratulations," a Jordan Marsh executive told him. "I see you are president of Federated." "What?" said Zimmerman. "It's in *The Wall Street Journal*," came the reply.

Burden and Zimmerman were competent merchant/administrators, but neither was experienced at managing an entire company, much less one in which nine cents of every retailing dollar had to be devoted to paying off debt. In fact, both came out of the old Federated regime that during the takeover battle the Campeau team had characterized as inefficient and profligate. The whole idea was to install a cost-conscious new management to control the LBO. Now, according to the LBO logic, not only were the foxes running the henhouse, but the henhouse was completely in hock.

· · ·

In the spring of 1988, Campeau took off in the Gulfstream to tour the "best department-store company in the world," just as he had in Allied. He had a new pilot now, who, like the last one, was never sure when the boss was going to arrive at the airport or where they were headed from one day to the next. Often, Campeau brought along several suitcases. Cartons of Evian water and health food and crates of oranges (the oranges he insisted on peeling himself, to insure their freshness) were stacked up in the plane's bathroom. Once the pilot made an unscheduled landing so a passenger could get to a toilet.

Campeau toured his new properties by limousine and gave the employees rousing speeches. He was followed by a wary clump of Federated executives, who privately were wondering whether to bail out of the company or stick around and see what this brassy new owner would do. An entirely fresh audience heard about the "new dawn of retailing," the commission system, the motivated sales force, the upgraded inventory, the atriums, the commitment to excellence, his plans to centralize the back office, and his emphasis on private-label merchandise.

"At Rich's," says an employee from the Atlanta store, "Campeau came on strong, and got everybody fired up. This was a man with passion, not out of your everyday mold. Onward and upward, he made you believe everything was possible. After all, he'd just won the battle with Macy's. On the other hand, he forgot people's names, kept calling Rich's 'Rich,' and seemed not really to be aware where he was or what he was doing. We couldn't decide if he was crazy crazy, or crazy genius."

The private-label idea was nothing new; it was common practice for department stores to make their own line of clothing to sell alongside the brand-name merchandise they bought elsewhere. Private label was more profitable than brand-name merchandise, and many retailers had tried to increase the percentage of it in their "product mix."

But private label was an expensive and long-term proposition, in which the sellers of the merchandise also became the manufacturers, and had to put up the money to make the clothes—usually in the garment factories of the Far East—and then to ship them back and distribute them to the stores. "There were certain obvious draw-backs," says an ex-Allied executive, "that were well understood in

the industry. You couldn't have too much private label, or else it
would degrade your inventory. Also, if your private label didn't sell,
or if there were flaws in the manufacturing, you couldn't blame the
manufacturer, because you were the manufacturer.

"But Campeau saw private label as a panacea. Depending on his
mood, he'd tell one audience he wanted 15 percent private label.
The next speech, it would go up to 25 percent." In April, Campeau
had told the *Daily News Record,* a retailing newspaper, that he
wanted private label increased to between 35 and 40 percent.

On one of his earliest visits to Rich's in May, Campeau had flown in
to the Atlanta airport, where he was met by the dutiful contingent
of executives, including Jim Zimmerman, before Zimmerman was
elevated to his new post in Cincinnati. Campeau and the Rich's
contingent got into one limousine to drive to the downtown Rich's
store, while a second limo was dispatched with Campeau's clothes
to the hotel.

The first limo had hardly left the airport before Campeau turned
to Zimmerman and said: "Why don't we merge Rich with Goldsmith's?"—continuing his practice of calling Rich's Rich.

The idea of merging Rich's, the Atlanta division, with Goldsmith's, the Memphis division, had been kicked around since before
the takeover. There was considerable support for it. A lot of money
could be saved by combining the two operations and abolishing the
Goldsmith's headquarters, just as Campeau had abolished the Maas
Brothers headquarters in Florida. Zimmerman replied that it was
certainly something worth considering for the future.

But Campeau wasn't talking about the future. "I want to merge
Rich with Goldsmith's," he said, "right away."

"That's impossible," said Zimmerman.

"Get them on the phone," commanded Campeau, referring to
the two heads of Goldsmith's, "and we'll see."

By now they were on Interstate 85, with Zimmerman reluctant
to broach this sensitive subject with dire implications for the management of Goldsmith's from a car phone. "Look, if you want to talk
to them, then you talk to them," Zimmerman told Campeau, "but I
don't think this is the proper time."

Campeau told Zimmerman to dial the number, as there was no

time like the present, and Campeau himself talked to the two heads of Goldsmith's and instructed them to fly to Atlanta that very night after dinner, to work out the merger of Goldsmith's into Rich's.

Fearing they were about to be given the ax, the two men hopped a plane for Atlanta and checked into the hotel where the new boss was staying. As Campeau had gone out to a dinner party, they waited nervously in their rooms for his call. By eleven-thirty, having received no word from Campeau, they phoned Zimmerman at home to ask what had become of the urgent meeting to merge Goldsmith's into Rich's. "Where the hell is he?" they said. Zimmerman said he assumed that their meeting with Campeau already had taken place.

"Maybe he forgot," Zimmerman suggested. Campeau admitted as much when Zimmerman finally reached him in his hotel room. "We can discuss Goldsmith's later," Campeau said.

Zimmerman politely reminded Campeau that two top managers had been summoned to Atlanta for what they had been led to believe was an emergency session, and that having come this far they'd appreciate a response from him in person. Campeau agreed, and invited the heads of Goldsmith's up to his suite. Campeau opened his door—he in his undershorts, they in their business suits—and announced: "Goldsmith's will be merged into Rich," and then bid them goodnight.


Cutting the Federated budget by $240 million, a critical element in the company's survival plan, given the high price that Campeau paid for it, proved easier said than done. True, some 3,400 Federated employees, including 207 from Cincinnati and New York merchandising offices, 1200 from Lazarus, 494 from Abraham & Straus, 250 from Rich's, 320 from Burdines, lost their jobs by June. Most of these unfortunates had worked as middle-level managers, supervisors, buyers, and back-office functionaries. The flurry of pink slips added an estimated $98 million to Federated's income, which could be applied to paying off Campeau's debt.

But many of these cuts were short-lived, as the various Federated departments and divisions discovered that they couldn't function without personnel. Of the one hundred or so jobs eliminated from headquarters in Cincinnati by June, at least half were restored six months later. The public relations/public affairs department was a typical example. The staff of fifteen was summarily reduced to two, filing cabinets removed, computers pulled out, phones hauled away on gurneys like bodies from a morgue. The Campeau team had decided that the company's PR functions could be handled by Campeau's New York PR firm, Adams & Reinhart.

Within a month, however, that decision was reversed, and former department head Carol Sanger was rehired as a consultant. By December, the Federated PR department was reestablished with three employees, and new computers and office equipment had to be purchased to replace what had been removed in May. Files, data bases, all had to be re-created from scratch, since everything had been indiscriminately tossed out earlier.

The resurrected Cincinnati PR group had to serve three masters —Campeau Corp., Federated, and Allied. In addition to their other work, they were given a special assignment from the new boss. Campeau wanted a brochure. It was no ordinary brochure that the already overworked Carol Sanger, now vice president for corporate communications was asked by Campeau to produce. It was a leather-bound book with an embossed cover, encased in a stylish brown sheath with gold lettering that read, "Campeau Corporation," and contained more than one hundred pages with full-color photographs of Campeau properties, historical sketches of his newly acquired department stores, and an inspirational introduction that began: "Because we can be no more than what we aspire to be, we will aspire always to be more than the best of what we are."

This little project on the side cost nearly $250,000 to produce— and that after Sanger had cut corners to save $125,000—and the research and editing took 25 percent of the work time of the PR department for a month. Campeau insisted that his brochure be finished immediately, so he'd have it to take along on an upcoming trip to Russia with the Reichmanns, who apparently had published an equally elegant inventory of their real estate investments. The trip to Russia was subsequently canceled.

Similar things happened companywide. Sacked employees straggled back. There was always some fantastic new thing that Campeau wanted done, and his money-is-no-object impulses often clashed with his penny-pinching demands. Meeting with the Blooming-

dale's senior staff at Le Train Bleu restaurant in the New York
flagship store, Campeau called for a $50–60 million cut in Bloom-
ingdale's operating budget, at the same time he announced that he
was going to open two new Bloomingdale's stores—in Palm Beach
and Minneapolis.

Cost-cutting and streamlining also ran up against bureaucratic
resistance in Cincinnati. Burden the CEO and Zimmerman the president had no prior experience in operating an LBO, and no particular motivation to upset the Federated status quo to please Campeau
and his bankers.*

Morosky's reorganization plan was handed over to James Bloise,
a Morosky protégé, who was given an office in New York. Bloise
inherited all of Morosky's charts and notes, such as those about the
nine Federated stores dealing separately with Calvin Klein, and the
different prices and terms they'd worked out to buy jeans from Levi
Strauss.

Although Campeau had succeeded in merging the Allied merchandising office with Federated's merchandising office, eliminating
250 jobs in the process, the reorganization seemed to have had
stalled there. Even the relatively simple task of consolidating the
back offices of Bloomingdale's in New York and Stern's in New
Jersey to save an easy $15 million encountered stiff opposition.
There was always somebody in Cincinnati or in one of the divisions
to object to every move.

Whenever Bloise got Campeau to commit to something, the Federated management refused to go along with it, and Campeau would
end up siding with them. After a while, Campeau stopped talking
to his efficiency expert, and Bloise was reduced to playing with
organization charts for his own amusement.

For eight months, Bloise never heard from Campeau, and then
one night Campeau called him at 11 P.M., wanting to know the
phone number of the main switchboard at Abraham & Straus.

* The "leveraged spinoff" of the Ralphs grocery store chain was a different story.
The management team at Ralphs stood to make millions if their LBO succeeded,
so they were motivated in a way that the Federated executives were not. Also,
Campeau refrained from meddling in Ralphs. These factors, combined with the fact
that the California grocery business had not slumped like the U.S. retail business,
made Ralphs the lone winner in Campeau's debt empire.

Over at First Boston, a doctored version of the cover page of an Ann Taylor catalogue was passed around the office. It showed a woman skipping gingerly along a sidewalk while holding on to a straw hat, under a headline pasted over the original that read: "Look What We've Done Behind Your Back."

This in-house joke referred to the fact that the Allied bondholders had not expected Campeau to loot the Allied assets for the sake of the Federated deal, but he was doing just that. On May 18, he announced that he was selling the Ann Taylor division. This was the first news that Ann Taylor's president, Michelle Fortune, had heard directly from Campeau since the breakfast meeting at the Waldorf.

Campeau had vowed numerous times that he'd never sell Brooks Brothers or Ann Taylor. His sale of Brooks Brothers was unexpected, but acceptable to the bondholders, since he'd gotten such a great price and since the bulk of the proceeds was returned to the company to pay off its bank loan. The sale of Ann Taylor was both unexpected and unacceptable, because this time the proceeds were headed elsewhere. Campeau planned to use the money to pay off a part of one of his equity loans in Federated, the $500 million borrowed from two Canadian banks, the Bank of Montreal (Beemo) and Paribas.

Instead of getting the money for Ann Taylor, Allied bondholders were only going to get Federated stock, purchased from a Campeau holding company. The holding company would get the Ann Taylor money, and use it to repay the aforementioned banks. In effect, Allied would be making a $500 million investment in Federated, in return for the dubious privilege of owning nearly 50 percent of Federated's stock.

Campeau's hurry to find some extraordinary means to settle the Beemo-Paribas loan was understandable. It carried the highest interest rate of any of his loans, it was due to be paid back in a year, and it was one of the few that was secured directly by his Canadian real estate. By selling Ann Taylor to retire it, he was, in effect, transferring risk from himself to Allied.

This maneuver didn't need the approval of Allied's bondholders, since the original junk-bond covenants agreed to by Citicorp and First Boston allowed it.* Campeau did, however, need the approval of Allied's reigning commercial lender, Security Pacific.

Sec Pac, as you may recall, had replaced Citicorp as Allied's lender when Citicorp wouldn't go along with an earlier Campeau machination. Now, in the summer of 1988, the roles were reversed. This time, Sec Pac, still smarting from its treatment in the Federated deal, was in no mood to cooperate with Campeau and refused to grant his request to sell Ann Taylor out of Allied. But Citicorp was willing to let him do it. Approached by Campeau once again to refinance the previous refinancing of Allied, that glutton for lucrative punishment assured Campeau it had no objection to his shedding Ann Taylor to lighten his equity burden.

There seemed to be a correlation between a bank's tolerance for Campeau's improvisations and where it stood in the lineup for future deals. In June, Citicorp once again became the leading lender in Allied, taking out the Sec Pac loan, just as Sec Pac had taken out Citicorp a year earlier. This latest switch of banks brought another shower of fees, as Citicorp extended Campeau another $1 billion plus.

"By this time," a former Citicorp banker says, "the pressures to make money on LBO deals was so intense that Citicorp's top management jumped at the chance to get back in with Campeau, even though at the lower levels we thought it was a terrible decision. One of our auditors, in fact, kept saying he couldn't 'make the numbers work' on the new Allied loan. 'Maybe that's because the numbers don't work,' we suggested."

With an accommodating Citicorp at his side, Campeau was *almost* free to sell Ann Taylor. To assure itself and the bank regulators it was making a prudent decision to reinvolve itself with Allied, Citicorp wanted First Boston to provide a "valuation opinion" that the Federated stock Allied was about to buy at Campeau's behest was worth what Allied was about to pay for it.

First Boston had reservations about writing such an opinion. It was a tricky opinion to write. There were technical problems and

* When the Allied bonds were offered in 1987, there were few restrictive covenants on junk-bond deals in general, and the Allied covenants, such as they were, were viewed by the market as "tough."

political problems, such as First Boston's appearing to be one of the villains in the trashing of Allied for Campeau's benefit. There was the question of whether once again to help Campeau solve a loan problem without his having to sell any of his precious Canadian real estate (a remedy he'd often proposed but hadn't taken). But while the financing group at First Boston argued against providing this opinion, the M&A group and the higher-ups were swayed by the fact that rival firm Bear, Stearns, and also Wasserstein himself had reportedly volunteered to do it.

"Wasserstein was the magic word to the First Boston executives," says an insider. "Once they heard that Wasserstein might do it if they didn't, First Boston's writing the damn opinion was a foregone conclusion." The firm got another $2 million fee.

The famous prices that Campeau extracted from the buyers of the Allied divisions, most recently Lord Rayner, he was no longer able to get in the summer of 1988 or after. Was the serendipity gone? For months, the Ann Taylor sale was delayed because Campeau was insisting on the usual high premium. First Boston tried unsuccessfully to peddle Ann Taylor to Japan. With the stores in limbo and key personnel defecting, it wasn't until February 1989 that Campeau finally sold the company, for only $407 million—$100 million less than he had planned on getting.

Live ones were in shorter supply than they had been when Wall Street's own notions of the worth of things briefly corresponded with Campeau's optimistic valuations. When a management group offered to buy Federated's Gold Circle division for $350 million, a price at the high end of First Boston's range, Campeau turned them down. He told bankers in New York that Gold Circle was worth $500 million. Instead of raising their bid, as at least two buyers had done in Allied, the management group retracted it. Conditions at Gold Circle deteriorated until the division had to be liquidated for its real estate value: $240 million, in October 1988.

Filene's Basement fetched a decent price in July, but only in the sale of MainStreet was First Boston's divestiture team able to double the expected proceeds (from $40 million to $80 million) and this only because their original estimates were too low. In a Federated junk-bond prospectus, Campeau had said he hoped to sell Gold

Circle, MainStreet, and The Children's Place for a combined $727 million. In the end, he got only $562 million.

The news of the Ann Taylor sale, Morosky's departure, and the financial reports of July 1988 that showed Allied's sales volume was down by 2.6 percent and that Allied had posted a $107 million loss for the latest quarter contributed to the growing sense of unease about Campeau and his heavily indebted empire. Campeau himself told his annual meeting in Toronto that this had not been a good six months for retailing, although he didn't dwell for long on this negative. He used the occasion to announce a continuing joint venture with DeBartolo, in which they planned to build five to ten new shopping malls annually in the United States, starting in the near future. In addition, he planned to open sixteen to eighteen new Bloomingdale's stores in the next five years.

But retailing and shopping centers, banks and their covenants, Allied's performance and Federated's budget cuts, were not the only things on Campeau's mind. Since the spring, he had been involved in every detail of his Austrian dream house on the southern shore of Lake Attersee. "Mr. Campeau likes space," reported Andreas Moosgassner, the architect who suffered many headaches, to the *Toronto Globe and Mail*. "But he didn't want to wait years. He wanted to have the house now, right away."

The architects received a continuous stream of early-morning phone calls and late-night faxes in which Campeau introduced his design ideas and suggestions that the architects tried to ignore or tone down. According to the *Globe and Mail* report, he wanted exterior columns, stacked one atop the other, that would have given the Alpine villa a Tower of Pisa look, but without the lean. These columns the architects managed to eliminate, except for the two that flanked the front door.

A Paris interior design firm was retained and later released; the entranceway to the kitchen alone was rebuilt and torn apart five times; the final result, completed in 1990, had two minarets, cathedral windows, seven bathrooms, three guest suites, and a full-sized swimming pool installed on the top floor with a view of the woods and Lake Attersee. The exterior was tinted in the colors of the

Hapsburg family. Austrian president Kurt Waldheim resided on the other side of the lake.

Local businessmen, impressed with the scale of Campeau's villa and with what they'd read of his North American accomplishments, invited him to become the first non-European member of the exclusive International Salzburg Association.

In July, Campeau's public relations agents, who had tried unsuccessfully to get him to stick to prepared statements, were fretting about a forthcoming cover story in *The New York Times Magazine*. Campeau himself was ecstatic about the story; but Davis Weinstock, his communications consultant, was wary. This was a major profile —who knew how it was going to turn out?

Already Weinstock had gone through a lenthy and complex negotiation with *Life* magazine when *Life* wanted to interview Campeau, and the subject had refused to cooperate unless he could be guaranteed the cover. Then when the *Times Magazine* intimated that Campeau *was* cover material, Campeau not only agreed to be interviewed, but devoted some attention to the planning of the photograph. He wanted to appear in the front yard of his Toronto mansion, with the turrets in the background and his wife Ilse and two large dogs at his side. Weinstock advised him to leave out the dogs, which along with Ilse and the mansion made the whole scene look overly Teutonic.

But there on the first Sunday in July 1988 were Campeau, Ilse, and the dogs, posed Teutonically in front of the mansion under the headline: "The Man Who Bought Bloomingdale's." The story itself, written by Phil Patton, was an even-handed account of Campeau's financial triumphs and his rise from the working classes of Sudbury, but on the fourth jump was an eye-opening paragraph: "What not even his own children knew was that Campeau had been maintaining a second family in Montreal."

All across New York, investment bankers and lawyers who'd spent hours, days, weeks with Campeau and lent him billions were racing to their telephones to ask colleagues: "Did you see the *Times?* Did you know that Campeau had two wives?" In Westchester County, the wife of a Prudential executive turned to her husband

and said: "How could you all have lent $11 billion to a bigamist?"
Similar sentiments were expressed in breakfast nooks up and down
Park Avenue.

Campeau was not a bigamist, of course. Still, that it was almost
two years and two deals later before Wall Street discovered his grand
romantic duplicity made his backers wonder: How well did we really
know this man to whom we loaned $11 billion? * Not that romantic
duplicity had anything in particular to do with mergers and acquisitions, and if Wall Street ever applied a moral test to its clients'
private lives, it would have died for lack of assignments long ago.
But Campeau's amorous retrading in the 1960s bore an uncanny
resemblance to his recent negotiating tactics, and, coming as it did
on top of the other ominous news, the revelation in the *Times,* if it
didn't upset the financial markets, upset the weekend of a lot of
financiers.

As further evidence that New York bankers and financial journalists don't pay attention to the Canadian papers, the romance story
had already been broken in the Toronto *Star* on April 7, three
months before the *Times Magazine* article appeared. A courthouse
reporter in Toronto, Elaine Carey, stumbled onto it in the hall of the
courthouse, the scene of ongoing litigation between Campeau and
his children over the stock in their trust funds, a conflict as messy
and as drawn-out as any of his Federated or Allied equity disputes.
During both retail buyouts, Campeau had been involved in this
bitter fight with his family, one that his Wall Street advisers knew
nothing about. Carey's article, "Court Battle Pits Campeau Against
Son" explains the details:

"As retail king Robert Campeau celebrated his latest takeover,
the pain and drama of a multi-million-dollar battle with his alienated
son were revealed yesterday in a Toronto courtroom.

"Campeau, 63, and his eldest son, Jacques, have not spoken for
eight years and, according to documents filed with the Ontario Supreme Court, Campeau has never met his only granddaughter, now
a year old.

"Campeau is trying to stop Jacques from gaining voting control

---

* The Federated board may have known about Campeau's two families, since it
hired a detective agency, Kroll, to do a background check on Campeau during the
later stages of the bidding war, and Kroll has said that it knew about them.

over 1,994,438 shares of Campeau Corp., worth an estimated $50 million. The shares were to revert to Jacques from a family trust when he turned 35 last December.

"Campeau says Jacques is entitled to the shares, but not to voting rights of the stock, which, by an implicit agreement, is to remain part of a unified family voting bloc.

" 'The issue is whether Jacques or his father is entitled to vote those shares,' John Brownlie, lawyer for Campeau, told Ontario Supreme Court Judge J. Elmer Smith yesterday.

" . . . Court documents show a bitterly divided father and son, venting their anger and pain through the legal system. Jacques was one of three children from Campeau's first marriage in Ottawa to Clauda Leroux. They had a daughter Rachelle and adopted two boys.

"Robert Campeau divorced Clauda in 1969 and married his second wife, Ilse, in 1971. They also have three children, the oldest, Robert Jr., was born in 1963.

" 'My father had two children by Ilse before he separated from my mother,' Rachelle Campeau Archambault said in an interview. 'We didn't know about this until the divorce three years later.'

"Jacques, his sister Rachelle, 41, and brother Daniel lived in Ottawa after the divorce. Campeau eventually moved to Toronto with Ilse and their children.

"Jacques worked for his father for eight years, but he left bitterly in 1980, a month after Clauda died after a three-year battle with cancer. Campeau never came to see his ex-wife before her death, Rachelle said.

"In August 1961, Campeau set up a trust fund for his three eldest children, giving each an equal number of shares that would become theirs when they turned 35. . . . After the dispute with his father Jacques went to court in 1983 to try to get the shares right away. The Ontario Supreme Court denied his claim, but said he would have the right to immediate possession when he reached 35. . . .

"Rachelle got her shares with no restrictions six years ago, Jacques' lawyers argue. But Campeau went to court on Jacques' 35th birthday, last Dec. 7, to prohibit him from getting the stock until the court case is settled.

"Campeau also argued the stocks should be held up because

Jacques' estranged wife, Carolyn, and his year-old daughter may have an interest in them." *

There were other complications—a new trust to supersede the old trust; an earlier court battle with another son, Daniel. As these matters were mired in litigation, the Campeau children were unable to cash in on the rise in the value of Campeau Corp. stock, which in 1987 had hit an all-time high of $26 a share.

"It is all very regrettable," Campeau said later, referring to the squabbles over the trust funds.

Campeau was disturbed by the profile in *The New York Times Magazine,* and particularly by the references to his home life, which he felt had nothing to do with the real story, his triumphs on Wall Street. Soon after the article appeared, he summoned Davis Weinstock, his communications consultant, to the mansion in Toronto. Weinstock was installed in the library, surrounded by the leather-bound first editions of Balzac, where for a full day Campeau and Ilse reviewed with him the offensive material, paragraph by paragraph. They seemed, Weinstock recalls, obsessed by it.

First Boston was worrying about the subtle negative effects that Campeau's bad publicity would have on the sale of the Federated junk bonds, the existence of which Campeau had denied back in April. As one unsettling detail after another was coming out, the calendar of junk bond issues was also beginning to get crowded.

Although the calendar didn't seem to pose any big problems through early September, First Boston foresaw a possible backlog after that, creating a buyer's market. In a buyer's market, the institutions that otherwise gobbled up all sorts of junk might become more selective—deciding, say, to bypass Campeau paper in favor of RJR Nabisco paper that was coming to market soon. It didn't help that many of the junk-gobbling institutions already were stuck with Allied junk, the value of which had begun to diminish. Allied bondholders were frustrated by Campeau's stinginess with information (only under prodding from First Boston had Campeau's team both-

* Reprinted with permission from the Toronto *Star* Syndicate.

ered to hold meetings to give progress reports) and infuriated by the trashing of Allied.

With all this in mind, First Boston, sitting uncomfortably on its huge junk-bond bridge loan along with Paine Webber and Dillon, Read, recommended strongly to Jim Roddy that the junk bond prospectuses be filed posthaste.

Roddy had a different agenda. He wanted to prepay a big piece of one of Citicorp's bridge loans by completing the mini-LBO of Ralphs grocery stores, itself requiring $400 million in junk bonds. Campeau could have sold Ralphs for an estimated $1 billion, but instead had opted for First Boston's more creative proposal to "LBO" Ralphs. In this maneuver, Campeau and the current management of the company would buy it with proceeds from bank debt and the sale of junk bonds. Among other advantages, the Ralphs' LBO would defer about $250 million in capital gains taxes that would otherwise have to be paid on a straightforward sale of Ralph's.

(Flashing back to Campeau's shopping-center schemes, Citicorp briefly wondered if Campeau was trying to steal Ralphs out of Federated, but on further investigation of the details, decided he wasn't.)

First Boston implored Roddy to get the bigger Federated junk bond deal done first, before tackling the less-important Ralphs. If Federated sold well, the firm argued, there shouldn't be a problem in financing Ralphs, but selling the Ralphs junk first was the tail wagging the dog. Roddy disagreed. His view was that if First Boston did Federated first, it would get back its huge investment in the Campeau bridge loan and would have no incentive to finish Ralph's quickly. Also, Roddy theorized that doing Ralphs first would remove a major uncertainty in the Federated financing. "I refuse to discuss the overall Federated junk bond deal any further," Roddy told Rothfeld, "until Ralphs is completed, and I'm instructing my people to do the same."

"Here was an example," a First Boston source recalls, "of Campeau's people beginning to think they were the investment bankers who knew how to handle the financing of these deals. In Allied, they listened to us, but in Federated, they began to prefer their own amateur advice to ours."

Under its bridge-loan agreements with Campeau, First Boston had the power to force Campeau to do the Federated junk bonds first, but while some in the firm argued for that course, the directors of M&A overruled them. They were afraid, they said, to annoy Roddy and by extension, Campeau, in case Campeau wanted to do another major takeover deal. Campeau and his advisers, they'd heard, were now talking about acquiring a Texas S&L!

So Ralphs junk and not the Federated junk went first, and the results were abysmal. The junk-bond market "threw up"—as First Bostonians put it—on the Ralphs deal, which then had to be restructured. Having just seen Campeau loot Ann Taylor from Allied, prospective buyers of Ralphs paper demanded tighter covenants that restricted Campeau from taking any assets out of Ralphs.

This restructuring of the Ralphs financing delayed that deal until mid-August, and meanwhile the Federated junk bonds hadn't gotten any closer to the market. It wasn't until late September that First Boston's $1.1 billion Federated offering was officially launched. By then, the Federated junk had to compete with a $60 billion on-slaught of everybody else's junk, including RJR's.

In spite of an elaborate road show, led by Federated CEO John Burden, to tell the Federated story to potential bond buyers in several cities, the Federated junk was shunned by the normal crowd of takers. One of the problems was that the Allied junk was currently trading at eighty-one cents on the original dollar with an interest rate of 15.45 percent, while the interest rate on the Federated junk had been pegged at between 13.25 percent and 14.75 percent.

The bond market didn't understand why First Boston had put a yield on the new Campeau junk that was lower than the prevailing yield on the old Campeau junk. First Boston, of course, couldn't tell the bond buyers that Campeau had demanded this strategy. On the road show, Campeau representatives explained that the Federated junk was protected with stricter covenants. This caused Allied bondholders to wonder why they hadn't been better protected in the first place.

Even after improving the yields by a percentage point or so on October 27, First Boston still couldn't sell the Campeau junk. So the firm pulled the issue from the market. This was an unusual event. A junk deal for Southland Corp. was postponed after the 1987 stock-market crash, but Federated was the first case in recent memory where an issue was so unpopular on its own merit that it had to be pulled.

On November 1, First Boston brought a smaller version of the

Federated offering to market, $750 million worth of junk bonds at drastically altered terms. The interest rates were raised to levels that were higher, even, than the rates on Allied junk—either 16 percent or 17½ percent, depending on which of two types of Federated bonds a buyer chose.

"We were oversubscribed," First Boston's David "Greg" Malcom told *The Wall Street Journal* (November 4, 1988) of the truncated junk-bond sale. "Everybody is very pleased. The company is pleased. It falls into their game plan, and it seems everything is working out."

True, the $750 million issue sold out, but this left a $400 million shortfall in the proceeds that would otherwise have paid back the three investment banks for their Campeau bridge loan. First Boston, Dillon, Read, and Paine Webber were now stuck holding $400 million in Campeau paper themselves, which is not what they'd had in mind when they'd first volunteered the use of their own capital.

Wasserstein's new era of merchant banking, which began with the revolutionary Allied bridge loan that inspired other investment banks to advance their firms' capital to a succession of similar bridge loans, met its Waterloo here. Having left First Boston, Wasserstein himself wasn't suffering any consequences, but his old employers were in the hole for $255 million. And Paine Webber, which only recently had recovered the $6 million that Campeau owed it in a settlement of a legal action, was stuck for another $95 million. Dillon, Read was in for the remaining $50 million.

Campeau's passionate "I won't have junk" remark had turned out to be somewhat prophetic, for unexpected reasons. The junk-bond market had half agreed with him.

Shall we shed a tear for the three investment banks who were personally strung out with their own capital on the latest Campeau bridge? All along, they had assumed they would be rescued by the institutions that regularly invested in junk, yet now it was they who had unwittingly become long-term investors to Campeau. Behind the scenes, First Boston held discussions over how to extricate itself and its two partners from this unexpected fate.

In its negotiations for the Campeau bridge loan back in February, First Boston and the other lenders had agreed that if the loan was not repaid by the maturity date, January 1989, it could under certain circumstances be repackaged as "exchange notes." These exchange notes, similar to junk bonds, could then be sold by the lenders to get their money back. First Boston added a special provision that required Campeau to give up 20 per cent of Federated's stock in the event he couldn't repay the bridge loan by the above date, thus triggering its transformation into exchange notes.

Knowing how anxious Campeau was about equity, the authors of the 20 percent provision figured that it would give Campeau strong incentive to obey the terms and covenants of the bridge loan. The suspicion that he might not was based on general observation and on the fact that Finkelson had joked during one of the meetings: "You can write whatever covenants you want but it doesn't mean I'm going to follow them." First Boston negotiators thought this was a curious bit of comedy coming from an attorney and a director of Campeau Corporation, as Finkelson had become.

At first, Jim Roddy, who had never liked the 20 percent provision regarded it as a sneaky way for First Boston to get hold of Campeau's precious equity. "You could pretend," Roddy speculated, "not to make your best effort to sell the junk bonds just so you could get your hands on some of our Federated stock." After some heated debate, First Boston's Rothfeld was able to convince Roddy that such was not the case, and that First Boston was not in the business of botching a junk-bond sale in order to get its hands on a client's stock. In the end, the 20 percent provision was agreed to by Campeau.

In November, after the junk-bond sale had in fact flopped, First Boston proposed to Roddy that the remainder of the bridge loan ($400 million) be repackaged as exchange notes, along with 7 percent of Federated's stock, prorated to correspond to the amount of the bridge loan still outstanding. But then First Boston agreed *not* to sell the Federated stock along with the exchange notes, because the Campeau people didn't want to lose the stock. First Boston expected to sell these exchange notes (paying 13.75 percent interest) to private parties. In spite of Campeau's recent public relations difficulties, First Boston believed that this investment opportunity would be attractive to somebody—most likely a big insurance company.

Roddy went off to get permission from Campeau's commercial

banking syndicate, which had to agree to the change in the status of this debt from bridge loan to exchange note. Citicorp said it wasn't inclined to help First Boston solve its little $400 million problem, but eventually agreed. Its co-agent in the Federated deal, Sumitomo Bank of Japan, held out for an additional fee.

First Boston, no stranger to demanding fees for everything, was nonetheless furious at Sumitomo for what it regarded as Sumitomo's nasty, self-centered bit of profiteering at First Boston's expense. But Sumitomo insisted on the extra fee, and along with Roddy, First Boston worked out an arrangement by which Campeau would pay it, later to be reimbursed by First Boston, depending on what happened to the sale of the exchange notes to private parties.

Far from the discipline that the leveraged buyout was supposed to bring to Federated and its former sloppy management under Howard Goldfeder, there was sloppiness and intrigue in Cincinnati. Everything seemed to be up for grabs. Campeau was rumored to have promised Marvin Traub's job at Bloomingdale's to Frank Doroff, formerly of Bullock's, unbeknownst to Traub. In Chicago, at the grand opening of a Bloomingdale's there, Campeau had chided Traub to his face: "Marvin, you're a great retailer, but I'm going to teach you how to be more profitable."

Federated was being run half from Cincinnati, where Zimmerman, the president, had transferred; and half from New York, where Burden, the CEO, remained, flying a triangle route from Manhattan to Cincinnati to Sanibel Island, Florida, on one of the four planes in Federated's Air Force.

The success of the LBO had fallen on the shoulders of Federated executives who weren't trained in LBO management, and it wasn't First Boston's job to teach them how to make the numbers come true. Anyway, Burden and his colleagues, impressed at first by Campeau's enthusiasm, had developed a growing antipathy toward the boss. Such incidents as the Rich's-Goldsmith's instant merger and the Traub remark had taken their toll.

Campeau had managed to gain and then keep the respect of Allied's division heads, who favored him over the penny-pinching and indifferent Macioce, but he never really caught on at Federated. At the annual Campeau picnic held in Bermuda in the summer of

1988, the Federated group stood aside and merely tolerated Campeau's joyous sing-alongs and fish-fork waving. They winked knowingly at the news of Campeau's incredible hole-in-one, which helped win him the golf tournament. They appreciated the generous salaries that Campeau was paying far more than they appreciated the paymaster.

In style and temperament, Federated's management resembled the Toronto Establishment that Campeau had tried and failed to impress in the early 1980s. "Federated was just as clubby as Toronto," a Campeau aide says, "and Bob didn't have much luck winning over the Federated people, either. Here he'd taken over two companies in order to get Toronto's respect, and then to run the companies he chose Burden and Zimmerman, who basically thought he was a jerk, especially after the rebate thing. There was a sense of Federated's going through the motions just to placate Bob."

The "rebate thing" was Campeau's latest creative response to the challenge of making Federated more profitable. In a meeting with his managers in Cincinnati, he observed that in the construction business, the major suppliers of building materials were often asked to kick back a percentage of their profits to the developer. Why not, then, make the same demands of the major suppliers of merchandise to Federated and Allied stores?

The Federated hierarchy was nearly unanimous in its opposition to passing the cup. True, the clothing manufacturers on Seventh Avenue were often hit with surcharges and "take backs" from the department stores for merchandise that didn't sell, but that wasn't the same thing as demanding a 5 percent rebate from Dan River, L'Oréal, Fieldcrest Cannon, Revlon, and others for merchandise that did.

Burden in particular was appalled at the rebate idea, but Campeau was flogging it with near-maniacal persistence, and nobody at headquarters could talk him out of it. Hoping that the marketplace would send a message here, Burden and Frank Doroff, who was put in charge of Federated's New York buying office, agreed to make some tentative inquiries with the CEOs of some of Federated's biggest suppliers.

This got nowhere. After several outright rejections, as well as abortive appointments that Campeau either canceled at the last minute or simply forgot, Burden decided he'd had it with the rebates and refused to knock on another door. Campeau's New York advisers thought the best way to handle this crisis was to tell the boss that the rebate problem would be more "effective" if he would ask for the rebates by himself.

Up and down Seventh Avenue at perfume companies, towel companies, and ready-to-wear companies, people were calling each other to ask: "Has Bob Campeau come to see you yet?" The owner of a giant retail conglomerate stopping by personally to solicit discounts was not an everyday occurrence. At J. P. Stevens, Dan River, West Point–Pepperell, and Fieldcrest Cannon, Campeau was met with cordial fascination by executives who were forewarned and had already prepared their responses. Dick Williams of J. P. Stevens reportedly told Campeau: "Bob, you're asking us to give you a rebate if you sell more of our merchandise than we anticipated. If you sell less than we anticipated, then do *we* get a rebate?"

The rebate idea was soon dropped.


While Federated's survival, in this critical phase of the buyout, depended on cutting expenses and maximizing the cash flow, under Burden's lame-duck leadership the division heads had a different mandate—filling the shelves with basic merchandise. Burden was known as a basic-merchandise man, and increasing supply was a key element to his retail strategy. To comply with Burden's wishes, the Campeau divisions in both Allied and Federated spent millions to increase their stocks of towels and sheets, underwear and socks, etc. in what amounted to an all-out millinery buildup.

At the Bon Marché in Seattle the normal annual budget of $25 million to replace basic inventory was doubled to an estimated $50 million a year. At Lazarus in Cincinnati, an unprecedented $100 million was spent; at Jordan Marsh, another $100 million. Campeau's franchises not only were choking on debt, but also on towels, sheets, underwear, and socks.

Federated had a $158 million loss for the nine months that ended in January 1989 on sales that were only marginally higher than sales from a year earlier. At both franchises, the budget-cutting and the "synergies" had not achieved the expected results. "We'd take out $240,000 in one place, and $70,000 of it would be put back in another," complained Roddy.

Campeau had chosen Morosky, the operations man, to rein in the Federated merchants, then dumped him in favor of those same merchants. The disappointing sales and the budgets out of balance had begun to alarm his bankers and to rankle him. Soon, he was casting around for another operations man to rein in the Federated merchants, just as Morosky had planned to do in the first place. The new Morosky was none other than Jim Roddy, whose only previous experience in retailing had been with People's Jewelers in Canada.

In an effort to shake up his retailers, Campeau earlier had asked Roddy to stop in at Federated headquarters on his way to the grand opening of a DeBartolo-owned racetrack in Oklahoma, to bring some discipline to the wayward operations. Then, in November 1988, Campeau began toying with the idea of giving Roddy a formal role as a fiscal and organizational watchdog. In December, he announced the plan publicly, which was the first time Zimmerman and Burden had heard of it. The retailers were taken aback.

On a ski trip with Finkelson, in January 1989, Campeau elaborated on his concept of a Federated ruling triumvirate, with Burden and Zimmerman as the merchants and Roddy as the cost-controller. By late February, he had expanded the committee-of-three into a committee-of-five, including himself and also Ron Tysoe. Burden and Zimmerman both were violently opposed to this managerial pentagon, and Roddy wasn't thrilled with it, either. Sensing that he was likely to become the next Morosky, another casualty of a fickle Campeau commitment, Roddy told Campeau he wasn't interested in the new assignment. Zimmerman reminded Campeau that he'd promised complete freedom to Zimmerman and Burden to run the company as they saw fit. Anything less, they said, and the two of them would quit.

Campeau backed down, as he often did when faced with opposition from his merchant princes. He treated them with much more deference than he treated his moneylenders. The five-man committee to run Federated was finished before it got started.

The first-quarter Campeau Corporation report for 1989 was released in a four-color pamphlet that featured a snazzy couple holding a shopping bag, flying through a firmament of shoes, earrings, and Campeau real estate on what appeared to be a linoleum magic carpet. "Dear Shareholder," the text said: "During the first quarter of 1989, our retail operations . . . generated solid increases in net sales and operating cash flow. These results are the strongest indications yet that our total retail strategy is working and working well."

First Boston's attempt to sell its $400 million hung bridge to private parties was getting nowhere. Campeau already had alienated the big insurance companies that First Boston identified as possible investors. The Prudential, his mortgage holder in Allied, was mad at him for the Ann Taylor sale, among other things. The Equitable was suing Campeau over an alleged breach of its contract with Allied to remodel a shopping center in Massachusetts, the terms of which Campeau allegedly had attempted to revise *ex post facto*. This litigation did nothing to endear The Equitable to a private-placement investment in Federated. One of its executives, Ben Holloway, would later refer to Campeau as "a man who in my experience didn't always tell the truth." The Travelers was an unlikely candidate as well, since it owned Dillon, Read, one of the investment banks that was stuck with part of the junk-bond bridge.

First Boston internally debated what to do next. One idea, promoted by the junk-bond experts, was that the Federated equity that Campeau was obligated to turn over to his lenders could, in combination with the exchange notes, be sold at a discount to bottom fishers. In the worst case that the finance people could imagine, First Boston might lose $15–20 million, a pittance as compared to the $250 million in fees and other income the firm already had made from Campeau's deals. And First Boston; Dillon, Read; and Paine Webber would have most of their money back.

The M&A group argued against the plan on the grounds that Campeau wouldn't like it. Campeau, they'd heard, didn't want to part with his 7 percent equity in Federated, even though he was legally required to do so, and the M&A group was reluctant to force an issue that might disturb a "valued client of the firm," which is what the new First Boston CEO, Bill Mayer, had taken to calling Campeau.

At least one First Bostonian who'd had regular contact with Campeau since Allied, Mike Rothfeld, had for months been reminding the M&A group and Bill Mayer of Campeau's reneging on agreements, and other bothersome behavior, such as having amnesia for agreements, but his superiors had just as regularly reminded him: "He's a valued client of the firm, Mike."

The "valued client of the firm" clause, a relic of the bygone era when investment banking houses lived by the gentleman's code and all their clients were large and conservative corporations with whom they had a long-standing and gentlemanly relationship, was now anachronistically applied to Campeau. Behind it was the implicit understanding that a client of the firm would continue to do business with the firm and generate more big fees for the M&A department and therefore deserved to be treated with a perpetual and cordial benefit of the doubt.

"How can you call him a client," Rothfeld told his more tolerant partners after it became clear that First Boston had decided not to displease Campeau by selling the exchange notes with his precious equity out from under him, "and want to do another deal with this man after everything he's done to us? Even if you did want to do a deal with him, he can't do another deal. He's already tapped out."

The debt overhang from the two acquisitions was beginning to un-settle even the secured creditors in Campeau's commercial bank syndicate. The commercial bankers expected Campeau to reduce some of his high-interest short-term Federated takeover loans by replacing them with a conventional long-term mortgage loan, as he'd done already in Allied.

In its usual cooperative spirit, Citicorp offered Campeau such a mortgage for Federated, for $1.1 billion, which would have relieved some of the debt pressure as well as his bankers' anxiety.

Campeau's trio of advisers, Roddy, Tysoe, and Buck Luce, agreed that taking the $1.1 billion from Citicorp was the reasonable course of action. But Campeau didn't want a conventional mortgage. He envisioned a more spectacular solution, a giant super mortgage for $4 billion, which would give him enough money to repay the Citicorp mortgage bridge, as well as First Boston's $400 million junk-bond bridge. That way, he wouldn't lose the 7 percent in Federated equity that First Boston was entitled to sell out from under him.

The super mortgage Campeau had in mind would revolutionize

real estate lending in the United States. He got this inspiration from the Reichmanns, who apparently had participated in a creative financing of some Rockefeller Center property. In return for a lower interest rate, the lenders were given an equity stake, or "piece of the action" in the buildings. Applying this concept to Federated, Campeau expected to wangle favorable terms by offering his lenders a chance to benefit from Federated's "upside."

Once more, Campeau had drifted out to the frontiers of wishful thinking. Not only was the concept unconventional, but $4 billion was more than double the appraised value of the Federated properties. Once more, his staff could only hope that the marketplace would send Campeau the proper message. With the budget problems in Cincinnati, the shortfall in the asset sales, the shortfall in the junk-bond sale, this hardly seemed the time to propose a great experiment. How the staff yearned for a simple, boring mortgage to refinance at least some of the costly short-term acquisition debt, for which Campeau was paying as much as 17 percent interest.

But Campeau hadn't gotten this far on the simple, boring path. He headed for Prudential, the same Prudential that had declined to participate in First Boston's private placement of the junk-bond debt, to pitch the super mortgage.

"Bob," a Prudential spokesman advised, "you have to realize it's not going to work. Our appraisals indicate that Federated couldn't possibly support a $4 billion mortgage loan."

"That's not true," Campeau retorted. "You are being too conservative."

Unfazed by this rejection—as if he hadn't even heard it, really—Campeau sent Tysoe over to Prudential, where he got the same message. After that, Campeau turned to The Equitable, where there was also nothing doing, not surprisingly, considering that The Equitable was involved in the lawsuit against Campeau mentioned earlier. Campeau was oblivious, according to his advisers, to the idea that his own behavior could come back to haunt him.

During late 1988, Campeau had flown off to Japan to try out the fantasy mortgage concept there. Nobody on his own staff wanted to accompany him, but Joe Perella, Wasserstein's sidekick, agreed to come along as a personal favor and also because Perella liked to go shopping in Japan. Campeau also brought along his son Bobby Junior. His staff had advised him that in Japan a close-knit family makes a favorable impression. Bobby Junior read wrestling magazines and practiced his electric guitar on the long flight to Tokyo.

In the offices of Nomura securities (which had invested several hundred million dollars in Wasserstein, Perella), Campeau startled a group of Japanese bankers by blurting out: "You ought to be grateful to America. It's rare that a conqueror treats a conquered country as well as you have been treated." Jaws dropped, and after Campeau left, Perella lingered to apologize for Campeau's impolite remark to the largest investors in his firm.

After his trip to Japan, Campeau called on Kevin Haggarty at Cushman & Wakefield, the largest real estate brokerage house in America, but not to pitch a super mortgage—he told Haggarty he already had one. A Japanese group, Campeau said, had approached him about doing a $4 billion deal at 6 percent interest. He wanted to hire Cushman & Wakefield to do the property appraisals.

Haggarty was a sociable Irishman who tended to be optimistic when it came to real estate, and he'd seen the Japanese pay amazing prices for buildings in New York. But he couldn't conceive of even the Japanese offering Campeau a mortgage at 6 percent interest when the prevailing rate at the time was 11 percent.

"Either you aren't hearing correctly what they are saying," Haggarty told Campeau, "or else somebody is just making promises in order to get you into their office. In either case, what you describe is impossible."

Campeau insisted that what he described not only was possible, but that a formal agreement with the Japanese group was imminent, and he was flying to Cincinnati for discussions between him, the Japanese group, and his Federated staff. "Meet me at the airport," he said. "I'm hiring you as an adviser." Haggarty went along.

At Federated headquarters, Haggarty discovered that the group to which Campeau was referring was Eastdil/Nomura, partly owned by the Japanese. Other real estate firms were also in the audience, as Campeau's retailers were brought out to give a hastily prepared dog and pony show, emphasizing Federated's exciting potential, how overhead was being reduced, how sales were on the rise, and so on. A slide presentation by CEO Burden was followed by Campeau's animated description of the "participating mortgage concept," as he had named it, a wonderful opportunity for a smart lender to "unlock a higher percentage of market value" by sharing in Federated's future profits.

As far as Haggarty could tell, Eastdil/Nomura showed no sign of having already agreed to lend Campeau the $4 billion at 6 percent interest, as he had intimated in New York. (Campeau expressed his disappointment about this later, by hanging up on Eastdil's Steve Karp.) Another large firm, JMB Realty, was similarly unenthusiastic.

"Before you leave," Campeau told Haggarty after the meeting had broken up with no apparent takers for the participating-mortgage concept, "I want to hire you as an ongoing consultant."

Haggarty, who still wasn't sure why he'd been invited to Cincinnati in the first place, was reluctant. "Look," he said, "I wouldn't mind being your consultant, but you already have First Boston. Don't you already have a contract with them to do financings and acquisitions? What do you need another consultant for?"

"I want somebody on my side of the table," Campeau explained.


Prudential said no to the super mortgage, JMB turned it down, The Equitable had no interest, and both Citicorp and Eastdil had volunteered to do a conventional deal instead. The realities of the marketplace were sending a strong and clear signal for once, but not strong enough. To the dismay of his advisers, Campeau had gotten a couple of maybes to keep him interested in the latest farfetched scheme. One was from Haggarty. The other, oddly enough, was from First Boston.

Hired at a hefty fee to be Campeau's private mortgage consultant, and challenged to "think creatively," Haggarty was trying to give Campeau his money's worth. In fact, he came up with a financial concoction of which Campeau himself would have been proud: a three-tiered super mortgage with three different levels of risk and reward, conventional at the bottom, unconventional at the top, and half-and-half in the middle, a sort of wedding cake of interest rates.

Although not entirely convinced that this wedding-cake super mortgage would appeal to lenders, Haggarty felt it had a better chance than Campeau's original concept, which was one-dimensional. "Whatever you do, you've got to do something to get away from your short-term loans at 16 percent-plus," Haggarty advised. "Even if you could get a blended 13 percent interest rate with the three-tiered mortgage it would be an improvement on what you've got."

Expecting that the Germans might be interested in the three-tiered mortgage, Campeau flew to Frankfurt, where he met with Deutschebank, but nothing resulted. Haggarty pursued some off-shore banks, but nothing there either. From Haggarty's point of view, these visits to banks were somewhat futile to begin with, since he assumed that First Boston had the exclusive right to handle Campeau's real estate deals. "Look, Bob," he asked one day, "what are we going to do? First Boston is supposed to be involved here. I can't be out marketing this."

"Get together with First Boston and work it out," Campeau said.*

Finally, in February 1989, Haggarty met with First Boston's chief real estate man, William Dickey. They had dinner together and continued their discussion of Campeau mortgages on a street corner outside the restaurant.

"I don't think it will work," Dickey was reported to have said, referring to the super mortgage. "It's crazy. There are problems you don't know about: title for the properties, financing restrictions, existing mortgages, tax problems. Campeau would get killed with the taxes. I think it's nuts."

"OK," said Haggarty. "I don't have the background information yet. I am just trying to suggest, 'Here's a concept. We should refine it together.' "

"We'll bounce it around in the office and I'll get back to you," Dickey said. But Dickey never did get back to Haggarty, and soon after their meeting, Haggarty stopped hearing from Campeau, who prior to this had been ringing him up at all hours. Months later, Campeau's secretary phoned Haggarty to say that Campeau was sorry he hadn't been in touch and would be calling in a few days, but he never did.

---

* Contrary to Haggarty's belief, First Boston and Campeau had never signed an engagement letter authorizing First Boston to do a mortgage financing for Federated.

With Haggarty out of the picture, the First Boston real estate group had Campeau to themselves. In spite of whatever Dickey had told Haggarty about the idea being nuts, First Boston itself was lobbying to do a scaled-down version of the super-mortgage deal.

An internal First Boston memorandum dated January 10, 1989, suggests that Dickey's real estate group really didn't believe that Campeau's $4 billion concept had a gnat's chance of attracting takers. It outlined broad areas, in fact, in which Campeau's expectations differed wildly from the realities of the marketplace, as follows:

1. Campeau thought that Federated real estate was worth $120–140 per square foot; while First Boston's real estate group thought it was worth $75 per square foot maximum. "Campeau may be correct, but the market will take time to recognize it," is the delicate way that Dickey, the author of the memo, described this schism. The memo was being sent to Campeau's staff.
2. Campeau claimed that every square foot of Federated property could be mortgaged; First Boston estimated that only 60 percent was "currently mortgageable."
3. Campeau expected to pay 7 percent interest on the mortgage loans, with a 10 percent "yield to maturity" that included a share in Federated's profits; First Boston said he would have to pay at least 8 percent interest, with a 13–14 percent "yield to maturity."

In conclusion, First Boston's real estate group was giving only one-in-ten odds that Campeau could find a lender for the $4 billion super mortgage that had become his great passion. This did not stop Bill Dickey, in February 1989 from telling Bill Mayer, the newly appointed president of First Boston, that there was a high probability that Campeau's unusual mortgage would work, if not for $4 billion, then for something less.

Getting into the Campeau spirit itself, the Dickey group had concocted its own version of the super mortgage, in which all of Federated and Allied properties would be rolled up into a single realty company that would lease the real estate from the operating companies. This mortgage package even outdid Haggerty's for its complex bafflement: there were at least five tiers here, including senior zero-coupon bonds, subordinated zero-coupon bonds, a conventional mortgage loan, a participating mortgage loan, and equity. "Formula and priorities of sharing cash flow are not clear," Dickey wrote, in trying to explain how all this would work.

Roddy and Buck Luce, who desperately wanted Campeau to drop the fantasy mortgage and get a more realistic grip on his problems, stood by and watched with weary fascination as First Boston, which by now had ample reason to sever its ties to Campeau altogether, instead played along with him on this most farfetched of all proposals. A firm "no" from First Boston, Buck Luce thought, and Campeau might give up this silly idea and take the conventional mortgage to reduce his huge debt.

It was in the best interest of First Boston—stuck with the $400 million bridge—to urge Campeau to be more realistic and reduce his huge debt. But this self-interest was competing against the real estate group's desire to serve as Campeau's mortgage agent, for which First Boston would be paid another big fee. The most profitable course, the higher-ups decided, was not to alienate a valued client of the firm by disagreeing with him, and possibly lose that fee as a result.

Throughout the winter and into the spring of 1989, First Boston tried to coax the valued client into signing an engagement letter giving it the exclusive right to handle the Federated mortgage deal. But Campeau kept changing the terms. Several drafts of a proposed agreement had to be revised, and the delays kept everyone in suspense.

At the same time that First Boston was stymied on this future bit of business, it struggled with the problem of what to do with the $400 million bridge loan still left hanging. The firm had yet to take action on selling its exchange notes with the Federated equity to the bottom fishers, because this, too, would have alienated Campeau.

First Boston's two partners in the bridge loan, Dillon, Read and Paine Webber, were beginning to worry about not getting their money back. A First Boston insider recalls that the meetings were not pleasant. "Dennis Friedman of Paine Webber was ripshit, really pissed off, that First Boston was diddling around on this issue. Steven Fenster of Dillon, Read wasn't too happy, either."

From mid-February into April, a series of meetings were held in

Bill Mayer's office on the forty-third floor of First Boston, beyond the models of clipper ships in glass cases, where the financing group argued, "Sell the exchange notes with the equity and let's be done with Campeau," while Bill Dickey of the real estate group along with the M&A group led by Jim Maher protested, in effect, "No, not that. We would upset a valued client of the firm." Mayer, the CEO, sided with Dickey and Maher on this point.

Even into April, First Boston sat on the exchange notes instead of selling them to pay itself back the $400 million from the hung bridge loan. And Campeau still hadn't signed a real estate engagement letter.

# Fourteen

•

A casual investor in Allied or Federated bonds who read the quarterly reports would have been lulled into a sweet and sound sleep by the procession of cheery statements coming out of Toronto and Cincinnati. Here is a sample of this reassuring litany.

1. From the 1988 report to Federated bondholders, published in December:

    While sales for the comparable divisions were essentially flat for the quarter as anticipated during this transitional phase, the company's earnings before interest and taxes were up about 6 percent from last year . . .
    The principal reason for this improved performance was the company's cost reduction and streamlining programs . . . The company's liquidity continued strong throughout the quarter. . . .
    Let us emphasize that streamlining is over and morale is back on track. We believe the entrepreneurial spirit and corporate resolve will make us winners.

2. From the April 28, 1989, quarterly reports, in which the company noted that net sales for the preceding nine months were unchanged, or "flat," relative to net sales from a year earlier:

We are pleased to report that in this transition period, a period during which flat sales were anticipated, the retained divisions of Federated produced stronger than expected fourth quarter sales. . . .

We also are pleased with the level of operating cash flow, which reflects the considerable progress of restructuring the company and increasing operational efficiencies.

3. From the June 13, 1989, quarterly reports, when Federated announced strong increases in net sales and operating cash flow:

We are pleased with our progress in the first quarter. . . . The substantial increase in our operating cash flow reflects solid sales growth in our retained divisions.

In every report, there seemed to be a great deal to be happy about—good cash flow, successful streamlining, funds more than adequate to cover working capital needs, etc.—while potentially disquieting factors such as flat sales were always "anticipated," bad news of any kind was always appended to a reminder that "more than half of the annual retail profits traditionally are produced in the fourth quarter," and increases in administrative expenses were always described as "enhanced selling services."

A fog of accountancy fell over the balance sheets of leveraged buyouts, especially in cases such as this one, where so many divisions had been sold off that the performance of the new, efficient Campeau Federated and the sloppy, old, mismanaged Federated could not easily be compared. In the spring of 1989, with hardly a year of continuous operation of the new Federated, it wasn't clear even to professional analysts how well the successor company was doing relative to the old.

In the various quarterly reports filed with the SEC, we find a frequent use of the phrase "much of the data is not comparable to last year due to the changes related to the company's restructuring." The accounting rules for corporate reporting made it difficult for even the most earnest readers to discern the true picture.

"Unfortunately, on-going results are hard to see," a report on Allied and Federated bonds from First Boston's high-yield research department noted in May. Holders of such bonds, however, would be more reassured than alarmed by the generally positive tone of the review.

In March 1989, believing that all was well in Cincinnati, Buck Luce took $125 million out of the working-capital fund (money used to pay for merchandise) in order to prepay part of an asset sale bridge loan from Citicorp, and save on the interest. But in April, just after the latest cheery corporate reports had been released, Campeau visited Paul Reichmann at Reichmann's office in Toronto with a desperate request for cash.

"If I don't get it, I don't know what I'm going to do," Campeau reportedly told Reichmann in seeking a $150 million infusion. Reichmann was taken aback by this sudden and urgent request after all the good news that he and everybody else had been hearing and reading about the new and restructured Campeau retailing empire. If things were going as well as reported, why the need for an emergency loan?

In any event, Reichmann wasn't interested in investing directly into Federated, which is what Campeau proposed. As an alternative, he proposed to make a $75 million loan to Campeau, if Campeau would put up his remaining half interest in the Scotia Plaza building in Toronto as collateral. The other half of Scotia Plaza Campeau already had sold to the Reichmanns during the Allied takeover.

By now, the Reichmanns had sunk a total of $335 million into Campeau deals, all of it secured by real estate and the assets of Campeau's Canadian corporation, and insulated from the retail ventures that the Reichmanns had said all along they didn't understand. Real estate they understood. Still, Paul Reichmann was mystified enough by Campeau's plea that he hired a financial investigator to figure out what was really going on in Cincinnati.

The bond market must also have smelled trouble in spite of the recent financial reports because by the end of April, the Allied 11½s of 1997 were selling for sixty-one cents to yield more than 22 percent, and the Federated 16s of 2000 had dropped to eighty-seven cents, yielding 19 percent. The marketplace was rapidly losing confidence in Campeau.

Campeau had made no progress at getting a mortgage, fantasy or otherwise. Having lost some patience in March, First Boston was pressuring Campeau to do a mortgage deal with its real estate group by threatening to sell the exchange notes with the precious Federated equity if Campeau continued to hold out for impossible terms. "There's always the schmuck factor," Bill Dickey had conceded to colleagues about the difficulties of working with Bob, yet Dickey and his superiors seemed unable to stop dickering with him.

Once again, what might have been a simple ultimatum was convoluted by Campeau's exotic wangling on the one hand, and First Boston's insatiable appetite for fees on the other. The result was that First Boston agreed not to sell the exchange notes before September 1989 if Campeau paid the firm $10 million and got a definite mortgage commitment by July 1, with a closing no later than September 1. (The mortgage money would enable Campeau to repay the First Boston bridge loan, among other things). If Campeau failed to close on time, then he would have to pay First Boston yet another $10 million fee, and First Boston would be free to sell the exchange notes on the open market. This basic plan was tentatively agreed to by both parties on April 19.

On April 20, Campeau was busily redefining these terms. Browbeaten into submission as usual, First Boston agreed to change the July 1 deadline date to August 1, and the September 1 deadline date to November. Campeau demanded more changes after that, and the retrading continued until April 24, when First Boston couldn't stand it anymore and sent Campeau a notice indicating it was exercising its rights to call in the equity reserve with the intent of selling the exchange notes on the open market.

On April 27, Bill Mayer, the most vocal proponent of the "valued client of the firm" philosophy, had a meeting with Campeau and his entourage at Campeau's suite at the Waldorf Towers. Buck Luce and Roddy were there; Buck Luce, normally radiant, looked haggard and tense after a recent series of banking problems and a run-in with Campeau in Florida. She'd heard that Campeau had been bad-mouthing her to Citicorp and to First Boston, and she'd flown to Florida to confront him with the allegation, which Campeau had denied.

Campeau was telling Bill Mayer he wanted to change a few more terms in the agreement about the mortgages. Mayer finally lost his patience. "Bob," he said, "my mother taught me to count to ten whenever I get angry, and I just have." With that, Mayer got up and walked out. Calling out, "No, Bill, no, don't do that," Campeau followed him through the door.

If this were a novel, Mayer's blowup would have led First Boston to sell the exchange notes and get its money back and be done with its noisome client forever. But in real life, the brouhaha resolved nothing. A further series of negotiations with Campeau about the mortgage agreement and more First Boston debates about whether or not to sell the exchange notes followed. An agreement was finally signed on May 10.

In the interim, Campeau had sent Roddy to meet with First Boston and further argue his case. Roddy was ushered into the office of George Weiksner, managing director who had taken over as Campeau's "relationship manager" from Ken Colburn, who, with considerable relief, was being transferred to the Boston office. Roddy told Weiksner and Mike Rothfeld that the threat to sell the exchange notes was all a bluff, since "if you guys at First Boston really had wanted to sell them, you would have done it already." Assured that it wasn't, Roddy got up, looked Rothfeld and Weiksner in the eye, shook their hands, said "God bless," and left the room. From First Boston, Roddy headed straight for Campeau's suite, to deliver the resignation speech he'd already prepared.


Exit Jim Roddy and Buck Luce, along with Tysoe Campeau's closest advisers and financial jugglers, who for two years had maintained corporate relations with dozens of banks, sometimes shielding the bankers from Bob, sometimes vice versa. Both had expected the Campeau acquisitions would make them multimillionaires. Both had pleaded with Campeau to take out a conventional mortgage for Federated and reduce the debt, but he'd carried on with the fantasy mortgage and to date had showed no sign of giving it up.

Buck Luce blamed her recent miscarriage on the pressures of trying to mediate between her difficult boss and the lenders, of holding the bank agreements together when every point was stretched to the limits of the lenders' patience, and of tempering Campeau's rages. Roddy was astute enough to recognize a sinking ship. By the first week in May, after a final try at convincing Campeau to get a regular mortgage, both had resigned.

A press release from Campeau Corporation announced these startling changes as a "corporate restructuring that culminates a 12-month process of operational reorganization." Ron Tysoe was named president of Campeau Corporation, to take over where Jim Roddy had abruptly left off.

At the July 20, 1989, annual meeting of Campeau Corp., Campeau, his glasses bobbing off his paisley tie, strode to the podium with a copy of *The Wall Street Journal* clutched in his hand. A standing-room-only crowd of reporters, analysts, and shareholders had assembled in the large room at the Royal York Hotel in Toronto to hear the latest update.

The *Journal* once again had published an irritating article on the day of Campeau's scheduled public appearance, this time suggesting that his retail acquisitions were in trouble and questioning whether his companies could continue to service the debt. "We've been tried, we've been hung and given reprieves so many times from all the newspapers and analysts in this country that it's just amazing we're still around," Campeau snorted, while flapping the *Journal* in the air.

He went on to lambaste the critics for getting their numbers wrong, and for focusing on immediate results. "A quick glance at the bottom line of the balance sheet will not give you a complete picture," he said. "It is more important by far that we seek to produce performance—that we refuse to succumb to the Wall Street–Bay Street approach that sacrifices long-term results for short-term profits." Campeau called his retail holdings "second to none in North America." "Now," he said, "no one can stop us but ourselves."

Burden and Zimmerman followed Campeau with upbeat forecasts to support his claim that revenues would reach $12.5 billion in 1989, more than enough to enable the company to survive the decline in retail sales that Wall Street analysts were expecting. Burden emphasized that only the most conservative forecasts of consumer retail spending were used as the basis for the company's plans.

Then Brian Allumbaugh, the chairman of Ralphs grocery stores, gave a heartening report on the activities of that successful mini-LBO, illustrated with slides of luscious California fruits and vegetables.

"Can we expect to see a Bloomingdale's in Toronto?" someone asked Campeau from the audience. "Will you sell Bloomingdale's?" someone else wanted to know. "Why would I sell the most wonderful retailing chain in the world?" Campeau replied.

At a press conference after the meeting, Campeau lectured the assembled reporters on the differences between Canadian and U.S. societies and the advantages of U.S. free enterprise. He offered the Canadian government unsolicited advice on how to cut its deficit, and warned that Canadian workers would need to improve their productivity to compete with the United States and the Japanese.

The April 1989 quarterly report for Federated, had stated that "funds from operations will be adequate to cover the working capital needs." In early July, First Boston was still sending out favorable research reports on Allied and Federated bonds. But in the report filed in September for the second quarter, which ended July 29, Federated suddenly told a different story: ". . . Cash needs during the third and fourth quarters will be significantly in excess of amounts expected to be available (from) working capital and funds from operations. . . ." In other words there was a serious cash shortage at the company.

The Allied quarterly report was more straightforward: "Campeau Corp. has agreed to provide Allied with a $100 million credit line for seasonal working capital needs . . . however, Campeau has advised Allied that it is currently unable to provide funds pursuant to such a credit line. . . ."

"Never in my experience had a company presented itself as looking so good and then turned out to look so bad in so short a time," said a Toronto analyst who had recommended Campeau Corp. stock —and therefore prefers to remain anonymous.

Why were even the company's own executives taken by surprise? Not because of a slowdown in sales certainly; Federated sales were up 5 percent in the July quarter over the previous year; Allied's were running ahead as well. Getting people to buy things in Campeau's stores was not at this stage a problem.

No, it was the business outside the stores, the business of the LBO itself that had left no margin for error, and yet a year after the latest acquisition had created several errors that were beginning to compound.

The first was Campeau's initial overpayment for Federated, which he himself had estimated at $500 million and might even have been more, depending on the degree to which he was bidding against himself in the latter stages of the auction against Macy's.

This overpayment had whittled the margin for error down to a sliver, on which the entire enterprise was precariously balanced.

The second was the inability of the Federated overseers to cut costs, reduce expenses, and sacrifice personnel in drastic enough fashion to satisfy the debt god, which loomed over their operations. In spite of the much-ballyhooed streamlining as described in the quarterly reports, the management expenses in the new, efficient Federated were actually higher, as a percentage of total sales, than they had been in the fat, sloppy, old Federated.

Third was the inventory buildup, which resulted from Burden's mandate to fill the shelves with towels and socks. It had gotten to the point that the new Federated, with only 43 percent of the sales of the old, much larger Federated, was stocking 65 percent of the merchandise. In the July quarter, mentioned above, while sales at Federated were up 5 percent, inventories were up 26 percent, as the spending spree had continued unabated through the spring and into the summer of 1989. The Lazarus store around the corner from Federated headquarters in Cincinnati was clogged with basic goods —even under the noses of corporate management, things seemed to be out of control.

The fourth was the misguided decision in March to borrow $125 million from the working-capital line to pay off part of a bank loan that wasn't even due at the time. Hard cash, a commodity that was showered in abundance on the stockholders and the dealmakers who got their remarkable fees, was now, a year later, in short supply, forcing Campeau to search for quick infusions from the Reichmanns.

The fifth was Campeau's continual foot-dragging on getting a conventional mortgage to bring down his debt, with a big Citicorp bridge loan coming due in January.

Thus, the synergy between the LBO and retailing had become far more consequential to the future of Campeau's enterprises than the synergy between real estate and retailing to which he had initially alluded.

In spite of their antipathy to the boss, the top executives in Cincinnati continued to "want to believe"—in the words of one of them—in the Campeau magic. Apparently, they were focused on the small picture to the exclusion of the bigger one, with Campeau promising to take care of the finances if they took care of the retailing, which is why as late as May, the chief financial officer, Russ

Davis, told the newspapers that "we're on solid financial footing now," and Burden and Zimmerman made rosy pronouncements in July.

Like old-fashioned housewives kept in the dark about the family budget until the day that creditors arrive to repossess the furniture, Burden and Zimmerman professed to be shocked. They were merchants, not accountants, who had, they said, relied on Campeau and his financial people for information about the big picture. "You take care of the business, I'll take care of the rest," they said that Campeau had often told them, and infected by his enthusiasm, they went along.

Federated did, however, have a well-staffed treasury department and a sophisticated corporate accounting system that kept track of such things as inventories, accounts receivable, and cash flow. Whether the controllers were ignoring the numbers, or were not sending them along to Burden and Zimmerman, or Burden and Zimmerman were too busy to read the internal reports is a matter of some speculation. In any event, the top managers at Federated did not suspect that in July the words "bankruptcy" and "Chapter 11" would soon be part of their daily vocabulary.

The Reichmanns suspected it. Their behind-the-scenes investigation, commissioned in April, led them to the sad conclusion that Campeau's retail divisions, as presently organized, could not generate enough cash to pay both the regular bills and the interest on the debt. Debt was eating up $1 of every $11 spent in an Allied or a Federated store. Bankruptcy seemed almost a foregone conclusion to the Reichmanns by midsummer.

On September 14, in public filings with the SEC, Campeau disclosed a more serious cash shortage than had been anticipated in late July. The company hinted that the Allied units might miss a payment on their junk bonds. On this news, the price of the bonds dropped $10 overnight, raising the yield to 32 percent. Macy's bonds fell in sympathy, as did the junk market in general.

Campeau's shocking announcement was the latest in what had become the unpleasant junk-bond surprise of the month: Integrated Resources ran out of borrowed money in June; Southmark filed for bankruptcy in July; Resorts International suspended interest payments in August; and Lomas Financial defaulted on notes in September.

Campeau was having a noticeable impact on the American economy, but not the kind that he had hoped for. Investors in junk were having trouble finding buyers. The market was so discredited that those who did sell were taking refuge in Treasury bills, finding relative solace in the U.S. government's balance sheet.

Rumors circulated on Wall Street that junk-bond trading desks had suffered big losses, that First Boston had stopped bidding altogether, and that Merrill Lynch had pulled out of the market. Merrill Lynch issued a "we have no junk-bond losses" denial.

Meanwhile, First Boston, which during the recent Campeau M&A follies had taken the opportunity to merge itself with its European Crédit Suisse affiliate and had attracted new investors in Japan, was trying to explain to these new Japanese investors why it was a holding a huge bridge loan in a Campeau enterprise. Jack Hennessey, the CEO of the First Boston parent company, was traveling around Tokyo, answering questions about Campeau's latest problems. "Capitalism is messy," Hennessey informed the Japanese bankers.

It was now the Reichmanns' turn to be surprised, but not about the cash crunch. They had discovered an interesting fact about Campeau's guarantee on the equity loan from DeBartolo—the DeBartolo guarantee also involved Canadian assets. If Campeau's U.S. companies failed, it was possible that DeBartolo would have a superior claim on these assets, which would wipe out the value of the shares and debentures in Campeau Corp. in which the Reichmanns held at least a $260 million stake.

The Reichmanns were wondering what to do about this disturbing little revelation about the DeBartolo guarantee, which changed the pecking order and made their investment in Campeau Corp. more risky than they had assumed, when Campeau again asked for more money. In August, he flew to Switzerland to plead in person with Paul Reichmann, who was on vacation and preferred not to be disturbed. Reichmann agreed to meet him in the chalet where he was staying.

There, Campeau told Reichmann that his retail units needed

another $250 million in working capital to survive the fall season and to pay for Christmas merchandise. Coolly but firmly, Reichmann told Campeau he had concluded that Campeau was fighting a lost cause, and would be better off filing for Chapter 11. That way, Reichmann reportedly advised, at least Campeau would get out with some of his Canadian assets. If Reichmann put in more money, as Campeau was requesting, all of Campeau's remaining real estate, including shopping centers, office towers, and business parks, would have to be offered up as collateral. Did Campeau want to risk everything? Perhaps it would be better if he thought it over first.

Campeau went away to think it over, but not for long. He told Reichmann that Chapter 11 was a death sentence for retailers—that no major retail chain had ever made it out. The two met again in London, where Reichmann was working on his huge Canary Wharf project which, if completed as planned, would relocate the entire downtown farther up the Thames River. An elaborate new bargain was struck—Reichmann would guarantee a $250 million line of credit so that Allied and Federated could buy their Christmas merchandise. In return, Reichmann would get another $250 million worth of Campeau Corp. debentures, backed by all the company's remaining assets. If and when the Reichmanns converted their debentures to common stock, they would have a 38.6 percent ownership in Campeau's company. Campeau, at that point, would have only 38.8 percent himself.

In addition, Campeau agreed to give up three seats on his company's governing board to new directors appointed by the Reichmanns. Also, a restructuring committee would be formed to deal with Campeau's U.S. problems. The chairman would be Lionel Dodd, the manager of the Reichmanns' investment portfolio. Campeau would be excluded from membership.

These moves were calculated to isolate Campeau from his failing U.S. operations and to give the Reichmanns more control of the outcome. The real estate developers who from the beginning had avoided investing in businesses they didn't understand were now helping to run one. And Campeau, who from the beginning had avoided selling any of his precious Canadian real estate for equity in his takeovers—preferring to borrow the money, instead—was now faced with the prospect of losing it all.

The announcement of the $250 million Reichmann bailout in mid-September elated Campeau's worried bankers and lifted the price of Campeau Corp. stock. Speculation about the Reichmann's motives ran in opposite directions: (1) that the loan was a calculated, mean-spirited ploy to gain control of Campeau's real estate; and (2) that it was selfless, humanitarian assistance to a fellow tycoon in distress. In truth, it was neither. Having already sunk nearly a half-billion dollars into Campeau enterprises, Paul Reichmann saw this latest investment as a chance to protect his earlier investments by exerting greater influence on Campeau's affairs. The Reichmann representatives on the restructuring committee and on Campeau's board could protect the Reichmanns' interests in any pecking-order dispute with DeBartolo that might arise from a Campeau default.

Whatever the Reichmanns' motive for the September bailout, Wall Street figured that the richest developers in the world were too smart to be throwing good money after bad, and therefore that Campeau's predicament must not be as dire as it looked. What the bankers didn't know was that the Reichmanns already had concluded that an Allied/Federated bankruptcy was inevitable.

In September, the Wall Street story became a Seventh Avenue story. The garment industry located along New York's Seventh Avenue began to wonder about Allied and Federated stores. The result of two years of fancy corporate finagling had George Grossman asking himself: If I ship the merchandise, will I ever get paid?

Grossman was a small manufacturer of women's clothing. His company was named Party Line.* He had grown up in New Jersey, apprenticed in the showrooms in the garment district in the 1950s, and then gone into business for himself. For eighteen years, he had supplied blouses to the better stores.

* The names George Grossman and Alberto Rubino and their respective enterprises, Party Line and Julie's Choice, are fictitious, although the characters and the businesses described here are real. People in the retail trades hurt by Campeau's bankruptcies were generally more reluctant to talk openly than the bankers who engineered the deals.

Grossman didn't operate in walnut-paneled headquarters. He came to work in an open-collared shirt and split his time between a small showroom on Seventh Avenue and a warehouse around the corner that had all the elegance of an auto body shop. Invoices and remnants were piled everywhere. His couch was sprouting springs. He employed thirty people overall, including a couple of designers, salespeople, and accountants. The blouses were designed in New York and manufactured offshore. He ran the business on primitive economic and social principles, such as Don't Spend More Than You Can Afford, and Loyalty Is Always Rewarded.

Allied and Federated department stores were among Grossman's most reliable customers. He sold both companies blouses and swimwear on the usual Seventh Avenue arrangement: the merchandise went out, and if the bill was paid within the first ten days of the following month, then the buyer would get an 8 percent discount. Generally, there were no problems getting paid, except at Bloomingdale's, with whom Grossman had an ongoing dispute over past due bills. He'd filed a lawsuit against Bloomingdale's, which Bloomingdale's had agreed to settle.

Beginning in late fall, Grossman read *The Wall Street Journal* articles about Campeau's troubles and heard the Seventh Avenue gossip that Federated/Allied lacked the wherewithal to pay both their suppliers and their lenders. Having shipped $40,000 worth of blouses to the Campeau stores in October, Grossman naturally was concerned. He talked to representatives from Burdines in Florida, Rich's in Atlanta, and Federated's New York buying office. Everywhere, he was told not to worry, that business was proceeding as usual.

In November, having received payment for the October shipments, Grossman shipped more blouses to Federated/Allied, because "we couldn't walk away from our good customer, and we wanted to stick with them for the betterment of the whole." In December, having been paid for November, again he sent blouses, and the bill for these was due and payable on January 10. "They told us, 'Thank you, we will never forget you,' " Grossman recalls.

To ship or not to ship: Alberto Rubino was asking himself the same question over at Julie's Choice, his line of party dresses. Rubino's mother was a seamstress; his father had died young; he'd come to Seventh Avenue as a teenager, worked his way up, started his own business. In 1989, he employed thirty people and did $10 million a year in gross sales.

"You keep shipping and they always owe you money," is how Rubino described the normal relationship between supplier and department store. "Eventually, you agree to a settlement for less than the full amount, giving them allowances for unsold merchandise and things they've marked down."

Bloomingdale's was historically one of Rubino's most reliable customers, but by the fall of 1989, his accountants were warning him about Campeau's credit problems. Rubino shipped more dresses anyway. "We're an optimistic bunch," he says. "Besides, who else were we going to sell them to?"

Up and down Seventh Avenue, dressmakers and suit makers, perfume suppliers and handbag manufacturers were faced with the same dilemma. Not just small-timers like Grossman and Rubino, but big-timers like Bud Konheim weighed the value of their long-standing relationships with Federated and Allied against the increasing likelihood that they might not get paid.

Konheim, the owner of Nicole Miller, a major ready-to-wear line, had seen "signs of trouble" at Burdines and Jordan Marsh, two of Campeau's Florida divisions, earlier in the year. "They didn't seem to be able to make decisions about what they wanted anymore," Konheim says. "They couldn't decide on an order—whether they wanted it or they didn't want it—and they couldn't write a confirmation." He stopped selling to both divisions, but he still shipped to Bloomingdale's, because "Bloomie's was a viable retail spot, Traub did a good job, and Traub was in control."

Seventh Avenue's worries extended beyond the manufacturers to the factors, the neighborhood bankers of the rag trade.

Since Colonial days in America, and since the Middle Ages in Europe, there had been factors. Factors loaned money to the people who made things or grew things, enabling the makers and the growers to stay in business while waiting for their customers to pay up. For this service, factors charged a percentage point or two of the amount loaned. In return, they took the risk that the money might not be collected.

Dozens of small factoring companies had sprung up around the garment trade in New York, and many of these mom-and-pop banks were still in existence as late as the 1960s. After that the number steadily declined until by the 1980s only thirty or thirty-five were left. The top twenty or so had been bought by large commercial banks. The Bank of New York had a factoring outfit, CIT Factors was owned by Manny Hanny, Heller Financial by Fuji, Republic Factors by Irving Trust.

That some of the banks that lent money to the Campeau deals also owned factoring companies that lent money to the retail suppliers created some fascinating conflicts of interest. A story made the rounds that Fuji Bank was trying to unload Allied and Federated bonds and was telling potential customers how solid and reliable those two companies were, while its factoring division, Heller, was warning *its* customers about the perils of shipping to Allied and Federated stores.

There was speculation that the Reichmanns would invest another $800 million in the Campeau rescue as soon as a restructuring plan was developed. In September, Merrill Lynch was hired to devise a plan. (It's about time Merrill Lynch was brought into this. With Goldman, Sachs; Paine Webber; Shearson Lehman; Kidder, Peabody; Dillon, Read; First Boston; Salomon Brothers; and Drexel Burnham Lambert all employed on one side or another in the two takeovers, Merrill Lynch was the last of the major firms to have gotten in on the action.)

But the restructuring plan devised by the Reichmanns and by Merrill Lynch foundered on two provisions. The first was that the Allied/Federated bondholders would volunteer to settle for seventy cents on the dollar for their battered investments, in return for future equity in the company. The future-equity concept excited nobody. Also, the Reichmann reputation for infallibility had convinced some bondholders that the company's problems would soon be solved, and that Campeau and the Reichmanns were using their well-publicized troubles as a convenient opportunity to steal back the bonds. Why accept less than full value, bondholders told themselves, for something into which the powerful Reichmanns were putting more of their own money? The signs for Olympia & York, the

Reichmanns' real estate company, were as prevalent in New York's financial district as the Medici balls had been in Renaissance Florence.

The second problematic provision of the restructuring plan was that Campeau would sell Bloomingdale's, his latest favorite franchise. Federated was desperate for quick cash, and Bloomingdale's was the most likely place to get it. Already there were offers in the $1.2 billion range, and Marvin Traub not only was seeking buyers on Campeau's behalf but was trying to buy the place on his own. Campeau, as usual, was expecting to get higher prices. He'd said Bloomingdale's was worth $2 billion. The reality of the desperate situation that he'd described to Paul Reichmann in Switzerland apparently hadn't sunk in.

Moreover, some of the brilliant complications from the Federated closing came back to haunt the players in this post-LBO crisis. In a restructuring such as the one the Reichmanns proposed, some of the tax deferrals that made the original deal possible would be lost. If a division such as Bloomingdale's were sold, the seller, Federated, would be stuck with a heavy capital-gains liability, thus further reducing the funds available to pay off debt. Other negative tax consequences would result from any buyback of junk bonds at a discount.

In the topsy-turvy of the tax laws, corporate raiders were rewarded with big tax breaks for doing LBOs, but were faced with huge tax disadvantages if their LBOs failed. This made it harder to work out of messes.

Bondholders' and bankers' hopes were dashed in mid-October, when it became clear to Wall Street that the restructuring wasn't going to work. Bloomingdale's wasn't sold, the bondholders had rejected the buyback conditions, and the Reichmanns weren't investing more. They felt they'd been lied to about Federated's condition earlier in the summer, fed misleading sales forecasts and estimates, and now, after they had tried to help Campeau anyway, he was blaming them for his problems.

"Where Campeau had once flattered and cajoled Reichmann," wrote Peter Foster in Canada's *Saturday Night* magazine, "now he accused him of bad faith. Reichmann, Campeau claimed to anyone who would listen, had promised to come up with a restructuring proposal and had not done so. Furthermore, only $175 million of the promised $250 million had been forwarded by the Reichmanns to the U.S. operations. . . ."

Before the end of 1989, the Campeau-Reichmann relations had gone the way of the Tom Randall, Paine Webber, Tom Macioce, Bob Morosky, Ben Riggs, Security Pacific, Prudential, Jim Roddy, and Carolyn Buck Luce relations, to name just a few.

On Friday, October 16, the news of the troubling developments at Campeau headquarters sent the junk-bond market into another tailspin, and the stock market with it. The Dow Jones industrial average suffered its biggest one-day loss since the 1987 Crash. For several hours, trading in what had become a $200 billion junk-bond market was almost nonexistent. The managers of junk-bond mutual funds had no place to dump their holdings to raise cash for the anticipated redemptions from frightened clients.

The prices of Allied bonds fell to thirty-two cents on the dollar. By mid-December, when the Federated/Allied restructuring committee was formally disbanded and Campeau Corp. was hinting that its retail units might have to file for bankruptcy, the bonds fell even further. The Allied 11½s of 1997 were quoted at $9, and Federated's 16s of 2000 at $17. First Boston, having put its money where its mouth was, owned $125 million worth of both.


For retailers, the 1989 holiday season was the most depressing yet. Overloaded with basic merchandise from the Burden millinery buildup and grasping for cash, the Campeau stores cut prices drastically. These frantic markdowns forced the other major retailers from Macy's to Neiman Marcus to follow suit; discount signs appeared everywhere, 20 to 50 percent off. For the first time, shoppers were introduced to the post-Christmas sale before Christmas.

The effects of Campeau's twin buyouts were now visible at the clothes rack. *The New York Times* had earlier observed that the Bloomingdale's on Fifty-ninth Street, the flagship store where Campeau had been honored at the Hooray for Hollywood! party, was looking shoddy and disorganized. The pizzazz that had taken twenty years to develop was lost in six months; suddenly it wasn't so smart to shop at Bloomingdale's, it was smart to shop at discount stores that carried the merchandise that would otherwise have been sold at

Bloomingdale's but now was dumped on the market by vendors afraid to ship to Campeau's companies.

The billions in loans showered by the banks on Campeau and the millions in fees that Campeau showered back had produced a nationwide retail deflation. Industry analysts were predicting that shopping patterns had changed forever. And after seventy-five years of continuously solvent operations, Allied and Federated were being driven to the poorhouse by an interloper.

That the department stores would have reached this same sorry state soon enough on their own, even without Campeau, was the educated opinion of of Bud Konheim, the manufacturer of Nicole Miller dresses:

"It was going to happen anyway. The department stores were dinosaurs; look how many have gone: Orbach's, Wanamaker, Best and Company, Bonwit. I could go on. The retail surge of the early 1980s, all the money, the popularity, Traub's picture on magazine covers, it was camouflage, camouflage for the fact that there were too many stores going into too many malls.

"In 1976, there were maybe a thousand malls in America and by 1990 there are twenty thousand malls. It's all because of the rise of the real estate developer as a factor in shopping centers. You could install a big department store in a mall to 'anchor' the mall, get in at low rent, it seemed like a no-lose proposition. But soon they'd put malls everywhere, including the North Pole, and when nothing was selling at the North Pole, the department store would come back to the manufacturers and blame them for making the wrong kind of dress or the wrong style of suit. They'd say to the manufacturer, 'your styles didn't do so well this year on the North Pole. We've got to put them on sale.'

"With more stores, and more and more square feet in which merchandise didn't move, it took theatrics to get customers interested, now there had to be a sale, and even if there was a sale, people would say 'So what?' You could roll a bowling ball down the aisles of department stores and not hit anybody. Pretty soon, 10 percent off had to be 40 percent off to get people's attention. What the department stores ended up doing was teaching the entire nation never to pay regular prices. That's how the dinosaurs killed themselves."

It was Campeau, though, who delivered the stunning blow.

At the outset of 1990, he still hadn't obtained a Federated mortgage, the three investment banks hadn't unloaded their $400 million in bridge debt, and one of the Campeau loans from Citicorp, the "mortgage bridge" was due and payable by mid-January. Campeau and the Reichmanns weren't talking, the newspapers were saying that bankruptcy was imminent, the factors weren't factoring, Seventh Avenue worried about getting back its money for Christmas shipments, and Campeau was in Austria, working on his house.

Bloomingdale's had $100,000 worth of Alberto Rubino's party dresses on the racks, a significant amount given the size of his company. Bloomingdale's also had $300,000 worth of Bud Konheim's inventory, which hadn't been paid for, and $30,000–40,000 worth of George Grossman's blouses were spread among Bloomingdale's, Rich's in Atlanta, and Burdines in Miami.

Grossman shipped his last order to Federated on December 20. Since this order wasn't factored, the financial risk was entirely his. His bill for the December shipment was due and payable January 10, but "after they received our merchandise, they changed the payment date to February 10, which is when we began to think we might be in trouble."

All the bankruptcy talk caused Grossman to call his buyers at Burdines, Rich's, and Bloomingdale's for assurance that he'd be paid. Each one thanked him for his loyalty to Federated and said that checks would soon be in the mail. Thousands of other vendors, many of whom had stopped shipping by January but still had bills outstanding from December, were getting the same answers.

At Nicole Miller, Konheim smelled trouble when he heard that Marvin Traub was making a personal appeal to vendors to accept a voluntary delay in his payment so Bloomingdale's would have time to solve a "liquidity problem."

"From then on, I was halfway hoping for the bankruptcy," says Konheim. "Not because I wished ill on anyone, but because bankruptcy at least would put all the creditors on an equal footing. Otherwise, I suspected they'd pay big vendors like Liz Claiborne right away, and the rest of us could be screwed."

On January 12, all the vendors who collectively were owed $100 million from the December period were relieved to learn that they could pick up their checks from the various Federated/Allied outlets. Konheim was doing a television interview with the FNN network from his Nicole Miller showroom when he received this news. He'd just predicted Campeau's imminent bankruptcy when he was interrupted by a buzz on his desk—his secretary said the Bloomingdale's accounting department was on the line. With the camera still rolling, the call was put through, so three million viewers could hear Konheim being advised to come down to Bloomingdale's and pick up his check.

"How do I know it's good?" he asks, on camera.

"Do you think we'd be stupid enough to send out checks that bounce?" the woman in accounting says.

What loomed over Campeau that was about to drive his companies into bankruptcy was the remaining $1 billion on the Citicorp asset bridge loan, due in January but extended into March. If he'd gotten a conventional mortgage, he could have paid off this loan. Perhaps, with the latest cash infusion by the Reichmanns, plus an extra $50 million advanced by Citicorp, he could have survived his liquidity crisis, had the overall situation been different.

At the end of 1989, the bottom line was that Federated had generated an operating cash flow of only $500 million. This was far below the $740 million projected by the Campeau number crunchers in early 1988, a spectacular performance in the annals of miscalculation. Technically, the $500 million was enough cash to pay the interest bills of $490 million, but it was far from a healthy circumstance. With an emergency austerity program at Allied and Federated, more effective cost-cutting, more pink slips, better control over rampaging inventories, and refinancing the Citicorp mortgage bridge, perhaps the debt gods might have been placated.

But all of these perhapses could not be divorced from the man Wall Street had installed in this predicament. Bankers who patronized Campeau's every pecuniary whim, capitalizing on his maniacal grasp at every passing opportunity, could not now expect, in a crisis, that he would suddenly become more realistic. After two fantastic purchases and so many favorable messages from the marketplace, such as the recent humoring by real estate financiers, was it any wonder that Campeau had continued to hold out for a fantasy mortgage, when the situation demanded a conventional fix?

By the end of 1989, even the bankers who had abetted Campeau through both deals were tired of haggling with their contentious borrower. Also, the publicity of Campeau's liquidity troubles was having a ruinous effect on the stores. Retailers and their factors who had generally gone along with the company and shipped merchandise into December were not about to continue shipping into January, with the future so obviously insecure. In fact, many of them had begun to root for the bankruptcy as the only way their interests could be protected. Even Citicorp, the mother of all Campeau lenders, was not in the mood to cut further slack.

At Bloomingdale's at Fifty-ninth and Lexington, a large crowd packed the underground corridor that connects the main store to the business office. Alberto Rubino, owed $30,000 for his dresses; and Konheim, owed $300,000 for his dresses, sent their emissaries, who were joined by a crowd of other emissaries from perfume companies, furniture companies, shoe companies, greeting-card companies, tie makers, sock makers, hatmakers, standing patiently on line in this quiet, first-ever run on the pay window of New York's favorite department store.

Management sent an employee down to usher everyone along and keep them calm in the heat and the dead air of the passageway; there was a two-hour wait from back to front. A rope-fence maze, the kind used for waiting lines in theaters and banks, was the final obstacle. Beyond the maze, checks were handed out from large file boxes, organized alphabetically.

All of Wasserstein's fancy ploys, First Boston's bridge loans, Citicorp's secured loans, the pile of briefs, contracts, and agreements from Campeau's lawyers at Cravath, the equity schemes, the juggling of assets, the two years of nonstop strategizing on Campeau's behalf ended in this human traffic jam in the Bloomingdale's passageway.

Some of the more clairvoyant suppliers to Federated/Allied, who tended to be the larger suppliers with access to corporate jets, flew directly to Delaware, Philadelphia, or Atlanta, to cash the checks immediately at the banks on which they were written. A Seventh Avenue tactical air group scrambled to the outlying banks on Friday, January 12.

The smaller and/or more naive suppliers, including Grossman, Rubino, and Konheim, deposited the checks at their own local banks, which meant the checks wouldn't clear until Tuesday at the earliest. This was unfortunate, because on Monday, January 15, Martin Luther King, Jr.'s Birthday holiday, Federated and Allied stores filed for bankruptcy. All the checks that hadn't been cashed on Friday bounced when the banks opened on Tuesday.

Grossman was screwed twice. In addition to the $20,000 check for the merchandise he shipped in December, the check he'd finally received as settlement for his earlier lawsuit with Bloomingdale's also bounced. "I still believed that the instrument, the check, was good," said Grossman, in wonderment that at the great Federated Department Stores, a complicated leveraged buyout had produced this all-too-understandable result.

"My dresses are still in Bloomingdale's and they haven't paid for them," marveled Rubino after the bankruptcy was declared and his check, retrieved from the Bloomingdale's passageway, likewise bounced. "But if I went in to get them, I'd be arrested for stealing."

# *Postscript*

•

Room 440, in the federal courthouse in downtown Cincinnati, is devoted to the exhibits, claims, and pleadings of the Allied/Federated bankruptcy. It is the first time a bankruptcy in Cincinnati has required its own private room. There is space for expansion should things drag on, as they already have, for eighteen months.

The hallway leading into Room 440 is poorly lit, and passing through it is like passing through a dark forest that opens into the sunny clearing of the bankruptcy records, arranged behind a long white countertop.

Two clerks work full-time as the curators of the Allied/Federated pecuniary artifacts. None of it is computerized. The ill-fated creations of Wall Street's number crunchers and dealmakers in their Quotron-equipped offices have found their final resting place in surroundings that resemble a nineteenth-century museum.

In an area to the left of the white countertop are two wooden tables, on which ten fat clipboards are laid out, open for public inspection. These ten clipboards hold all the relevant documents filed within the last month. Alongside are two stacks of additional documents too thick to bind.

Beyond the tables are two long rows of flesh-colored metal shelves, each eight feet high. These hold the 135 linear feet of Allied/

Federated petitions, motions, responses, orders, applications, and affidavits from the 50,000 creditors' claims.

The statements of financial condition and executors' contracts alone fill 29 volumes, and each of those is 2,020 pages long. The transcripts of court hearings run more than 3,900 pages. There are 250 docket sheets that list 4,500 separate filings with the court, beginning with Document 1, the original 6,000-page petition for Chapter 11 protection filed on January 15, 1990.

The 50,000 creditors from a single bankruptcy filing is a record in financial history. The number includes Bud Konheim, Alberto Rubino, and George Grossman, plus thousands of other vendors and merchandisers, plus bankers, real estate companies, factors, bondholders owed principal and interest, and the IRS, which seeks $600 million in federal income taxes.

There are six official committees that represent the secured creditors (mostly banks), the unsecured bondholders, and the unsecured creditors (mostly vendors and manufacturers), in both Campeau enterprises. All are fighting for their mutual and competing self-interests, and meet bi-monthly to map out strategy.

Heading the list of unsecured creditors is First Boston, with a total of $526 million in unwise Campeau investments, including the Federated bridge loan that was never repaid, as well as more than $100 million worth of Allied and Federated junk bonds that First Boston bought of its own accord, mainly from other institutions that had helped get the Federated junk deal sold.

Paine Webber, owed $102 million from its Campeau misadventures, is also a member of the Federated bondholders committee, which gives the firm more of a voice in the ongoing Campeau affairs than it ever had when Wasserstein was running things. Wasserstein, once again proving his brilliance, is not a Campeau creditor.

The biggest secured creditor is Citicorp (who else?) followed by Sumitomo. The eight pages of banks who joined the Citicorp-Sumitomo syndicate reads like a Who's Who of Japanese finance: Sanwa Bank, the Long-Term Credit Bank of Japan, the Bank of Toyko, the Fuji Bank, the Hokkaido Takushoku Bank, the Industrial Bank of Japan, the Kyowa Bank, the Mitsubishi Bank, the Nippon Credit Bank, the Tokai Bank, and the Dai-Ichi Kangyo Bank. An Arab bank, two German banks, a Brussels bank, and a Scottish bank—but not a single Canadian bank—are represented in this international funding of Campeau's secured debt. "I wouldn't doubt that this is the largest loan problem that Sumitomo has ever had in the United States," says John Garnet, a former Sumitomo banker.

Among the biggest holders of junk bonds was a familiar name from the savings-and-loan bailout: Columbia Savings and Loan, which bought $98 million worth of Federated junk bonds. Now that Uncle Sam has taken over Columbia on the public's behalf, we've become a nation of creditors in Federated. Several insurance companies, including Metropolitan Life and the now-defunct First Executive of Los Angeles, also own Federated bonds.

Of the vendors and suppliers, Crystal Brands is stuck with $5.6 million worth of unpaid claims; Liz Claiborne, $5 million; Chanel, $3.8 million; American Greetings, $5.8 million; Sara Lee, $2.9 million; Reebok, $2 million; Polo Ralph Lauren, $2.5 million; two big factoring companies, Heller and CIT, $4.1 million and $9 million respectively; and Ohio Mattress, $2 million.

CIT Factors is an interesting situation because it is 40 percent owned by Manufacturers Hanover, a bank that after the Allied deal refused to have anything further to do with Campeau, and yet still managed through its factoring arm to be stiffed by Campeau's companies for $9 million.

Ohio Mattress is another interesting situation because it has so much in common with the debtor. It, too, received a big bridge loan from First Boston that it couldn't repay after the junk-bond market balked at buying Ohio Mattress bonds. Here, then, is a case of one First Boston client stiffing another, and both of them bridge loan fiascoes from the great era of merchant banking that First Boston had so zealously promoted. What went around also came around in the venturesome M&A department, run by Jim Maher.

Of the real estate creditors, JMB and affiliates have filed 500 different claims, mostly having to do with joint ventures with Federated to develop shopping malls. The DeBartolo Company has filed 150 claims, based on a host of overlapping agreements with numerous parties, not the least of which is the $480 million equity loan secured by the stock in Ralphs grocery stores, a separate entity that is not part of the aforementioned proceedings.

There are $8.2 billion in total claims.

The Campeau bankruptcy is an industry in itself. Already it has outlasted Campeau's Federated, and may well outlast Campeau's Allied in the end, providing steady employment to lawyers, accountants, advisers, the private firm hired to send out notices and mailings, the printing company that prints the notices. The bankruptcy court alone has approved $70 million in payments out of company funds to its professional helpers, a figure that is sure to be exceeded by the amounts paid to lawyers, accountants, etc., by creditors and debtors themselves.

A Cincinnati law firm, Jones Day, representing Federated/Allied, has received $14.9 million to date; its co-counsel, Frost & Jacobs, $2.9 million. The lead auditors, Peat Marwick, have received $4.5 million; the accountants to the secured creditors, Ernst & Young, $2 million; the Allied bondholders' lawyer, Coudert Brothers, $2.6 million; the Federated unsecured creditors' lawyer, $1.6 million; the Federated bondholders' accountants, Arthur Andersen, $1.6 million. These are just samples of the secondary bonanza that is making Campeau a darling of the American bar, and a legend in accounting circles. In mid-1991, the Frost & Jacobs law firm billed the court for 347,000 photocopies at fifteen cents a page, or $52,189. And that's only one firm's bill for three months' worth of Xeroxing.

Shearson Lehman has been hired by the court as the chief Federated/Allied financial adviser, for which it is paid $250,000 a month, its bill already exceeding $3 million. Back in 1985 in Canada, Shearson was engaged by Campeau to find him an S&L, when Campeau disappeared, which turned out to be a very lucky thing for Shearson. Otherwise, the Campeau megatakeovers might never have happened, and Shearson would have been out three big fees: one for representing DeBartolo in the Allied defense, another for representing Federated in its own defense, and a third for representing the bankruptcy. For all three fees, Shearson has Campeau to thank, and they more than make up for the finder's fee that Campeau had neglected to pay in the search for the S&L, from which he was distracted by his face lift.

As yet another financial adviser to Federated, Salomon Brothers is paid $150,000 a month; Lazard Frères gets $150,000 a month for advising the Allied bondholders' committee; Smith Barney, only $100,000 a month to advise a second group of bondholders, who have petitioned to raise the amount to $150,000. The Blackstone Group was recently hired to represent the Federated bondholders for $125,000 a month plus expenses, and Eric Gleacher has been approved as the adviser to the secured creditors at the going $150,000 rate. Gleacher wanted a guarantee for $1.2 million minimum, but that was scratched.

A list of other law firms representing the creditors and debtors runs several pages, as a wide range of lawsuits has been contemplated. Most worrisome to Wall Street has been the possibility that the Allied bondholders will file a "fraudulent conveyance suit." All along, they have contended that Allied assets, particularly the Ann Taylor division, were looted by Campeau to pay for Federated, and that his bankers helped him do it. First Boston, which wrote Campeau's valuation opinion on which the Ann Taylor sale rested, has been nervously awaiting this likely litigation.

In April 1991, the bankrupt company filed its long awaited plan of reorganization, in which the $8.2 billion total claims against the company can finally be paid off. Not in cash, of course—who has that kind of money?—but in some combination of a little cash and a lot of paper, i.e., stock. As of this writing, it is uncertain how many creditors will agree to be paid in paper, the value of which is based on numerous number-crunching assumptions, which the company itself admits "may not materialize."

If the reorganization is approved, the new Allied/Federated, to be known as Federated Department Stores, Inc., will go public again, so in addition to the large number of creditor/shareholders, other investors will be able to buy the stock.

The eleven remaining Campeau divisions, including Burdines/Florida, Jordan Marsh/Boston, Jordan Marsh/Florida, Maas Brothers/Florida, Rich's/Atlanta, Lazarus/Cincinnati, Abraham & Straus/New York, Stern's/New Jersey, the Bon Marché/Seattle, and Bloomingdale's/ New York have kept doing business throughout, although twenty stores have been closed (two new ones have been opened) and Jordan Marsh has been put on the block to raise cash. The Goldsmith's in downtown Memphis, the Rich's in downtown

Atlanta, the Bon Marché in Eugene, Oregon, the Bloomingdale's in Dallas, and a Lazarus in Grand Rapids, Michigan, are among the casualties.

All four planes in the Federated Air Force were sold off. The Gulfstream went to the Deluxe Check Printing company in Minnesota; separating Campeau from his favorite jet was not a pleasant task. Campeau ordered his pilot to bring it back to Canada, but the plane reportedly was locked up in a Cincinnati hangar to prevent its abduction.

The retail operations were handed over to Alan Questrom, lured back to his old company with a $2 million signing bonus and a five-year $12 million contract. If Campeau hadn't come along, Questrom would have remained at Federated, where he had been expected to be tapped as Goldfeder's successor. But Campeau did come along, and Questrom took his golden parachute and escaped to Neiman Marcus. The bankrupt Federated offered him more for his services than a healthy Federated would have paid. Even Questrom has Campeau to thank for making him richer.

Questrom was so sought after that the Reichmanns agreed to fund his salary in advance of the court's formal approval and to guarantee a $7 million payment if the bankruptcy judge refused to appoint him to the job.

In accepting the "challenge of restoring Federated and Allied to profitability," Questrom was joined by G. William Miller, former Secretary of the Treasury and therefore well versed in debt financing, who was paid $1 million annually to serve as the chairman and CEO of the new holding company, Federated Stores, Inc.

Cash to buy new merchandise came from a new revolving credit line provided by the ubiquitous lender: Citicorp. Satisfied that once again they'd get paid for new orders with checks that didn't bounce, thousands of vendors who had stopped shipping to Campeau after December 1989, began shipping again, even though they still were owed money.

Ron Tysoe, the last of Campeau's key advisers not to have quit or been fired, continued on the job at Federated headquarters, doing his best to help straighten things out. Jim Roddy and Carolyn Buck Luce joined forces in a new venture—advising U.S. and Canadian corporations on mergers, acquisitions, and restructurings. They are well prepared to deal with every possible complexity or foul-up.

Back on Wall Street, First Boston itself had to be bailed out, barely surviving two years of the new era of merchant banking it initiated. Having invested its own capital in several unfortunate bridge loans for which the Campeau bridge loan set a precedent—to AMI International, to Jerrico, to Ohio Mattress—the troubled firm turned to its richer parent, Crédit Suisse, for a $650 million rescue.

The write-offs that First Boston took on the Campeau loans wiped out all the big fees it had made on Federated and Allied. The result of all its dealings with Campeau was a $100 million loss.

Of the principal advocates of the two Campeau deals, William Mayer was relieved of his duties as CEO and subsequently resigned; Jim Maher, who replaced Wasserstein as head of M&A became a vice chairman; Greg Malcom, who headed the junk-bond group, left the firm at the end of 1990; Bill Dickey of the real estate group was transferred to California and then also left the firm; and Ken Colburn, the relationship manager, continued to work in the firm's Boston office, where he asked to be transferred in 1989.

Of the Cassandras of the deals, Kim Fennebresque resigned to become a general partner at Lazard Frères, and Mike Rothfeld quit in July 1989 to accept an offer from an old-line private investment firm.

Wasserstein's M&A firm, Wasserstein, Perella, was having its own problems making ends meet. Though Wasserstein never loaned money to Campeau, as his most notable adviser he got more than his share of negative publicity in the aftermath, none of which was good for business.

Citicorp, which lent money to every side of both Campeau deals, was one of the largest creditors in the bankruptcy, in spite of the fact that just before Campeau filed for bankruptcy, Federated paid off $250 million of one of the Citicorp bridge loans. But the Campeau loans were the least of Citicorp's problems, although it could be argued that they were symptomatic.

Since Citicorp was saddled with $8.6 billion in bad loans to Latin America and a variety of other bad investments, including another $2 to $2.5 billion in nonperforming real estate loans, its earnings dropped from $5.36 a share in 1988 to $1.16 a share in

1989, and its stock lost two-thirds of its value. Disgruntled investors sold it down from a high of nearly $30 to a low of $10.75. Adding insult to its debits, Citicorp was chastised by the Federal Reserve Board for taking too active a role in the buyout of Del Monte foods through its venture capital group, thus overstepping its bounds as a commercial bank. The Fed forced Citicorp to turn the deal over to Merrill Lynch.

By the summer of 1991, Citicorp was scrambling to raise money and reduce losses, to meet the government's capital requirements. "All big companies get sloppy," its chairman, John Reed, told the press. "We're no exception."

The Sumitomo Bank of Japan, the co-manager of Citicorp's syndicate for Federated, sufferd a culture shock from the bankruptcy filing. Sumitomo, along with other Japanese banks, was skeptical of the leveraged-buyout concept to begin with. Initially, its representatives took the position that the LBO idea made no sense, only to be convinced otherwise by their sophisticated American counterparts.

When the news of Campeau's filing for Chapter 11 reached Tokyo, it caused great agitation in the Sumitomo boardroom, where the directors regarded bankruptcy as a disaster and a public disgrace. It took several phone calls from Sumitomo's emissaries in New York to convince the home office that in America, bankruptcy was as common as hiccups, and no more frowned upon and that a company that filed for Chapter 11 could continue to function as before.

Allen Finkelson, Campeau's lead attorney and beauty-contest organizer, continued to practice merger law as a full partner at Cravath, Swaine & Moore, which in 1990 ranked ninth among U.S. law firms in gross revenues, with 288 attorneys bringing in $213 million.

Boyd Jefferies, the man who sold Campeau 25.8 million shares of Allied stock the morning of the Street Sweep, has since pled guilty to parking stock illegally for Ivan Boesky. After getting his probation, Jefferies took a job teaching golf to troubled children.

Robert Morosky, Campeau's temporary retailer, returned to live in Columbus, Ohio, and commute regularly to Wichita, Kansas, far from the merchant princes, where he runs Safelight Auto Glass, a company that makes windshields.

John Burden III continued to split his time between New York and Sanibel Island, Florida. Howard Goldfeder retired to California.

Bud Konheim, a $300,000 Campeau creditor, continues to operate Nicole Miller, the dress manufacturer, and to ship to the new Federated. After Campeau's filing, Alberto Rubino, a $100,000 creditor, was forced to lay off 10 percent of his work force—three employees—and to cut back on expenses. He resumed shipping party dresses to Bloomingdale's. And George Grossman, a $30,000 creditor, is still shipping his blouses.

Tom Macioce, the Allied CEO, died in 1990.

Ed DeBartolo, the shopping center magnate, was hoping that his equity stake in Ralphs grocery stores and his guarantee from Campeau Corporation would someday enable him to recover his $480 million investment. The Reichmanns, owed $650 million, watched the value of their collateral—Campeau Corp. shares—drop from a high of $26 to a low of fifty cents on the Toronto Stock Exchange. Campeau had blamed the Reichmanns' "half-hearted" rescue for much of his troubles. He and the Reichmanns were no longer speaking.

The Canadian bankers who were reluctant to lend to Campeau when this odyssey began were, in the end, the only ones who were dealing directly with the man. The National Bank of Canada was trying to recover the $150 million it had loaned Campeau in 1987 so that he could buy back his own company's shares. The collateral for this loan was the shares themselves, now worth closer to $4 million than the $150 million the bank had advanced.

In late 1990, Campeau, whose misfortunes had not diminished his capacity for optimistic connivance, made the National Bank an incredible offer—he would take these shares off its hands for $80 million. This not only would limit the bank's loss to only $70 million, it would enable Campeau to regain control of his company by getting his shares back. The bank was intrigued—but where at this stage was Campeau going to get $80 million?

For weeks, Campeau held the bankers in suspense over a series of private meetings with a so-called "mystery investor," who Campeau hinted had already agreed to provide the $80 million. Articles about the mystery investor appeared in the Toronto papers, the entire financial district wondered who it could be—certainly not the Reichmanns or DeBartolo or First Boston—but perhaps an Arab, or the Vatican once again, or a recent lottery winner?

In the end, the mystery investor turned out to be Paul Desmarais, the Canadian developer who had bought Campeau's company after Campeau's nervous breakdown in the early 1970s and then sold it back to him a few months later. This second Desmarais rescue had a historic and an emotional appeal—twenty years later, the man who took away Campeau's original company returns to help him recover the upgraded version. As it turned out, however, the eagerness of the mystery investor to actually put up the $80 million was greatly exaggerated. The deal never took place.

Meanwhile another Canadian bank, the Bank of Nova Scotia, was attempting to recover the $10 million mortgage it held on Campeau's Bridle Path mansion. Campeau had agreed to put the place up for sale, but the effort had stalled over the price. Local real estate agents estimated that the house might sell for $3–4 million. Campeau reportedly wanted more.

His last appearance as CEO and chairman of Campeau Corp. was at the August 1990 annual meeting in Toronto. Wearing a gray suit, a blue-and-white shirt, and a snazzy red tie, Campeau entered the conference room at the Hilton Hotel to subdued applause from three hundred shareholders.

"I truly sympathize with all of you that have incurred losses," Campeau said. "I know how you feel . . . the time has now come to focus on the future . . . hindsight gets better all the time . . . we have to remember that at the time we were looking for acquisitions in the frenzy of Wall Street . . . it was a deal that made sense to our investment bankers who gave us numbers . . . to support our projections . . . and we proceeded on that basis."

In the question-and-answer session, someone from the audience asked Campeau about his role in the company, and he snapped back, "I am the chairman and CEO of Campeau Corporation. Next question." But it wasn't long before Campeau was stripped of those titles, and of any position of influence in his own company, by his creditors and his rescuers, the Reichmanns and the National Bank of Canada. The bank had seized its share of Campeau Corp. stock, the collateral from the defaulted personal loan to Campeau, and together with the Reichmanns, it now owned a majority of the shares.

Campeau's untiring efforts to insulate one asset from the other and to maximize every advantage had backfired in a sad and spectacular way. At the end of his two glorious leveraged buyouts, he himself had suffered their fate, his various possessions sold off for cash, his real estate empire dismantled. His Campeau Corp. shares, which in 1988 were worth $500 million, were reduced to $10 million by 1989. His debts far exceeded these assets, his net worth was less than zero.

To overcome Campeau's desperate resistance to selling assets voluntarily, the banks sued to force him into involuntary personal bankruptcy. In May 1991, his own Campeau Corporation (although, by then, "his" in name only) sued him for $12.7 million and asked him to return some paintings and cars, and $5,200 worth of telephone equipment from his Toronto chateau. The company also said it would no longer pay the salaries for his chauffeur and his household staff, or his travel bills and club memberships.

He will be left, apparently, with a house in Florida and the mansion in Austria, and no obvious way to pay for the upkeep at either one. Although the Austrian mansion was purchased with a loan from Campeau Corp., which in turn had borrowed the money from the Bank of Nova Scotia, it seems that the property is owned by a Liechtenstein foundation, called a *sifttung,* which has existed for centuries. Campeau may have bought a controlling interest in the *sifttung* in his wife's name. Technically then he is a guest on his property, and the banks may have trouble taking it away from him.

After spending most of 1990 in Toronto, where acquaintances said he appeared to be cheerful and buoyant in his rare public appearances, in 1991 Campeau was more frequently found in Austria. In March, his lawyers informed the Allied bondholders and other litigants that Campeau would not be coming to court or giving depositions "on the advice of his physician." Rumors were rampant that he'd had another nervous breakdown.

# *Conclusion*

•

It is not clear at this writing how well the Federated and Allied remnants will survive the Campeau ordeal, saddled as they are with the fees of bankruptcy, which are proving to be as burdensome as the fees of the LBO that got them into this mess—and paid out generally to the very same people. The retailers' best hope to emerge from default into solvency is once again to issue stock in which individuals can invest with confidence, if any such can be mustered. Among the various rights in corporate society is the right to go private and then public and back to private again, reversing the process as many times as necessary. There is nothing to keep LBO victims such as Allied and Federated from going public to save themselves now, eventually to be taken private in the next heyday of leveraged buyouts, once people have forgotten the consequences and enthusiasm for the LBO procedure is restored.

Nor is it clear how Campeau can raise himself up from the bickering and the lawsuits in which he is now embroiled. With his telephones and his paintings about to be stripped from his house on the Bridle Path in Toronto by his own Campeau Corp., he has suffered what amounts to a corporate eviction at the hands of his own creation, as cruel a fate as being thrown out on the street by one's own family, except in this case instead of the street he has the mansion in Austria from which to repair himself and make a comeback. There is evidence of rejuvenation already in the recent report that he has tried to do a real estate deal on some property around his Austrian lake.

In their bitterness over having landed two solid companies in Chapter 11, both Campeau and his bankers have tended to blame each other: the bankers emphasizing that their calculations would have proven correct had they not been subjected to the distorting antics of Campeau and his hirelings; while Campeau has thanked Wall Street, and particularly Bruce Wasserstein, for leading him into a losing and overpriced proposition.

A more sympathetic and high-minded point of view is that Campeau and his bankers were victimized not by each other, but by the hopeless romance that caused them to fall into each other's arms. To have a hopeless romance, of course, you have to have passion, Campeau's drive for self-aggrandizement in this case being fully matched and then some by his bankers' drive to earn fees. Hopeless romance also requires great faith—in this case, the bankers' faith in their own calculations, which was more than equaled by Campeau's faith in his own marvelous ability to work miracles part-time.

This romance between Campeau and the lenders cannot be separated from the period in which it flowered, the 1980s, which after all was the decade for high leverage and mystical accounting not only for corporations but also for the national government. It was during this decade that the country passed from being a creditor to being a debtor nation, with the government not only the biggest borrower of all, but the ultimate guarantor of the bankers and their romantic sprees.

In the end, the public—you and I—will end up paying for these sprees, in the case of the troubled banks, via some sort of gratuity in the form of new taxes the government will levy to bail out the various romanced lenders, added to the extra taxes it will have to levy to pay for its own fanciful borrowings. Hopefully, the great bargains that have recently been found on the shelves of department stores, thanks in part to the Campeau markdowns, will enable us all to save enough money to make our required contribution to the banking rescues. Think of it every time you buy a shirt or a dress on sale.

# Photo Credits

•

1. *Ottawa Star*
2. UPI/Bettmann
3. John McNeil/*The Globe & Mail*
4. Erik Christensen/*The Globe & Mail*
5. Edward Regan/*The Globe & Mail*
6. Tibor Kolley/*The Globe & Mail*
7. Jeff Wasserman/*Financial Post*
8. *The Globe & Mail*
9. James Lewcun/*The Globe & Mail*
10. Peter Freed/Picture Group
11. UPI/Bettmann
12. AP/Wide World Photos
13. David Lubarsky
14. Federated Department Stores, Inc./Allied Stores
15. Chris Nichols
16. Andrew Popper/Picture Group
17. Michele Singer/Outline
18. *New York Times* Pictures
19. Carolyn Schaefer/Liaison International
20. UPI/Bettmann
21. *Cincinnati Enquirer*
22. John Chiasson/Gamma-Liaison
23. UPI/Bettmann
24. Brooks Brothers
25. *Cincinnati Enquirer*
26. John Chiasson/Gamma-Liaison
27. John Chiasson/Gamma-Liaison
28. David Lubarsky
29. Campeau Corporation
30. Rick Friedman/Black Star
31. Diana Nethercott/*Financial Post*
32. Peter Sibbald
33. Nomi Morris/*Financial Post*
34. Peter Redman/*Financial Post*

# Index

•

# FOR THE BEST IN PAPERBACKS, LOOK FOR THE

In every corner of the world, on every subject under the sun, Penguin represents quality and variety—the very best in publishing today.

For complete information about books available from Penguin—including Pelicans, Puffins, Peregrines, and Penguin Classics—and how to order them, write to us at the appropriate address below. Please note that for copyright reasons the selection of books varies from country to country.

**In the United Kingdom:** For a complete list of books available from Penguin in the U.K., please write to *Dept E.P., Penguin Books Ltd, Harmondsworth, Middlesex, UB7 0DA.*

**In the United States:** For a complete list of books available from Penguin in the U.S., please write to *Dept BA, Penguin*, Box 120, Bergenfield, New Jersey 07621-0120.

**In Canada:** For a complete list of books available from Penguin in Canada, please write to *Penguin Books Canada Ltd, 10 Alcorn Avenue, Suite 300, Toronto, Ontario, Canada M4V 3B2.*

**In Australia:** For a complete list of books available from Penguin in Australia, please write to the *Marketing Department, Penguin Books Ltd, P.O. Box 257, Ringwood, Victoria 3134.*

**In New Zealand:** For a complete list of books available from Penguin in New Zealand, please write to the *Marketing Department, Penguin Books (NZ) Ltd, Private Bag, Takapuna, Auckland 9.*

**In India:** For a complete list of books available from Penguin, please write to *Penguin Overseas Ltd, 706 Eros Apartments, 56 Nehru Place, New Delhi, 110019.*

**In Holland:** For a complete list of books available from Penguin in Holland, please write to *Penguin Books Nederland B.V., Postbus 195, NL-1380AD Weesp, Netherlands.*

**In Germany:** For a complete list of books available from Penguin, please write to *Penguin Books Ltd, Friedrichstrasse 10-12, D-6000 Frankfurt Main 1, Federal Republic of Germany.*

**In Spain:** For a complete list of books available from Penguin in Spain, please write to *Longman, Penguin España, Calle San Nicolas 15, E-28013 Madrid, Spain.*

**In Japan:** For a complete list of books available from Penguin in Japan, please write to *Longman Penguin Japan Co Ltd, Yamaguchi Building, 2-12-9 Kanda Jimbocho, Chiyoda-Ku, Tokyo 101, Japan.*